Garrison Keillor

Studies in Popular Culture
M. Thomas Inge, General Editor

Garrison Keillor

A VOICE OF AMERICA

Judith Yaross Lee

UNIVERSITY PRESS OF MISSISSIPPI
Jackson & London

Copyright © 1991 by the University Press of Mississippi
All rights reserved
Manufactured in the United States of America
Designed by Sally Horne

94 93 92 91 4 3 2 1

The paper in this book meets the guidelines for permanence and durability
of the Committee on Production Guidelines for Book Longevity of the
Council on Library Resources.

All excerpts from archived recordings and scripts at Minnesota Public Radio
have been reproduced by courtesy of Minnesota Public Radio and Garrison
Keillor. All excerpts copyright © Garrison Keillor.

Library of Congress Cataloging-in-Publication Data

Lee, Judith Yaross, 1949–
    Garrison Keillor : a voice of America / Judith Yaross Lee.
        p.   cm. — (Studies in popular culture)
    Includes bibliographical references and index.
    ISBN 0-87805-457-X (cloth). — ISBN 0-87805-473-1 (paper)
    1. Keillor, Garrison—Criticism and interpretation. 2. Lake
Wobegon (Imaginary place) 3. Minnesota in literature. I. Title.
II. Series: Studies in popular culture (Jackson, Miss.)
PS3561.E3755Z76 1991
791.44'092—dc20   90-24702
                                                                 CIP

British Library Cataloging-in-Publication data available

FOR MY JOES

WITH LOVE

CONTENTS

PREFACE

From Lake Wobegon
I get my voice.
—Garrison Keillor
to Diane Roback (1985)

In working on this book, I have enjoyed the excitement of writing for readers as well as for scholars, and I have therefore taken pains to look out for the needs of my new friends as well as to fulfill my obligations to my colleagues. A few words are in order, therefore, about terms that have different meanings for humor scholars than for people who simply like to laugh, and about my transcriptions of oral material.

First, the *comic pose* refers to an attitude that a narrator or speaker adopts temporarily for narrative purposes; although the term has evolved from the ordinary sense of pretending, the comic pose does not involve deceit, because its artifice is part of a joke. In the scholarly study of humor, a comic pose describes the way that a humorist communicates with the audience at a particular moment. As a vehicle for humor, a pose is a good, perhaps even inevitable, undertaking. Humorists may well discover their most successful poses in inspired moments of narrative instinct, but a pose need not be premeditated to be either identifiable or exploitable. Using a pose consistently, by design or by accident, constitutes a comic strategy.

Second, *cracker-barrel philosophy* and its twin, *homespun wisdom*, apply to all lessons delivered by a colloquial speaker who has no professional authority to deliver them. Unlike a teacher, parent, or other personages in a role superior to the audience's, cracker-barrel philosophers derive their moral authority from personal experience and the innate virtue of their ideas, not from book-learning, social status, or professional standing. Except in the case of an ironic narrator (the Confederate sympathizer Petroleum

V. Nasby, for example), cracker-barrel philosophers usually advance admirable sentiments. In any event, for the student of American humor, and throughout this book, *cracker-barrel philosophy* and *homespun wisdom* lack any negative connotation. In giving up the right to speak, an audience raises a storyteller to a status higher than its own. Unlike lecturers, who use this status for authority, humorists need to adopt poses of inferiority or of only modest superiority (to artificially reduce their status to equal to or less than the audience's) in order to dispense homespun wisdom.

Finally, *rhetorical strategies, techniques,* or *tactics* are simply devices of storytelling. Everyone who tells a story at a dinner party aims at some effect: impressing the audience, garnering sympathy, getting a laugh, and so on. Successful raconteurs intuit the devices needed for the job. Their techniques will always appear in clearer outline to a historian, who has the benefit of hindsight, than to the storytellers or their audiences. Whether chosen consciously or instinctively, the devices are nonetheless put to deliberate use. All narrators *exploit* their material in the interest of what they perceive to be a good story.

Transcriptions of speech from *A Prairie Home Companion* are my own, made from audio or video recordings as cited parenthetically or in notes. Citation of a date always indicates a transcribed quotation; quotations from written texts are identified by title. Such marks of oral speech as "um" and "uh" or "doncha know" and "ya know" are included here only in a few examples, and then solely to illustrate the colloquialism of a particular set of remarks. Otherwise I have, as a general rule, silently eliminated the hesitation markers and used normal spelling. I aimed first of all to avoid the conventional association between dialect spelling and southern speech, since (unlike Huckleberry Finn) Garrison Keillor speaks standard midwestern English, with less noticeably round o's, for instance, than many other Minnesotans. But I also wanted to avoid the implication that spelling alone can represent an oral performance, which in fact exploits a great many other elements not so easily rendered in print: the duration of pauses, rising and falling inflections, variations in pace and stress. (Philologists and anthropologists, of course, have their own orthographic conventions for these and other subtleties.) I have represented pauses with the dash (—), reserving ellipses to indicate omitted material. I have indicated the short stop by a comma, the full stop with a period, and the combination of a long pause and a shift in direction with a new paragraph. I tried to balance the sometimes conflicting needs for visual clarity and aural accuracy.

In addition, my research into the historical development of *A Prairie Home Companion* is based mainly on a sample of two or three programs from each of its thirteen years. This procedure was necessitated by both the volume of material (about twelve hundred hours of programming, which must, after all, be examined in real time) and the relative inaccessibility of some archival tapes, which exist only as masters. A few bonuses offset the obvious disadvantages of this method. Certainly the process of sampling several shows a year clarified shifts in direction and patterns of continuity even as it blurred the exact moment when a pattern appeared for the first time.

Working on such a productive (indeed, peripatetic) subject presented certain problems, not all of which have I solved to my satisfaction. Finishing the book required setting an arbitrary stopping point for it, and the publication of *Leaving Home* offered the most compelling one. This third volume of Keillor's works marked in print the conclusion of his live broadcasts of *A Prairie Home Companion*, and so represented a convenient and logical turning point in the humorist's career in two media.

On its way to publication, this book has indebted me to a good many people. My biggest debt is to Garrison Keillor himself, who took several hours to talk with me about his work, pointed out factual errors that only he could identify, opened his Prairie Home Companion Archives to me, and granted permission to quote from copyrighted material. Rosalie Miller of Minnesota Public Radio, formerly associate producer of *A Prairie Home Companion* and presently producer of the rebroadcast series, has been continually gracious and helpful—sending me tapes, tracking down names and dates, digging out dusty materials from the basement (twice!!), rescuing me from mistakes, and generally helping me find the paths that I wanted to explore. Except for the obvious problems of dealing with an enormous mass of material, especially nonprint material and documents not considered valuable until recently, I could not have been more fortunate in my research and in being given assistance without interference.

Also aiding my work in Minnesota were Lois Hendrickson of the University of Minnesota Archives and Marcia Pankake, bibliographer for English and American literature at the University of Minnesota Library. Thomas Kigin, general counsel of Minnesota Public Radio, generously shared his recollections of the development of *A Prairie Home Companion* and the American Public Radio network. Donna Avery of Rivertown Trading offered her interpretation of Keillor's public appeal. My dear friends Frederick Langendorf and Marian Rubenfeld generously provided housing, office space, a computer, and an introduction to Twin Cities life. I am grateful to Bob Jansen, librarian for the *Minneapolis Star Tribune*, for photocopies of Keillor's newspaper columns.

This book began when my colleagues and students at the University of Helsinki, particularly Jim Johnson and Markku Henriksson, assured me that other people were indeed interested in the development and rhetoric of Keillor's humor. Seetha Srinivasan of the University Press of Mississippi and Tom Inge, series editor, offered patience and encouragement all along the way; Judith Bailey brought a fresh eye to the difficulties of the manuscript. I am also grateful to Sandra Hanson and Judith Halden-Sullivan, who encouraged me to present my work in progress to my colleagues at LaGuardia Community College of the City University of New York.

John Bryant and Joseph Slade read more of the manuscript than they probably wanted to, and offered valuable advice—some of which I didn't take. Those are the parts that are wrong.

Garrison Keillor

CHAPTER I   **The Matter of Minnesota**

An Introduction

I thought I'd like to talk for a hobby. I'd like to say funny things that couldn't be edited, that no researchers would examine.—

Garrison Keillor to James Traub (1981)

"I want you to know that I've never believed in doing brave and cheerful farewells," Garrison Keillor announced near the beginning of the last broadcast of *A Prairie Home Companion* on Saturday, 13 June 1987. "When I go—I'm sure I speak for all of you—when I go, I want people to throw themselves prostrate—down on the floor, the dirt—whatever's down there—and I wanna hear—I wanna hear weeping and howling, and I want people to throw their arms around my ankles and beg me to stay." The humorist came remarkably close to having his wish come true, certainly closer than anyone at Minnesota Public Radio could have envisioned when the weekly variety hour began in 1974 as what Keillor called a "casual enterprise."[1] The announcement on 14 February of his retirement from radio was national news,[2] and the final program attracted a huge audience. An estimated twenty-two thousand requests for tickets to what became known as the Farewell Performance came pouring into St. Paul's World Theater (renovated especially for the show), far in excess of the theater's capacity.[3] In addition to the 915 winners of the ticket lottery who attended the last show, 4 million regular listeners to the local affiliates of American Public Radio (the network founded to syndicate *A Prairie Home Companion*) heard it on radio, and millions more Americans watched it on the Disney (cable) Channel. The United States Information Agency treated Europe and Scandinavia to a thirty-five-minute excerpt over *The Voice of America*. Australians heard the show two weeks later, and folks who missed the event entirely could order an audio cassette from Minnesota Public Radio or a videotape produced by Disney Home Video. Radio, once dismissed as a dead medium, again captured people's hearts.

No wonder. In the years after Garrison Keillor put Lake Wobegon, Minnesota, on the map, his tales of small-town America bore witness to the childhood idyll of the baby boomers (the postmodern, postgraduate, postpartum generation), reassuring the disillusioned. Keillor's voice, at once sincere and seductive, transported them back to the good old days. When he spun his dreams and conducted what he called his séance on *A Prairie Home Companion* each week, even sushi addicts drew comfort from the smell of tuna hot dish, soul food of the fifties, emanating from the Chatterbox Cafe. In Lake Wobegon the elm trees still flourished, impervious to the Dutch elm disease that denuded the rest of the Midwest. In Lake Wobegon the living was so easy that Main Street had just one traffic light— usually green, at that. In Lake Wobegon, after all, Keillor reminded the nation each week in closing his monologue, the climax of the two-hour variety show, "all the women are strong, all the men are good looking, and all the children are above average."

Although the host had received some two thousand "please don't go" letters,[4] the audience in the World Theater for the Farewell Performance did not rush onstage to grab his ankles and beseech him. Fans did, however, find other ways almost as doting to declare their adoration. The Minnesota Historical Society acquired his suit, autoharp, and other memorabilia, and after Keillor left for Denmark, the curators also asked for his trademark red socks (his assistant could only find half a pair).[5] More predictably, the University of Minnesota Library sought his private literary papers, and devotees across the nation poured into bookstores all summer to reserve copies of *Leaving Home* (1987).[6] After its publication in October, this collection of Lake Wobegon monologues remained on the best-seller list for twenty-two weeks despite equivocal reviews; by 1990 more than two million copies were in print—quite a respectable record, although nothing like the success of his mock-autobiographical *Lake Wobegon Days* (1985), which was on the *New York Times* best-seller list forty-four weeks in hardcover, twenty-one weeks in paperback, and had nearly four million copies in print within five years.[7] And Lake Wobegon loyalists continue to listen to *A Prairie Home Companion*, denying reality by tuning in the reruns aired over 248 stations in forty-four states and the District of Columbia and, for a time, three dozen more in Australia.[8] In rerun, the Old Scout broadcasts more than five hundred hours every week.

This book explores the comic imagination that has inspired such devotion from the normally sedate audiences for public radio and comic fiction. Keillor's popularity places him among our yarn-spinning giants. Not since James Thurber (1894–1961), another mid-westerner turned *New Yorker* writer, has an American humorist so successfully juggled two media. Unlike his contemporaries among local-color humorists—including Roy Blount, Lewis Grizzard, and Fran Leibowitz—Keillor claims a national, mythic dimension for his locale. Like Will Rogers (1879–1935), he has attracted a wide audience for cracker-barrel humor, even serving as the official homespun philosopher for the 1988 Democratic National Convention. And like Mark Twain (1835–1910), Keillor has created a great deal of comic (and not so comic) confusion between his public persona and his private person.

The confusion is part of the story that *Garrison Keillor: A Voice of America* has to tell, and it has little to do with biographical facts. Most acolytes know that Garrison Keillor, born Gary Edward to John and Grace Denham Keillor of Anoka, Minnesota, on 7 August 1942, grew up in Brooklyn Park. His family belonged to the Plymouth Brethren, a fundamentalist sect that has caused the humorist's liberal commentators more discomfort than Keillor himself has apparently felt. By instinct or circumstance, although he enjoyed plenty of childhood companionship, young Gary was a loner during his school days—first in Brooklyn Park, then at Anoka High School (1957–1960), and continuing at the University of Minnesota (1960–1962, 1963–1966, B.A., English).[9] An able student, he channeled his energies into various school newspapers and literary magazines; at the university, where he edited the *Ivory Tower* and won the Academy of American Poets Contest, he also worked on campus radio stations WMMR and KUOM.[10] In November 1969 he began supporting his poetry by hosting *The Morning Program* at KSJR in Collegeville, Minnesota, the first station in what is now the eighteen-member Minnesota Public Radio (MPR) network.[11] Within five years he had achieved local fame as the host of *A Prairie Home Companion* morning show and national recognition as a regular contributor to the *New Yorker*; six years later, in 1980, his Saturday radio program lured a national audience. By 1985, with a best-selling book and a loyal corps of listeners, Garrison Keillor was well on his way to a spot on *Playgirl*'s list of America's ten sexiest men.

Early in his life he discovered his passions for writing, storytelling, music, and radio—not necessarily in that order—but he kept them largely to himself. One of his favorite autobiographical reminiscences, for example, recounts how as a young boy he hid in the closet to sing, imagining that his voice was being broadcast through the microphone represented by the handle of the family Hoover.[12] Although the anecdote has a touch of universality about it (who didn't have similarly grand childhood fantasies?), the image of young Keillor in the closet nonetheless provides an apt, and aptly comic, symbol of the shyness that became his trademark as the host of *A Prairie Home Companion* twenty years later. He veiled his ambitions to write somewhat differently from his desires to perform, but the same conflict over ambition may explain why as a child he wanted to write a book called *Pioneer's Revenge*.[13] In 1956, an eighth-grader "at a time when boys didn't write poetry," as he put it, Gary Edward Keillor adopted the name Garrison. "It sounded a little stiffer, a little bigger. Flags flying," he recalled thirty years later. "I think I was trying to hide behind a name that meant strength and 'don't give me a hard time about this.'"[14] With brief exceptions, including a stint as Garrison Edwards, he has stood (or hidden) behind it ever since, both in print and on the air.

He began radio announcing in 1960 during his freshman year at the University of Minnesota and, except for brief periods, continued until 1987. "Announcing is much easier than parking cars or washing dishes," he explained in 1985, reflecting on the differences among his various college jobs, "and yet it has a kind of status attached to it.[15] But although radio has won him renown and certainly provided an outlet for his writing, Keillor originally saw it mainly as a way to support his fiction and poetry. This sense of radio's subordinate role explains why he has quit broadcasting several times over the past twenty years in order to write full-time, yet never entirely stopped writing to devote more time to his radio broadcasts.

His college years set the pattern for juggling work in the two media. Almost as soon as he entered college he "stumbled into radio," as he put it, by joining the student radio station. A recent version of the story, which varies from time to time, holds that he was so infatuated by a Danish exchange student he had met in high school (she became his second wife in 1985) that in his freshman year of college, when he learned that the Danish Royal Ballet was performing, he went to the campus radio station and offered to interview all the girls for them. He recalls immediately beginning a daily fifteen-minute newscast in which he first imitated Edward R. Murrow's intonation and later David Brinkley's. By the following April he had become station manager.[16]

At the same time, he began participating in the lively literary scene at the University of Minnesota, whose faculty in the early 1960s included John Berryman, James Wright, and Allen Tate. Keillor has fond memories of a graduate poetry seminar that he took with Tate in his junior or senior year. The students wrote in traditional forms—the sestina, villanelle, and sonnet, for example—and met regularly to discuss their poems at Tate's home on Irving Avenue, where he lived with Isabella Gardner. Keillor also recalls studying with James Wright, who offered a humanities course and served as faculty adviser to Delta Phi Lambda, an honorary student organization. When Wright read the apprentice poet's "Nicodemus" at one of the club's workshops, Keillor recalls, "I died with pleasure and gratitude."[17]

The apprentice poet first appeared in print in the *Ivory Tower*, the monthly literary supplement to the *Minnesota Daily*, beginning with "My Child Knew Once Who He Was" in April 1962 and followed by regular contributions until April 1967.[18] His signed work for the college magazine numbers nineteen pieces—stories, book reviews, and poems. In addition, as *Ivory Tower* editor from the beginning of his junior year (October 1964) through the first half of his senior year (January 1966), he wrote at least thirty unsigned editorials and fillers. A surprising number of these early pieces bear the stylistic signature of his later writing. An unsigned story on university organist Heinrich Fleischer in November 1963, for instance, concludes with the sort of hyperbolic detail that often found its way into the Lake Wobegon tales: "He is a man for whom I would turn pages and stand by the pipes and sing 14-note Amens and Halleluiahs."[19]

Keillor resigned as editor in January 1966 to campuswide praise for his "unvarying good taste, journalistic skills, wide-ranging interests and whole-hearted commitment to excellence,"[20] although exactly why he stepped down was a matter of some speculation at the time. His resignation letter cited the need to study more, and he recalls resigning in an effort to stay in school after a series of *I* grades (incompletes) turned into *F*'s, driving his cumulative grade point average below 2.0 and threatening him with academic dismissal. (He averted disaster by earning straight *A*'s after quitting the magazine.)[21] He probably wanted to guarantee his eligibility for the poetry contest later that spring (he won first prize). And he may also have chafed at the recent recommendations of a faculty committee that all student publications receive closer supervision by professionals and governing boards.[22] Regardless of the reason for his resignation, Keillor's colleagues at the *Ivory Tower* were sorry to lose his leadership, and they lauded his "perceptive creativity."[23] By the time he left the University of Minnesota, in June 1967, a year after earning his B.A. in English but before completing the M.A. program, he had acquired nearly six years' experience in both radio and writing.

The range of these student writings might surprise fans who think of Keillor mainly as a comic writer and personality, for his *Ivory Tower* pieces run the gamut from aesthetically serious poetry to campus reportage to beatnik jokes. The earliest work has a strong didactic undercurrent. "My Child Knew Once Who He Was" (1962) mourns the commercialization of Christianity and Christmas, concluding, "My holy child is lost upon / a flood of chalky Jesus dolls." A deeply religious sensibility also pervades other early undergraduate pieces: "Sleepers" (1963), a poem indebted to Wallace Stevens's "Sunday Morning"; "God by Magic" (1964), an editorial attack on the Campus Crusade for Christ; and "Nicodemus" (1965), a highly original poem that won honorable mention in the 1965 American Poets Contest. The concern with ethical questions extends to secular subjects as well. "A Memo from Henry Boothe Luce to His Editors" (1963), for instance, chastises photographers from *Life* for invading J. D. Salinger's privacy. Although evident in the later Lake Wobegon monologues, particularly those of the mid-1980s, the religiosity of the student poems combines with an intellectual and literary earnestness that is rather submerged in the later writing and entirely unfamiliar to those who know Keillor only through *A Prairie Home Companion*.

His comic writing for *Ivory Tower* has a more familiar exuberance, but the pieces anticipate his later work more in their range than in their themes or forms. Few are extended fictions like "Frankie" (1966), a short story about a young man's first great love, or self-effacing personal narratives like "How Can I Be Happy When I Can't Play Hockey Like I Wanna?" (1967), whose subtitle "A Portrait of the Writer as a Young Mucker," might also have served as well for some of the Lake Wobegon monologues. Whether signed or unsigned, Keillor's comic writing in *Ivory Tower* generally sticks to the topical, which in the university setting usually means the academic. The most polished examples include three very different burlesques. "Correspondence: The Brian Cobb Incident" (1965), an epistolary narrative, coyly traces a professor's complaints about a flatulent student through the campus bureaucracy. The self-consciously pompous "Whom Are Us?" (1964) presents a mock interview with someone called "Us" on the purpose of college magazines. "Off to the Smut War" (1964), a fanciful editorial modeled on the *New Yorker's* "Talk of the Town," takes its inspiration from an old local newspaper story, "What Huns Would Do If City Were Captured." Thirty-five years later, Keillor drew on this student story in "How the Savings and Loans Were Saved" (1989), which imagines President George Bush's response to an invasion of Chicago by "vast hordes of barbaric Huns" (42). The revival of his old story points to the continuum between his apprenticeship on the *Ivory Tower* and his post-Wobegon career on the *New Yorker*.

Keillor's first professional credit as an author was a poem, "Some Matters Concerning the Occupant" (1968), published in the *Atlantic* a year after he left school, though he was still working for KUOM, the University's professional noncommercial station. A self-conscious, ironic lyric marked by legalese and religious imagery, the eighteen-line poem identifies threats to humanity in a commonplace notice to tenants:

> "Entrance"
> shall also be taken to mean
> "exit."
> No animals or children are allowed,
> occupant shall not disturb the air
> or drive sharp nails into his hands.
> . . . .
> The space shall be considered void.
>
> This Notice Shall Not Be Destroyed.

This serious, earnest poem differs in form and tone from the humorous fiction that Keillor would soon begin publishing in the *New Yorker*, but it nonetheless hints at what would become the hallmarks of his oral and written tales. Technically, the poem puts clichés and stock phrases in unexpected contexts; thematically, it blends ethical concerns with banal details. The poem is precisely crafted, and it thoroughly exploits the economy of the short form. Together the elements of the poem indicate that two years before the appearance of his first comic sketch in the *New Yorker*, "Local Family Keeps Son Happy" (1970), and some six years before *A Prairie Home Companion* began live broadcasts (1974), Garrison Keillor had begun to find his voice.

Or, rather, voices.

Over the course of nearly twenty years, the Minnesota humorist has spoken through dozens of narrative personas, only one of whom is the celebrated Garrison Keillor, semiofficial chronicler of Lake Wobegon. Nearly all his fifty-odd humorous publications belong to the American comic tradition that Walter Blair has called "a man's voice, speaking"—the mock-oral or vernacular tale whose first-person narrator has speech patterns so authentic and a psychology so realistic that the telling of the tale implies a fully developed character.[24] But seldom is it the same man's voice that is speaking. A few of Keillor's earliest narrators—the slangy baseball player, for example, of "How Are the Legs, Sam?" (1971) and the disc jockey who talks in rhymed country-western lyrics in "On the Road, Almost" (1972)—recall such classic mock-oral speakers as Huckleberry Finn. But Keillor also blends oral and written narrative techniques. His *New Yorker* fiction adapts mock-oral techniques to accommodate amateur *writers* as well as slangy speakers, and most of his tales imply such authors, whom we might consider vernacular voices once removed. In addition to the business reporter of "Snack Firm Maps New Chip Push" (1970), a burlesque promotion of buffalo chips, the roster of these early voices includes an encyclopedia author in "Bangor Man" (1972), a newsletter writer in "Friendly Neighbor" (1973), and a U.S. Department of Agriculture extension sex agent in "Sex Tips" (1971). As the humorist continued toying with narrative voice, his personas encompassed both the sublime and the ridiculous: not only the familiar dramatic monologuists of "My North Dakota Railroad Days" (1975) and "Who We Were and What We Meant by It"

(1984) but also the hard-boiled narrator of "Jack Schmidt, Arts Administrator" (1979) and a confessional Snow White in "My Stepmother, Myself" (1982).

In the context of so many invented voices, remembering that "Garrison" Keillor is an invented signature becomes crucial. At the very least it is a comic mask, a sign of the humorist's public persona; in some instances, it might also serve as an assumed identity, a pseudonym to hide behind. The cacophony cautions against believing too much in any one voice and urges us to focus instead on the essential fictiveness of the storyteller, who continually reinvents himself while narrating the published stories and in the monologues of *A Prairie Home Companion*. The Lake Wobegon tales, whether published or spoken, have characterized Garrison Keillor as a genial yarn spinner who is so traditional that he merely substitutes microphone or typewriter for campfire or cracker barrel. Still, this image is as false as it is appealing.

Keillor himself has cultivated the fictive identity, abetted by innate differences between radio and print. The implied "speaker" of a short story presents few problems for the writer who wants to create a new teller for each first-person narrative. Writers easily shift from one narrator to another without raising doubts about their authorial integrity. On the other hand, the audible "I" of an oral tale implies a fully realized personality, identifiable as the person actually speaking to us and therefore not so easily exchanged. Radio enhances this phenomenon, which is essentially an extreme suspension of disbelief. Thus, in his notorious fictional newscast *War of the Worlds* (1938), Orson Wells was able to rouse listeners to panic about an invasion from Mars. And radio lent powerful credence to the characters of Jack Benny and Gracie Allen, who could never escape the comic personas they created.

In Keillor's case, the contrast between clearly distinct fictions and a continuing series of public performances amounts to a contrast between many represented (or implied) voices and a single persona incarnate, the host of *A Prairie Home Companion*. The Garrison Keillor who welcomed listeners and performers to the show and who told stories about growing up in Lake Wobegon is a performer himself, playing a role created and scripted (sometimes quite literally) by the Garrison Keillor who invented Lake Wobegon and composes stories. The distinction between the public and private Keillors, between performer and author, is as blurred as the distinction between Samuel Clemens and Mark Twain, but Keillor apparently likes it that way.

Keillor's career has more than a few superficial elements in common with Twain's. Both began as regional writers of short comic sketches, went on to write long fictional works drawing on their childhood memories, reaped great success from live performances, became mass-media celebrities, and enjoyed huge personal loyalty. And both have contributed to the American mythology of rural childhood: the image of young Gary aiming an overripe tomato at his sister's behind ranks with that of Tom handing over his whitewash and brush. The popular press was quick to hail Keillor as Twain's successor, and just in case anyone failed to connect the modern humorist with the giant of the past, *Time* photographed Keillor behind a white picket fence, a reminder of the halcyon days of *Tom Sawyer*.[25] The iconography notwithstanding, as a comic writer Keillor is no more the wholesome homespun philosopher than was Twain, whose abiding cynicism is documented in Hamlin Hill's *Mark Twain, God's Fool* (1973).

Keillor and Twain probably resemble each other most in their ability to market themselves as public and commercial properties. As Louis J. Budd demonstrates in *Our Mark Twain* (1983), Samuel Clemens deliberately strove to capitalize on the popularity of Mark Twain and gave careful concern to "the making of his public personality" in news articles as well as personal appearances.[26] Leaving aside whether Keillor's red socks (not to mention his white suit) represent the counterpart of Twain's favorite costume, the Minnesotan gave cause to view his public persona as a creative endeavor even before he began claiming Lake Wobegon as "my hometown." From the start of *A Prairie Home Companion* he made himself a subject of his narratives, and when in 1986 Keillor objected to the writing of his biography, he might well have quoted Twain himself, who protested similarly a century earlier: "I am sorry to object, but I really must. Such books as you propose are not proper to publish during my lifetime. A man's history is his own property until the grave extinguishes his ownership in it. I am strenuously opposed to having books of a biographical character published about me while I am still alive."[27]

One reason Twain objected to biographies was his desire to preserve his public persona from contamination by the facts. Twain didn't record his life story in *The Adventures of Tom Sawyer* (1876) and *The Adventures of Huckleberry Finn* (1885), but he wanted the public to think so and frequently boasted, "All my books are simply autobiographies."[28] But the main reason behind Twain's protest, as Alan Gribben has explained, was his conviction that a writer owns the details of his life as a commodity—that is, a commercial product. Indeed, Gribben maintains, Twain exploited his commercial potential so well that he "led the way in modern-day 'image-making.'"[29] In addition to the more ordinary ways of keeping himself in the public eye, he registered his pen name with the U.S. Patent Office as a trademark and lent it to a number of commercial endeavors, including a self-pasting scrapbook and a history game that he patented himself. More than seventy-five years after his death, the legacy of his commercial interest continues intact: Twain's work remains copyrighted by the Mark Twain Company to this day and will not enter the public domain for some time. Even more important, perhaps, a sizable portion of Twain's public still clings loyally to the image of the genial humorist who reinvented himself as Tom and Huck.

Some of Garrison Keillor's fans have fallen victim to the same temptation, confusing the invented with the real. At a seminar on radio at the Museum of Broadcasting in June 1988, participants insisted that the Lake Wobegon saga was a kind of *roman à clef*, and they dismissed as professional coyness its creator's assertions that Lake Wobegon was an imaginary place based on his experience of many small Minnesota towns—including Freeport, Marine on St. Croix, and Anoka—without representing any of them. Perhaps these listeners did not realize the degree to which their confusion insults the writer's imagination; perhaps they failed to see the humor of such confusion (the reason, as Mark Twain well knew, that newcomers were treated to tall tales as an initiation rite). In any event, the abundant comic incongruities and blurred distinctions of *A Prairie Home Companion* suggest that the confusion between the private writer and his public voice just adds one more joke to the list.

The format of the radio show, as Keillor conceded, was "a throwback."[30] More, it was a blend of elements revived from *The Grand Old Opry* and other programs of radio's golden age. In an era of videotape and satellites the live-broadcast variety hour, the melodramatic playlet with sound effects, and the golden-oldie sing-along were comic anachronisms. Together they signified an amateurism almost as outmoded as Mark Twain's lecture platform or Keillor's favorite costume, the bare-ankle trousers and loud red tie and suspenders of the classic hayseed. As a narrative counterpart to the hick's costume (irrelevant to radio in any case) Keillor exploited a pose of amateurishness that granted him the license to spin his Lake Wobegon yarns. Glitches in the live performances conveyed his authenticity and veracity; the absence of slick performance values gave the impression that he wasn't performing at all. Sincerity only becomes an issue, however, because Lake Wobegon is a fiction. As in all tall tales, the fun arises from the tension between the *appearance* of realism and the *awareness* of fantasy, as in the parodic noncommercial commercials for the Fearmonger's Shoppe ("serving all your phobia needs since 1954") and the nonnewsworthy, digressive "News from Lake Wobegon," a mixture of recent events and misty reminiscences set in "the little town that time forgot and the decades cannot improve."

The program took a while to reach its most familiar form, however. It began in November 1969 when Keillor took over *The Morning Program* at KSJR in Collegeville, the first station of Minnesota Educational Radio. In October 1971 Keillor and the program moved to KSJN in St. Paul, the new flagship station of MER. The miscellany of recorded music and disc-jockey banter was broadcast four days a week in the morning drive-time slot. At the same time the show began to be called *A Prairie Home Companion* and to carry "commercials" from such imaginary sponsors as Jack's Auto Repair of Lake Wobegon. Keillor left the show in November 1973 and returned in July 1974, when *A Prairie Home Companion* split essentially in two. Keillor continued to host the weekday morning program under the old drive-time format until April 1982, and he also launched the Saturday evening program, which featured live performances of music, skits, special acts, and topical humor.

Yet even after he had found his niche as the writer and host of the Saturday show, Keillor did not immediately discover the narrative potential of Lake Wobegon. Until 1976 it remained an insiders' joke, a woebegone place in "the outer boonies," as 1970s slang might have put it. The characters and situations had already begun to be sketched out in advertisements for Jack's Auto Repair and Art's Baits and Quiet Harbor. What Keillor needed was a perspective on his local-color material. That perspective lies at the heart of what we might call the Matter of Minnesota, with all due respect to Homer (for the Matter of Troy), Sir Thomas Malory (for the Matter of Britain), and Mark Twain (for the Matter of Hannibal).[31]

The Matter of Minnesota involves much more than locating stories in Minnesota towns, and it evolved differently in print and on radio. The mature radio monologue depended on four main elements: creating a distinctive place and cast of characters; developing incidents and following characters in real time, week by week and season by season; assuming a flow of events beyond the limits of the anecdotes themselves; and balancing distance or intimacy on a topic for the desired comic or sentimental effect. These elements did not appear all at once, however, and they continued to evolve over the life of *A Prairie Home Companion*. Keillor hit upon the basic eccentricity of Lake Wobegon when he invented Jack's Auto Repair, and from time to time he linked Jack's services and commercials to the passage of time and seasons, but only in 1976 did he begin to exploit fully the narrative potential of real time by touting Visitors' Day in Lake Wobegon and by reading letters from Barbara Ann Bunsen.

These two weekly features provided distinct points of view that later merged in the extended monologues of the mid-1980s. The announcement of Visitors' Day events allowed Keillor to speak about Lake Wobegon in his own voice, or that of the stereotypical radio announcer, and so to convey the humorous perspective of the outsider looking at the natives. Barbara Ann's letters, on the other hand, provided the more complex viewpoint of first-person narration from a native Wobegonian. Although "The News from Lake Wobegon" would appear to have evolved in a straight line from the weekly promotion of Visitors' Day, in fact Barbara Ann's letters contributed more directly than the newscasts to the development of the Lake Wobegon myth. Both formats justified reading a script in front of the studio audience, to be sure; the announcer's "report" or Barbara's "letter" provided an alternative to memorizing and reciting a story. But by 1977 Keillor evidently realized that epistolary narration offered a host of rhetorical advantages unavailable to the mock newsreader or chronicler. Either the announcement of upcoming events or the reading of letters could establish the illusion that Lake Wobegon coexisted in real time with the real world (two weeks in Lake Wobegon corresponding to two weeks of radio shows), but theoretically speaking, letters hold out far greater opportunities to convey the illusion of reality.

Barbara Ann (named for the heroine of the Beach Boys' hit song)[32] could assume that her readers knew the people and events she mentioned, and her letters to her parents, Clarence and Arlene, are accordingly allusive and incomplete. (The comic formula of her letters took the pattern to the extreme, since she characteristically signed off with a bombshell revelation thrown in as a minor detail.) The legacy of Barbara Ann's letters to Keillor's stories for his own voice, therefore, goes far beyond either the comic display of a naïve and eccentric Wobegonian confronting the outside world or the establishment of narrative routines such as "Everything is just fine, I am all right, so don't worry, everything is o.k." and "Hugs & kisses, Barbara Ann" followed by a "P.S." With these letters, recited at irregular intervals from June 1976 through January 1981, Keillor balanced affection and ridicule as he conveyed the impression that Lake Wobegon and its inhabitants had an ongoing life entirely independent of him. The letters implied that a whole community knew the town's history, which consequently acquired an aura of objective reality, and they hinted that he had simply chosen highlights of the saga to share. The strategy worked. Two radiologists from St. Cloud Hospital were kidding around when they suggested to Keillor that Father Emil try daily cancer treatments from their new linear accelerator; the listener from Midland, Michigan, who sent thirteen dollars to clean the pigeon droppings off the "Statue of the Unknown Norwegian in St. Paul" was not.[33]

Keillor concedes that reading the letters from Barbara Ann amounted to a "trick" borrowed from Cliff Arquette, who as Charlie Weaver on Jack Paar's television shows read letters from his relatives back on Mount Idy.[34] Trick or not, reading a letter instead of speaking from memory underlines the literariness of the early Lake Wobegon tales. It took time for Keillor to develop patterns of oral narration. As he did, the monologues grew in length and complexity. They averaged just three to six minutes long from 1976 until the show began regular national broadcasts on 3 May 1980. But then the Lake Wobegon stories began inching toward twenty minutes. Between 1984 and 1987, the monologues generally ranged from twenty minutes to half an hour.

Even as he was finding its use for oral storytelling, the Matter of Minnesota provided a bridge between Keillor's radio work and his writing. Some of his earliest tales for the *New Yorker* reworked characters and ideas from the morning version of *A Prairie Home Com-*

panion. In February 1973, just before "The Slim Graves Show" appeared in the *New Yorker,* the Minnesota Educational Radio program guide, *Preview,* carried a thumbnail sketch of "musical director" Graves, along with other Lake Wobegonians serving the Old Scout as "faithful laborers in the broadcasting vineyard whose reward too often (alas) is merely their proximity to the great."[35] The character in the *New Yorker* story, however, does not hail from Lake Wobegon, nor does he work on radio, though the story hinges on his intense involvement with radio as a listener. Similarly, *Minneapolis Tribune* columnist Will Jones recognized the radio origins of "Sex Tips" (1971), which featured Harley Peters, the U.S. Department of Agriculture extension sex agent whom Keillor said he had known since college days.[36]

His consistent juggling of the two media from his real college days onward suggests that Keillor discovered early in his career that neither medium by itself provided him an adequate creative outlet. "This has been an enduring conflict for me," he conceded in a seminar on radio at the Museum of Broadcasting. "Writers create something, and it goes on and it finds its own route when you're done with it. . . . [Written stories] are reprinted and remain as fresh or as interesting, we hope, as they were in the beginning. Whereas *A Prairie Home Companion,* . . . when it was over on Saturday night, it was all done. The liveness of it, the intimacy of it, were so much a part of the value of it that you couldn't separate them from it."[37] In the introduction to his first collection of stories, *G.K. the D.J* (1977), a slim folio of nineteen sketches "written *against* radio," he confessed that the very intangibility that attracted him to radio also left him feeling dissatisfied: "Radio eats everything, it eats constantly, and when you are done with your shift at the zoo, what do you have to show for it? *Nothing, dear God.*"[38]

Publishing recordings of selected monologues offered one solution. Putting his oral stories into print was another. Keillor did both—first in *A Prairie Home Album* (1972) and later in *Lake Wobegon Days* (1985). Together with the monologue texts collected in *Leaving Home* (1987) and the seasonal monologues recorded in *News from Lake Wobegon* (1983), a four-cassette set boxed to resemble Land o'Lakes butter, the series of publications put much of his best oral material into the hands of his audience. Since his retirement from *A Prairie Home Companion,* several more collections, both print and audio, have appeared.

Nonetheless, the Matter of Minnesota remained largely a Minnesota matter for several years. Minnesota Educational Radio continued to add stations—four between 1971 and 1975—expanding the audience within Minnesota and in neighboring states. In September 1974, shortly after Keillor's Saturday broadcasts began, MER changed its name to Minnesota Public Radio. In February 1979 MPR began offering the program to public radio stations throughout the country through National Public Radio. When NPR declined to offer the show a weekly slot, MPR decided to form its own network, using a satellite uplink acquired in the late seventies. MPR joined with other stations actively producing their own programs, including WNYC in New York, to found the American Public Radio network, which an MPR official described as "a cooperative venture," and made *A Prairie Home Companion* its primary offering.[39] On 3 May 1980 the American Public Radio network began weekly live broadcasts of the Saturday evening program, and Keillor's voice began to be heard regularly from coast to coast.

The first subscribers, concentrated in college towns, numbered sixty-five public radio stations in twenty-seven states. In the spirit of alternative broadcasting that nurtured *A Prairie Home Companion* in the first place, Keillor jokingly called the network the Powdermilk Broadcasting System, a bald poke at the Public Broadcasting System, also PBS for short. Four years later, as the program celebrated its tenth anniversary, the American Public Radio network had grown to 235 stations, and the Matter of Minnesota had become entrenched in American popular culture.

It remained visibly present there for the rest of the decade, claiming more and more Lake Wobegon boosters as Keillor's reputation as a storyteller spread. By the time Keillor left *A Prairie Home Companion* in 1987, his fictional little town had acquired a presence of its own. "Lake Wobegon (Fictional Town)" had been listed in the index to the *St. Paul Pioneer Press and Dispatch* since 1984, and was very nearly included on Minnesota maps of the American Automobile Association in the mid-1980s.[40] A 1987 study officially titled *Nationally Normed Elementary Achievement Testing in America's Public Schools: How All Fifty States Are above the National Average*, by John Jacob Cannell, M.D., became known as "The Lake Wobegon Report," and the marvel in question was dubbed "the Lake Wobegon phenomenon."[41] Less comically, we might consider the following local report to the national news pages of the *New York Times*, far from the cornfields of the prairie:

UTOPIA, Tex.—All the children of Garrison Keillor's fictitious Lake Wobegon may be above average, but that would hardly suffice here in Utopia. . . .

"It almost is what Sir Thomas More wrote about," said Ron Bownds. . . . "It's pretty much crime-free and drug-free. It's pretty close to perfect."

Utopia has at least as much in common with Sir Garrison as Sir Thomas. In some ways, it seems like a sprightlier Texas version of Lake Wobegon, transplanted to the rolling hills and maple and cedar groves of the Sabinal Canyon about 80 miles west of San Antonio.

Instead of the Chatterbox Cafe, there's the Lost Maple Inn, which people bill as the friendliest cafe in Texas. There are not many Norwegian bachelor farmers around, but there are the "Senior Seniors," who carry on a marathon domino game every day in a vacant storefront. It's hard to find any Powdermilk biscuits, but people [from] Uvalde or Bandera come for the deer sausage and jerky made at the Boyce & Davenport general store.[42]

With such evidence that Lake Wobegon has entered the American lexicon, it's no wonder that "Garrison Keillor Lake Wobegon" was the answer to a *New York Times Magazine* double acrostic puzzle,[43] or that the Taft Group in Washington, D.C., offered a prepublication copy of *The Directory of International Corporate Giving in America* to "Clarence Bunsen, Sons of Knute Temple, Municipal Building, Lake Wobegeon, MN 55101." Bunsen is, after all, one of the leading citizens of Lake Wobegon. In the late 1980s, Lake Wobegon had a claim to the geography of American humor much stronger than that of P. D. Q. Bach's University of Southern North Dakota at Hoople, if not quite that of Yoknapatawpha County, Mississippi, or Hannibal, Missouri.

As *A Prairie Home Companion* grew surprisingly successful, fans began actively participating in the fantasy, if only as a joke. The public response included not only the predictable correspondence from listeners (from as far away as Tasmania) who asked for the lyrics to a comic song or offered praise about a particular show but also a regular stream of gifts—both sincere and comic—indicating the listeners' imaginative investment in the Lake Wobegon mythology. Devotees sent letters reporting on recent visits to the town. Others, perhaps inspired by the "True Facts" section in *National Lampoon*, sent photographs of the Prairie Home Cemetery (for which the show was in fact named) and Bob's Bank, Hotel Minnesota and the Chatterbox Cafe—even the Woe-Be-Gone Forest. The usual purpose, as the correspondent who sent a photo of Jack's Tours put it, was evidence "that the truth is sometimes stranger than fiction."[44] One fan, inspired by Saul Steinberg's famous cover for the *New Yorker*, sent a full-sized drawing, "The Bostonian View of the World," locating Lake Wobegon between the Berkshires and the Pacific, just south of Canada and north of the rust belt. Keillor's spurious commercials inspired some listeners to send in suggestions for new products, but others made truth of the fictions. A box of Raw Bits cereal, stained bags of Powdermilk Biscuits ("in the big blue box with a picture of a biscuit on the cover"), official correspondence on Bunsen Motors letterhead, a needlepoint work announcing "Happiness is a Lake Wobegon Christmas"—all demonstrated the audience's desire to participate in this fictional world.

Public recognitions followed the private ones. The archives of *A Prairie Home Companion* contain dozens of elegant certificates, engraved keys to the city, and other testimonials. These include a pastel rendering of "A Good Night at the Sidetrack Tap" by cartoonist Michael Mitchell of the Hanna-Barbera Company, a resolution introduced before the Minnesota House of Representatives by Representative Gil Gutknecht of Rochester "directing the correction of the surveying and mapping errors that have continually resulted in the omission of the town of Lake Wobegon and Mist County from maps of Minnesota,"[45] and a proclamation from the Commonwealth of Kentucky Department of Agriculture designating "the Honorable Garrison Keillor . . . An Honorary Commissioner of Agriculture." Minnesotans had begun the proceedings long before Philadelphia and Los Angeles began receiving the weekly broadcasts. As early as 1976, when the live radio show was only two years old, Lieutenant Governor Rudy Perpich included a sample tape of *A Prairie Home Companion* in the Minnesota Time Capsule established by the state bicentennial commission.

Minnesota Public Radio and the staff of *A Prairie Home Companion* capitalized on the rising national interest and actively encouraged the audience to participate in the Lake Wobegon fantasy. The tenth anniversary show in July 1984 prompted the publication of a souvenir program complete not only with fairly conventional photos of bygone shows but also with the business cards of Lake Wobegon's primary merchants and display ads for Powdermilk Biscuits, Hotel Minnesota, and (with a nod to Ronald Reagan, then running for reelection) the Fearmonger's Shoppe ("Do you feel safer now than you did four years ago? Isn't it time you did?").[46] Tickets for the Friday concert or Saturday live broadcast of the tenth anniversary show were sold for $100, $50, and $25 and the proceeds used for the restoration of the World Theater; additional funds came from sale of T-shirts and buttons bearing the message "I SAVED THE WORLD (THEATER).[47] On other occasions, MPR fund-raisers also produced Powdermilk Biscuit T-shirts, Lake Wobegon sweatshirts ("Sumus Quod Sumus"), and bumper stickers hailing "Lake Wobegon: Gateway to Central Minnesota."[48] The bumper sticker went into orbit on the Space Shuttle Columbia for seven days, 12–18 January 1986, with NASA astronauts Pinky Nelson and James Buchli, who sent Keillor an aerial photo of Minnesota with the comment, "Unfortunately, Lake Wobegon is just off the picture."

Encouraging fans to become co-conspirators in the Lake Wobegon fantasy extended the basic joke behind the myth. Intensifying the joke made it funnier, but some people got sufficiently caught up in the fantasy that they began to lose sight of the basic lie. They started trying to locate the town in real geography and to uncover the real history and biography behind the tall stories. However charming as hero-worship, these efforts are basically faulty, and they miss the point about Mist County.

They also denigrate the storyteller's gift. Attempts to find the model for Lake Wobegon reduce an astonishing feat of imagination to the simple appropriation of history and geography. Pressed by one loyalist to confirm her suggestion that Lake Wobegon lies in a northern Minnesota county whose Indian name actually means "mist," Keillor patiently insisted, "My Mist County is a pun."[49] And while we have to consider the possibility that he might want to throw his fans off the track (a practice that delighted William Faulkner, for instance), Keillor truly seems less interested in protecting his fiction than in reclaiming it as a product of his imagination. The tall humor of "the little town that time forgot" depends on our recognition that time cannot really forget what never existed.

Furthermore, the biographical or historical elements of the Lake Wobegon saga have more to teach us about the fictionalization process than about the myth itself. Michael Fedo provides a case in point

in *The Man from Lake Wobegon* (1987) when he apportions elements of "the little town that time forgot" among the various Minnesota towns where the humorist lived. Fedo observes quite correctly
that the humorist lived in Freeport and Marine on St. Croix, whose
"combined populations barely exceed Lake Wobegon's 942 souls,"[50]
but these truths in and of themselves explain very little. Certainly
they do not account for the fictional census any better than Keillor's
birthdate, *1942*.

By contrast, a good many insights into Lake Wobegon and the
creative process emerge from considering the evolution of the Lake
Wobegon anthem, "The Song of the Exiles," which began in 1972
as a ballad for a show that Keillor did with Tom Art and Gregory
Bitz in Rochester, Minnesota.[51] The original verses describe leaving
his Freeport farm to get a city job. Keillor revised the ballad primarily
by substituting *Wobegon* for *Freeport* and *biscuits* for *oats*, but these
simple changes do not imply that Keillor considered the two towns
interchangeable. On the contrary, he rendered his sentiments about
leaving "my prairie home" a good deal more complex by replacing
Free-port's connotations of liberation with the ambivalence of *Wobegon*, which can signify either forlornness or the demand "Be gone,
woe!" In addition, the facts surrounding the revision—that unlike
much of his old material these verses remained in the files for him
to work on again, that he chose not to invent something entirely
new as the Lake Wobegon anthem, that he decided to transform
a poignant song of farewell to an ironic song of absence—all suggest
that the writer remained dissatisfied with his text until it expressed
feelings about a fictional place, a place other than Freeport.

For that reason, *Garrison Keillor: A Voice of America* offers critical analysis of humor, not biographical analysis of the humorist.
The historical development of *A Prairie Home Companion* detailed
in chapters 2 and 3 reveals that the Lake Wobegon myth was shaped
by two separate processes. On the one hand, the early, obviously
invented narratives about Jack's Auto Repair gradually became more
realistic, acquiring more concrete and banal details while moving
away from the outrageous or bombastic premise. On the other hand,
authentic details from Keillor's life underwent progressive fictionalization. Offhand comments about growing up in Anoka and Brooklyn
Park gave way little by little to set pieces about "Lake Wobegon,
Minnesota, my hometown." Chapters 4 through 6 focus on Keillor's

writing for print: *Lake Wobegon Days*, the short fiction, and *Leaving Home*. It is too early to appraise the writing in his fourth book, *We Are Still Married* (1989), a miscellany of short fiction, Lake Wobegon monologues, previously unsigned pieces from the *New Yorker*, and comic poetry (including a few verses formerly attributed to Margaret Haskins Durber, Lake Wobegon's poet laureate). *Leaving Home*, by contrast, contains a collection of Lake Wobegon stories drawn from the last few years of *A Prairie Home Companion*, and so forms a thematically and chronologically convenient frame for assessing the first stage of the humorist's career.

For many devotees, of course, the essence of Garrison Keillor's humor has nothing to do with the evolution of *A Prairie Home Companion* or the rhetoric of comic narration and everything to do with the Matter of Minnesota, the details of the Lake Wobegon stories themselves. Yet to focus on the Bunsens and Tolleruds as if they existed independently of the humorist's imagination is to gloss over the most astonishing aspect of Keillor's mythmaking: that he created Lake Wobegon and all its hosts, and found ways of giving them the spirit—if not the actual breath—of life. Unlike Thomas Pynchon, Robert Coover, and other American comic writers of the 1970s who also tried to construct what Philip Roth called "the passageway from the imaginary that comes to seem real to the real that comes to seem imaginary,"[52] Keillor did not mix fantasy with historical fact. Instead, he created an alternative world—a hybrid of fantasy and memory, satire and sentiment—where some saw themselves and others saw fools.

It is a strategy born of ambivalence, and it serves the same purpose as the footnotes in *Lake Wobegon Days* and the character doubling in *Leaving Home*: to manage conflicting feelings by dramatizing them. We cannot doubt that Lake Wobegon is "the little town that time forgot, that the decades cannot improve," but the description coyly begs and evades the crucial question: whether Lake Wobegon is already perfect or absolutely incorrigible. As an exercise in humor, this famous description doesn't differ very much from asking audiences to sing "Now I Lay Me Down to Sleep" to the tune of "Tell Me Why," in two-part harmony, as in fact Keillor did at *A Prairie Home Companion*'s Farewell Performance. The reassuring words of the children's prayer don't exactly clash with the sweet old song, but the combination has more than a tinge of comic incongruity.

The Matter of Minnesota derives its energy from just this conflict between sincerity and satire, keeping the Lake Wobegon tales lively and unpredictable.

The ambivalence is certain—it pervades all Keillor's local-color humor—but sincere feeling doesn't rule out comic playfulness. His humor, whether it draws on the Matter of Minnesota or the Matter of New York City (recently developed for his new radio show, *American Radio Company of the Air*), blurs the point where the admiration ends and the ridicule begins. Garrison Keillor embraces both. So he quite justifiably asserts that Lake Wobegon monologues don't aim at nostalgia, in part because such places as Lake Wobegon do in fact continue to exist but also because, as he insisted at the tenth anniversary performance, "I'm not nostalgic for them." The childhood of his monologues is a time of embarrassment and pain, best remembered from the safety of adulthood, although the intense pleasures of childhood endure as moments of rapture. It is this mixture of misery and joy that gives his memories such power, just as the blend of admiration and contempt gives the Lake Wobegon myth its ring of truth. Still, few of us would willingly exchange the powers and privileges of adulthood for the insecurities of adolescence, however unpleasant our burdens, although the fantasy of doing so has great appeal to a generation of baby boomers watching their children reach maturity.[53] Whatever wistful memories Lake Wobegon evokes of a happier time have to do not only with childhood but also with rural life, complete with narrow-mindedness.

Nostalgia is easy—"Nostalgia comes out of a faucet. You can get nostalgic like you run yourself a warm bath" (15 Dec. 1984)—but portraiture is hard, especially when the model exists only the imagination. That so many fans have sought Lake Wobegon in the real landscape testifies to Keillor's success, but credit must go to the writer's creativity, the performer's persuasiveness, and the fans' willing suspension of disbelief at least as much as to the author's own memories. Nevertheless, the confusion between the real and the imagined, author and performer, hints at a key reason for his success. Like Mark Twain, Garrison Keillor has come to embody his myth.

That is both an advantage and a liability as Keillor enters the next phase of his career, which promises a more equal balance between radio and print. Resigning from *A Prairie Home Companion* may not have made him homesick for Lake Wobegon, but it evidently made him long for radio, and the first few weeks of *American Radio Company of the Air* have shown that he will discover how to mine the Matter of New York City as he did the Matter of Minnesota—by trial and error as he goes along. Inaugurated on 25 November 1989, the new live variety show was broadcast by Minnesota Public Radio over the American Radio Network from the seedy annex of the Brooklyn Academy of Music, the Majestic Theater, a fitting successor to the run-down World of St. Paul. An urbanized version of *A Prairie Home Companion*, *American Radio Company of the Air* replaces country gospel with do-wop and soul music, and features radio dramas about New York characters and problems, performed, appropriately enough, by the Broadway Local Radio Theatre, an acting company named for a subway line. Lacing a familiar down-home atmosphere with cosmopolitanism provides a new context for his tales of Lake Wobegon as well as an opportunity to attract minority listeners to public radio. As an adopted New Yorker and an exiled Minnesotan, Keillor can speak intimately, confessionally, and critically about both places while he maintains a running comic contrast between them.

At the same time, he can attract local boosters in the audiences of both markets. Despite his response to charges that Lake Wobegon didn't have any African-Americans or other minorities (rural Minnesota doesn't have any), he has complained for some time that public broadcasting serves too small a segment of the American public: mainly white, college-educated fans of classical music. The title of *American Radio Company of the Air* avoids the regional specificity of *A Prairie Home Companion*, because the program was originally planned to rotate among a variety of cities in the quest for a more national image and a wider, more diversified audience. Nonetheless, the ticket holders at the Majestic Theater in the first six weeks largely remained the white, middle-class classical music fans who tune in to WNYC-FM.

Still, Keillor has come a long way from July 1974, when the theater audience for the first live broadcast of *A Prairie Home Companion* numbered only twelve. The first New York show sold out within a week, and although *American Radio Company of the Air* needs some time to find its identity, in his first monologue Keillor committed himself once again to the artistry of spontaneous performance. "I believe in that," he told the audience, describing how his parents pretended that the house was not really a mess when visitors arrived unexpectedly. "I believe in pretense. I believe that sometimes you just have to look reality in the eye and deny it" (25 Nov. 1989).

The broadcast schedule for *American Radio Company of the Air*—six weeks of live broadcasts followed by six weeks of reruns of *A Prairie Home Companion*—makes clear that Keillor will no longer allow radio to dominate his work. The alternating schedule protects his time for writing in both his media. And rightly so, since his stories for print give voice to a different set of gifts. Unlike the tall tales of western and southwestern humorists, Keillor's fiction doesn't rely mainly on a humor of character or situation, though the stories have wonderfully eccentric characters and a range of comically bizarre and banal situations. The humor of his fiction is verbal and literary, as befits a writer with aspirations as a poet. (He still reads and writes poetry and was discouraged by the reception of the poem that opens *We Are Still Married*).[54] He has yet to publish the novel that he was working on when he began the morning version of *A Prairie Home Morning Show* in 1971 and yet to fulfill the novelistic promise of *Lake Wobegon Days*. An energetic and prolific writer-performer for the last twenty years, he now has the time and financial freedom to write what he wants, and he can meet the apparently unending appetite of his fans for the Matter of Minnesota through recordings of old monologues, skits, and songs. As a result, Garrison Keillor enters the second phase of his career poised to exploit even further what he has called "a tremendous talent for lying" (25 Nov. 1989).

In my emphasis on the art rather than the artist, however, I do not mean to gloss over Keillor's ambivalence toward fame. Of course, we might have expected such a reaction from the author of the shy Americans' manifesto, "Shy Rights: Why Not Pretty Soon?" (1981).[55] Actually, however, it was a long time in coming. A former journalist himself, Keillor graciously gave interview after interview for a dozen years to publications as different as *Mother Earth News* and *Esquire*.[56] He took *A Prairie Home Companion* on extended tours through big cities such as Atlanta, Chicago, and San Francisco and small towns such as Red Wing and Mankato, Minnesota—burgs like his beloved Lake Wobegon. But he chafed at the less gratifying consequences of celebrity. When admirers began staking out his house in St. Paul and journalists second-guessed his love life, Keillor decided to return to what he called "the life of a shy person" by abandoning

A Prairie Home Companion and leaving Minnesota for a quieter (or at least less scrutinized) life in Denmark. But it wasn't satisfactory, and he returned to the United States a few months later, this time choosing the quintessential big city over the classic small town. Lake Wobegon's favorite son settled in New York and took up residence at the *New Yorker*.

His second relocation within three months startled his fans even more than the first. Those who considered Keillor the embodiment of homespun American values could forgive him for putting true love and family above his career, but they could not envision him amid the bright lights and sleaze of Times Square, much less in the company of the urbanely eastern literary magazine. The move was less surprising, however, to MPR colleagues and aficionados of the stories in *Happy to Be Here*. Staff members of *A Prairie Home Companion* saw the beginning of the end in the tenth anniversary show, attributing their feelings less to anything specific than to a general aura that the end was around the corner.[57] In fact, Keillor had already begun hinting at his dissatisfaction in his comic chronology for the souvenir program, whose predictions for December 1984 include this presage of doom: "GK takes job as afternoon DJ on 1000-watter in Biwabik, commutes on Saturdays until PHC is shifted to Mondays . . . and renamed 'Rural Feminist Forum.'"[58] Despite this apparent longing for the small-town idyll, however, readers of the *New Yorker* fiction could see Keillor's more jaundiced view of rural innocence, already evident in his debut story, "Local Family Keeps Son Happy," and very well developed by 1975, by which time "The Slim Graves Show," "Friendly Neighbor," and "My North Dakota Railroad Days" had all appeared. Generally speaking, fans of his Lake Wobegon material (including *Lake Wobegon Days* and *Leaving Home*) represent a different group from the admirers of his *New Yorker* fiction. Such details suggest that when Keillor characterized his move from St. Paul to Copenhagen as the "collapse of an American career," as he put it in the introduction to *Leaving Home*, he was not indulging in comic hyperbole or whining ungenerously about the celebrity's loss of privacy as much as he was acknowledging and mourning the conflict between public obligations and private desires, between the sentimental Lake Wobegon monologues, on the one hand, and satiric *New Yorker* fiction, on the other.

Keillor underscored his desire for privacy when Michael Fedo began work on The *Man from Lake Wobegon*, a biography so unauthorized that Keillor's attorneys discouraged Keillor's acquaintances from being interviewed and denied permission to quote published material.[59] Fedo himself took over the project from another writer, who decided not to proceed in the face of Keillor's protests.[60] Whatever the reasons for his objections (obvious possibilities include concern for his reputation and disapproval of that biographer), one salutary effect has emerged: the emphasis has shifted from the writer to his work. That is where I prefer to keep it, although Keillor has in various ways assisted my research. We have met only three times, when he reviewed his old University of Minnesota writings, answered questions about his work and career, and pointed out some errors of biographical and historical fact, but he has also been generous in permission to quote published and archival material. The writer's discomfort with fame has not imposed itself on this book.

Nonetheless, Keillor's ambivalence toward fame and anonymity has become a significant element of his career as a humorist. As we might have inferred from his farewell joke about being begged by his audience to stay, the author's desire for the quiet life conflicts with the performer's need for an audience. He joked about it again at the Second Farewell in New York City, 3–4 June 1988, when he told the audience that he had to return to the United States because he had no fans in Denmark. His ambivalence has also found expression in the other medium in which he works. *Leaving Home*, originally intended to complement Keillor's emigration to Denmark, appeared with fortuitous irony just after his return to New York. Six months later, in March 1988, came the announcement of the Second Annual Farewell Performance of *A Prairie Home Companion*, marketed with a comically equivocal slogan: "It was so much fun leaving, we're coming back to say goodbye again."[61] That April, the *New Yorker* published "Meeting Famous People" (1988), a black-humorous story about performers who crave and abhor hero-worship. Ten months after that, Keillor returned to the stage for a New York performance with the typically self-deprecating title "A Pretty Good Night at Carnegie Hall" on 9 February 1989 (following out-of-town previews in New Haven and other northeastern locations). A third farewell took place in Los Angeles, 9–10 June 1989, three months after the publication of *We Are Still Married* and amid announcements that Keillor would launch *American Radio Company of the Air* in the fall.[62] By June 1990, as the staff of *A Prairie Home Companion* geared up for the Fourth Annual Farewell, the company of the new show braced for its second season. In short, rumors of the humorist's retirement were highly premature and greatly exaggerated, and the conflict between Garrison Keillor's public and private lives has yielded to the more interesting struggle of finding appropriate media and satisfying material for his creative voice.

CHAPTER 2   *A Prairie Home Companion*

Companion

Homespun and Hip

We are not architects but companions, and I believe, as Scripture says, "here have we no continuing city." By this, St. Paul meant we should not use very much recording tape.
—GK the DJ, (1977)

Listening to a tape of the first live performance of *A Prairie Home Companion* would astonish fans-come-lately. Not that they would find it unrecognizable, despite the country twang and higher pitch of Keillor's voice, for the variety-hour format of music and humor was already fixed. The ninety-minute program broadcast on 6 July 1974 from Macalester College in St. Paul opened with the host's folksy rendition of "Hello, Love" and featured a combination of folk music performed by guitarist-singers Bill Hinkley and Judy Larson and once-popular songs by Vern Sutton and Philip Brunelle of the Minnesota Opera Company, all of whom returned regularly to banter with Keillor over the years.[1] (In a fine touch of symmetry, Sutton sang John Philip Sousa's "Stars and Stripes Forever" on the last broadcast as he had on the first.) Still, the absence of the mature show's signature element, Keillor's elaborate monologue detailing the lives of Lake Wobegon's citizenry, would surprise and disappoint admirers who had not followed *A Prairie Home Companion* from the start. Lake Wobegon had been a feature of Keillor's broadcasts since the fall of 1971, almost three years before he began the live show, but not until 1977 did it evolve into "the little town that time forgot," and nearly half a dozen more years passed before Lake Wobegon replaced Brooklyn Park and Anoka as "my hometown." In the early days, Lake Wobegon existed simply as the location for imaginary commercial sponsors of Keillor's morning program for public radio KSJN in St. Paul—that is, as an insiders' joke shared by Keillor's morning audience. Lake Wobegon helped define the playful character of the new show, whose joking tone expressed the spirit of the 1970s: self-consciously amateur, slightly politicized, and decidedly camp. The highly polished, staunchly sentimental performances of later years must be examined and understood in light of these early values.

The most important of the early production values centered on the live broadcast itself, which by 1974 represented an eccentric technique. High fidelity recording had long since displaced live performance, and radio was coming to depend more and more on automated "carts," the prerecorded tape cartridges introduced in 1960 for smooth integration of music, station identification, and commercials. In contrast to the technological leap represented by the carts, live broadcasting before a studio audience was more than just a "throwback," as Keillor has described his format.[2] It was an extreme departure from established practice for both the disc jockey and the station. (Of course, the very name *disc jockey* indicates the reliance on records and other storage media.) Unlike broadcasters of the thirties and forties—the heyday of live radio—KSJN did not even have a studio suitable for an audience.

Oddly enough, the live broadcasts grew out of the program's more conventional origins as a morning music program for KSJR in Collegeville. Keillor took over *The Morning Program* in November 1969. In an interview years later he said he first began talking about Lake Wobegon while he was at KSJR: "It slipped in gradually as a way of talking about my relatives. It created a little bit of distance.[3] *The Morning Program* mixed popular and classical music with humor in an eclectic format apparently encouraged by William Kling, the founder and president of Minnesota Public Radio, known as Minnesota Educational Radio (MER) until September, 1974. One version of the show's history credits Kling with the format—"Bill said: 'Why don't you play a little Joni Mitchell once in a while.' Garrison played the Beach Boys instead, and the rest is history"—but Keillor recalls that the head of MER was primarily interested in running a classical music station.[4] At any rate, the history nearly ended in 1971, during

Kling's stint with the Corporation for Public Broadcasting. An interim station manager offended the morning show host with a memo suggesting that his format was alienating affluent members devoted to classical music.[5] Keillor, who objected as much to the medium of this complaint as to its message, resigned in February and was not mollified for nine months.[6]

In October 1971 Keillor returned to *The Morning Program* when it began to be broadcast from KSJN, the new flagship station of MER, in St. Paul. Lake Wobegon became a feature of the show, now rechristened *A Prairie Home Companion*. In these early days, however, he called the place *Lake Woebegone* and set it a long, long way from paradise. Less a town than a downscale marketing concept, it was simply the site of Jack's Service Station and Men's Clothing Store, as well as Jack's Real Estate Office, all in the woods alongside what was essentially a very large puddle. True to the antimaterialist spirit of the late sixties and early seventies, Keillor kept his tongue firmly in cheek as he extolled the area's simple pleasures: wooded lakeside lots close to "Jack's Automotive Services" and unrivaled security for the kids. "Lake Woebegone is guaranteed safe for children," he insisted; "at no place is the water more than three feet deep. Don't risk possible family tragedy at other locations."[7] The "beautiful shores" of Keillor's woebegone lake were not yet the gateway to a mythical Mist (*missed*) County.

Keillor's successful narrative formulas arrived partly rather than fully formed, and extant manuscripts in the Prairie Home Companion Archives chronicle their development. By the time the live broadcasts began in 1974, Keillor concluded his mock commercials for Jack's Auto Repair with the formulaic "all tracks lead to Jack's, where the bright flashing lights show you the way to complete satisfaction." Yet scripts from 1971 reveal that he experimented with the tag line for well over six months. The oldest text, dated 6 October [1971], introduces the new sponsor and claims simply "All tracks lead to Jack's." Three days later, the apparently dissatisfied writer played around with the tone, settling for the wry "one look at Jack's and you'll say, here is where I can find complete satisfaction." Later in the fall, promoting Jack's winterizing service, Keillor experimented with a modicum of conventionality: "Tell him Garrison sent you, and Jack will give you a little thing, you wind it up and put it in your pocket, it makes you tremble all over. That's at Jack's, at Lake Woebegone."[8]

By the spring of 1972, Keillor had still not yet settled on a tag, but he had established a second element of the Lake Wobegon myth. Events at the fictional Lake Woebegone would exist in real time—not compressed or expanded fictional time—and, as a result, the lives of Lake Wobegonians and the radio audience would intersect. "Jack's Auto Repair is marking its sixth month with the Morning Program," Keillor wrote, setting up the audience for a humdinger of a misplaced modifier, "and Jack's wants to thank the hundreds of folks who have mentioned these stations when going in to get repaired." Now the tag evoked the outrageous, as did the commercial itself. Jack's spring tune-up included an examination of "nearly every moving part in your car's engine. . . . Especially the secret inner parts that other mechanics simply don't talk about—like the anomaly," and the script closed by praising Jack's as the place "where your shopping dollar will find a willing hand and a friendly smile, the one-stop shopping complex out on Lake Woebegone with the big flashing light visible throughout the five-county area, all roads lead to Jack's."[9] Surviving manuscripts don't indicate exactly when Keillor hit upon the trope that finally satisfied him, nor do they establish exactly what he said on the air about Jack's Lake Wobegon enterprises at any particular time, but still they allow us to glimpse the gradual, nonlinear process by which an exacting writer developed his material over time.

Even in 1971, however, KSJN listeners became hooked almost instantly. Will Jones, a critic for the *Minneapolis Tribune*, declared "the returned, revived, retreaded Garrison Keillor . . . a safety menace" in the 6:30 to 9:00 a.m. drive-time slot, claiming that he had nearly laughed himself off the road. Indeed, by all indications, the humor was wonderfully inspired. Jack's Auto Repair sponsored the Second Annual Chicken Music Festival—several hours of "chicken-themed music," including sixties' rock-star Tiny Tim singing "Chickery Chick," a recording by the six-foot star best known for his camp falsetto rendition of "Tiptoe through the Tulips."[10] The program was so successful and Keillor's hold on the medium so strong that his literary aspirations were soon eclipsed. Within a month, Jones proclaimed the host a "former poet," even though Keillor continued reading poems at the Walker Art Center, was at work on a manuscript titled "1871-2," and had already published nine stories in the *New Yorker*.[11]

"I set out deliberately to be warm and folksy and Middle America and down to earth," he protested shortly after his return to broadcasting, professing bewilderment at his growing reputation as an eccentric. "It's the most down-to-earth thing I've ever done, and I have to believe people are putting me on when they say it's far out."[12] More likely, however, the writer was protecting his warm, folksy persona and putting the reporter on at the same time. Keillor's burlesque writings through 1971 reveal an already well honed ability to walk the fine line between imitation and parody. So do key elements of the program. Considering its Twin Cities' commuter audience, A Prairie Home Companion had more than a touch of irony in its title, all the more since the companion was both the program and the host, and Prairie Home referred to a cemetery in Moorhead, Minnesota. The ambiguity demonstrates his taste in homespun humor half a dozen years before Keillor slyly characterized Lake Wobegon as "the little town that time forgot and the decades cannot improve." The style was popular from the start, and the station took little risk in expanding its offerings to include live broadcasts of a successful show, especially late on Saturday afternoons.

Before live broadcasts began, however, Keillor took a leave of absence beginning in November 1973. He asked for the leave partly because he had received an assignment from the New Yorker to report on The Grand Old Opry and because he wanted to devote more time to his writing but also because he had become dissatisfied with the "evanescence" of radio. In contrast to writing, doing a radio show often left him feeling that "we are wasting our lives feeding words and music into a goat."[13] This time, though, Keillor was taking a sabbatical, not resigning, and Kling felt confident he would return. In fact, by August 1973 plans were already afoot for live Saturday broadcasts. The Minneapolis Tribune reported: "'Keillor will be doing something else for us,' Kling said. 'We're not sure what.' One possibility is a Saturday version of 'Prairie Home Companion' specializing in live music from across the state, Kling said."[14] Although Keillor has claimed that he hit upon the idea for his variety show while reporting on The Grand Old Opry, Minnesota Educational Radio began considering the format even before he left for Nashville.[15]

In relation to the morning program, the live show was as much a spin-off as an experiment. Indeed, the Saturday program seems to have emerged as something of a compromise over the best format for the morning show. When Keillor began inviting folk musicians such as Judy Larson to the small KSJN studio, the demands of the drive-time formula (including regular reports on traffic, news, and weather) conflicted with the flow of the burgeoning variety hour. Station management had long since come to respect the sense of personal and professional integrity that had led Keillor to resign in 1971; a second show doubtless offered a happier solution. For Keillor's part, inviting performers to a live broadcast on Saturday afternoon provided a way to satisfy KSJN and himself as well.

It would be a mistake, however, to conclude that he disliked the morning radio show. After all, in 1976 he resumed hosting the daily program along with the Saturday broadcasts and continued to do so until 1982, when the Saturday show was nearly eight years old.[16] He seems to have given it up only after adding the job of writing *Lake Wobegon Days* to the production of weekly nationwide broadcasts. Perhaps more to the point is Keillor's explicit regard for the morning program, which offers insight into both the man and his art. "I loved broadcasting at that hour of the morning," he recalled in June 1988, describing how the show infused him "with a real sense of religious mission. . . . I loved the feeling of being the shepherd of lovely but temporarily unhappy people . . . who needed humor."[17] Part of his satisfaction stemmed from the sense of triumph over television; he noted with great pleasure that radio remains the mass medium in charge of waking people up in the morning and helping them greet the day.[18] A larger measure, however, arose from his bond with the audience.

That bond has special meaning for a writer. Poets can read their works to an audience, as Keillor often did, but for the most part writers create their readers in their own minds. Novelists and story writers seldom hear from their readers and even then only after the long interval between the completion of a work and its publication. The immediacy of radio allows an intense engagement with the audience that for Keillor can sometimes outweigh the insubstantiality of the medium, though he finds the difference between writing and radio "an enduring conflict."[19]

Spinning tales on the air stands midway between writing for publication and announcing on radio, and the development of the Lake Wobegon narrative suggests that the writer found radio storytelling a gratifying challenge. Years later, he recalled that his first effort at public storytelling "seemed like a long leap":

The story was a real departure. . . . I did tell it. The story was written; it was a real manuscript, more polished than monologues to come. It was a story in which the Bunsens were there; there was a family feud of some kind. It was kind of a dumb story, backing the car down the driveway. . . .

It was nothing distinguished. But it was such a departure that my boss spoke to me about it and asked me if I was going to do more of this. He gave us absolute freedom doing the show, but he felt this was a change. I told him yes, I absolutely was going to do this. I felt that I had turned a corner.[20]

However dramatic the shift seemed to Keillor and William Kling, evidence in the archives shows the extended Lake Wobegon tale, far more complex than the Jack's commercial, evolved even more slowly and less tidily. Keillor told an occasional story on the air in 1974 and 1975, and regularly reported the news from Lake Wobegon throughout the mid-seventies, when he also began reading letters from Barbara Ann Bunsen to her family. By the summer of 1977, when an estimated half million Minnesotans heard the weekly broadcasts,[21] the town had grown to include two churches and a post office, as well as a distinctive population of strong women, good-looking men, and "decidedly above average" children, yet even then, Keillor's narrative formulas and the town itself were still evolving. At that time Keillor was calling it "Lake Wobegon, Minnesota, the town that time cannot change" (27 Aug. 1977). As late as 1978, Keillor could still omit a Lake Wobegon monologue entirely, and not until 1979 did the elaborate Lake Wobegon narrative become a centerpiece of the weekly performances.[22]

What monologue there was in the first live broadcast of *A Prairie Home Companion*, as for most of the first two years, came at the beginning of the show, and it had less in common with what he would eventually call his "séance" than with the familiar patter of television's longest-lived host, Johnny Carson. To be sure, Keillor did not imitate Carson's barrage of one-liners, for Keillor is not a stand-up comedian, but neither did the Minnesotan spin a yarn about an imaginary town. Instead, he chatted about his guests and about recent events in the real world. On the first broadcast, he talked a bit about the show; six months later, he joked about the Watergate tapes and the Superbowl (though he would talk about the weather if nothing else turned up), and then he gradually wove his topic into a "Jack's spot," a commercial for one of the many goods and services on Jack's full and ever-expanding roster. One spot, for example, touted the Superbowl Withdrawal Program of Jack's Counseling Service: "Just call 949-949 in Lake Wobegon—or if you have a dial telephone, you could just dial the letters W-H-Y W-H-Y, which comes out the same" (18 Jan. 1975).

The first live broadcast gave little hint of the narrative potential of the Jack's spots. As Keillor demonstrated "the Jack's Autoharp, a musical instrument that is turning the Lake Wobegon music scene upside down," he talked up the accompanying book of songs. The humor of the spot centers on the backwardness of Lake Wobegonians, which the host conveyed as he described how the very titles of the songs in the book contained instructions for playing them. The songs included not only "Be C-ing You" but also the memorable "Hey, Your G-ns [jeans] Are in D-cent; G, G-minor ObC-n" (6 July 1974). This punning example (more effective heard than read) demonstrates that the Jack's ads did not contribute narrative techniques to the developing Lake Wobegon saga, but they nonetheless did provide a growing set of facts and, tied to those facts, a jaundiced perspective. Shortly after the show's second birthday in 1976, for instance, a particularly inspired spot praised the virtues of "warm clothes from Jack's Auto Repair Dry Goods Emporium in Lake Wobegon," and thus combined Keillor's now-standard satire of commercial rhetoric with a humor based on local facts (in this case, Minnesota winters) and pseudo-folklore:

> In the old days, as those of you know who've read your history books, the old trappers and the old hunters and the old scouts, to keep warm in those bitter winter months, would carry a bear around in their arms—to gain the necessary warmth to keep up the vital bodily functions—or some of them, anyway. And it was not so much that the bear's breath was warm, though it was, it was more the exertion of carrying that tremendous weight that helped them work up a little sweat and got them through the hard winters. It's from that same principle that Jack's developed the Warm Coat, and that's why it weighs a hundred and fifty pounds. It weighs a hundred and fifty pounds because it's lined with over a hundred pounds of Jack's Hot Rocks—the rocks that serve as insulation and also to take your mind off the cold if you should happen to touch them accidentally. (28 Aug. 1976)

With the gradual introduction of Jack's Fountain Lounge, Jack's School of Writing, Jack's School of Thinking, Jack's Protective Work Glove for the Guitarist, and Raul's Warm Car Service from Jack's, the commercials exemplified Lake Wobegon's literalist, retrograde, occasionally primitive approach to life. Their blend of formula and invention, realism and anomaly kept the inside jokes lively for quite a long time. So did the use of such staples of American humor as tall talk and bears.

Considering the importance of the Jack's commercials to the development of the Lake Wobegon saga, it is not surprising that some of the later Lake Wobegon landmarks began as Jack's enterprises. The Chatterbox Cafe, for instance, evolved from Jack's Toast House, the original "place to go that's just like home"—and for essentially the same reason. At Jack's Toast House in 1976, customers sat on torn kitchenette chairs after the Toastesses reminded them to enter through the back door (26 Nov. 1976); at the Chatterbox Cafe in 1979, customers were promised "one of Dorothy's big meatloaf and mashed potato specials . . . served family style, and the tables will be cleared and the dishes done family style, too" (12 May 1979). It was through Jack's various enterprises, in short, that Keillor first portrayed Lake Wobegon as an ironic alternative to the romantic, sentimental image of small-town life. In the early years of *A Prairie Home Companion*, at any rate, "just like home" wasn't much of a compliment. The satire of the Jack's commercials wasn't sufficiently intense or didactic to serve as a corrective to romanticism about home or rural life, but understatement was part of the point.

The most important contribution of the Jack's commercial to the Matter of Minnesota, however, was not long-term but immediate, and it grew out of the basic clash between commercial rhetoric and unmarketable products. For most of the 1970s, that category embraced only local flora and fauna, the unremarkable landscape and ordinary folks of Lake Wobegon. This ironic implication began to change in the late 1970s, and by 1982 the Jack's commercial gave way to ads for Bob's Bank ("Neither a borrower nor a lender be"), whose boasts of small-town friendliness veiled hints of nosiness and interference. In later years, Keillor took the mock-commercial rhetoric one step further, transforming the unmarketable into the precious. Items not worth having gave way to sentiments about what money cannot buy.

But in the days before the long narrative became a feature of the show, other elements yielded a similar effect: engaging the audience with the performance as a process. The early broadcasts called close attention to the live production, often making the audience itself the focus of the show. Through the content and structure of *A Prairie Home Companion*, Keillor emphasized the physical presence of the audience, the presence or absence of scripts, and the simultaneity of the performance and its transmission.

In the first live broadcast, as for years afterwards, Keillor used the audience itself as material. (The first live broadcast was not the first live show. Three concert performances, all taped at the Walker Art Center in Minneapolis on 7 April 1974, and broadcast subsequently, preceded the first live broadcast. Keillor continued to give concert performances for the next thirteen years.) Although he did not ask the ticket holders where they were from (as he would in the late seventies), or read messages from listeners to their friends and family (as he would in the eighties), he did converse with his live audience and invite their participation. In this context, the decision to open the show by singing "Hello Love" proved especially apt.

The 1970 song by Betty Jean Robinson and Aileen Mnich, which remained the theme song throughout the life of *A Prairie Home Companion*, celebrates the unexpected return of a prodigal lover.[23] Keillor jumped from the first verse to the fourth to shape the words to his task, omitting the details of a shaky romance and focusing instead on the couple's reunion. As a result the theme song recasts the relationship between audience and host: the intimate terms of the song characterize the pair as lovers and encourage listeners to bond with him one by one, rather than as part of a group. That in fact the Companion and his show have been absent, not the audience, undercuts the sentimentality of the lyrics a bit and gives the song a degree of comic incongruity appropriate to the program's tone. The success of Keillor's voice, his characterization of himself as a gracious host welcoming his listeners to his prairie home, stems partly from his effective exploitation of the show's rhetorical possibilities, beginning with his choice of a theme song.

Other nonnarrative elements of the program also established a bond between listeners and their radio Companion. The most obvious device for encouraging active involvement was the sing-along segment. Already present in the first live show, when Vern Sutton encouraged the audience to join him in the chorus of a not-so-golden oldie from 1900, "A Man Who Has Plenty of Good Peanuts," the sing-along took various forms over the years. "The Piano Bench," Sutton's contribution in the late seventies, found its inspiration in the tendency of families to store old sheet music—good, bad, and topical—in their piano benches. "The Department of Folk Song," run by Greg Brown in the early eighties, dredged up all sorts of oldies-but-goodies (including that alliterative day-camp classic, "Great Green Gobs of Greasy Grimy Gopher Guts") from nearly two thousand contributors, many of whom sent letters or tapes to make clear how their family sang a particular song.[24] Keillor himself took charge of the comic group singing, in which his interest seems never to have waned. In June 1988 at his Second Annual Farewell Performance at Radio City, the largely East Coast audience followed the lyrics printed in their programs as they sang "America," "Now I Lay Me Down to Sleep," and instructions for using airplane oxygen masks—all to the tune of "Tell Me Why."

Regardless of format, the rag-tag sound of group singing consistently accomplished several important ends. First, it emphasized the presence of an audience, whose participation could then give the radio listeners the sense of being in the hall themselves. Next, it helped build a wide audience by bridging generations and their different senses of the past. Only a few listeners were old enough to recall the heyday of "A Man Who Has Plenty of Good Peanuts," but those too young to remember the variety hours of the twenties and thirties had followed the famous bouncing ball of *Sing Along With Mitch* on NBC-TV in the sixties.[25] Still others could learn new lyrics to old tunes or apply familiar lyrics to another well-known tune. Finally, and probably most important, the segment emphasized the *process* of entertainment over the *product*. This aspect would have particular appeal to Keillor's peers, who came of political age in the sixties, singing in the antiwar movement. But *A Prairie Home Companion* encouraged its audiences, regardless of age, to have fun themselves and to take vicarious pleasure in witnessing others having fun, rather than to settle for the more familiar experience of viewing (or hearing) a rhetorically distant performance.

Showcasing homegrown talent also had the effect of drawing the audience close by inviting listeners to share something intimate and rare. Keillor has noted that the decision to hire local musicians had more to do with a low budget than anything else, but the show made a virtue of necessity.[26] As the National Endowment for the Arts apparently recognized when it agreed to begin funding the fifteen-month-old show beginning in September 1975, *A Prairie Home Companion* offered folk musicians a special opportunity to play for an audience wider than their family, friends, and coffeehouse regulars without sacrificing what might be termed the folk quality of their performances, as could happen in the more formal setting of a concert, for instance.[27] Even as the radio transmitted the music across the state (and later from coast to coast), the live audience sustained the original feeling of the small performance. In fact it *was* small for quite awhile: the show could accommodate an audience of only 82 from October 1974 to November 1975, when the capacity rose to 220; special performances aside, the audience seldom exceeded 600 for most of the show's history.[28] Without the limits imposed by an auditorium, however, audiences swelled impressively. An outdoor broadcast in the summer of 1979 drew a crowd of eleven thousand.[29]

A large stock of local jokes fed and benefited from the show's small-town feeling. The Lake Wobegon and Powdermilk Biscuit routines belong to this class of material; Powdermilk Biscuits burlesque the local Pillsbury industry as well as allude to Tennessee Ernie Ford's ads for Martha White Flour. But these jokes were relatively accessible to an audience outside Minnesota, compared to such truly inside jokes as jibes at Minneapolis charter reform, the bus system, and local celebrities. Keillor joked about charter reform in his opening monologue on the first live broadcast and continuously exploited any humor he could find in the current weather, but songs with local themes exemplify his local humor at its best. An early example, set to the tune from "The Streets of Laredo," explodes the idea that "it's a joke to grow up in Anoka":

> It may be an old town, and somewhat rococo.
> It isn't a focal point, goal, or plateau.
> It's not El Dorado, Valhalla, or Mecca.
> It's only our home, and as such apropos.
>   (18 Jan. 1975)

This song is more notable for contradicting the notion that Keillor had always claimed Lake Wobegon as his hometown than for its humor. But other songs illustrate the rhetorical potential of his local humor. Two prime examples from the late 1970s, the music tributes to Bombo Rivera of the Minnesota Twins and Barbara Flanagan of the *Minneapolis Star*, demonstrate particularly well how Keillor mined the Matter of Minnesota for his local audience. "The Barbara Flanagan Waltz" and "Bombo" exist almost exclusively to celebrate shared knowledge of local facts.

The "Waltz," which, for all its teasing, did not offend its subject, debuted at the Lake Harriet bandshell in southwest Minneapolis, a site that inspired Keillor to comment on Flanagan's columns on local beautification.[30] Expostulating that "she loves . . . little cafes—the kind with a lot of plants in them, a lot of macramé, the kind they don't have in Lake Wobegon exactly," he went on to explain that her interests arose quite naturally from her beautiful name, itself, he observed, "in 3/4 time." So he sang of Hennepin Avenue, the Como Park Zoo, and other local improvement projects and punctuated the verses with a chorus in a thumping waltz rhythm:

> With letters she's peppered
> The Como Park Leopard,
> To try redesigning its spots.
> Oh, the Barbara Flanagan Waltz
> the Beautiful Barbara Waltz,
> Style and beauty is everyone's duty. . . .
> (30 July 1977)

Unlike some inside jokes, these lyrics are not inaccessible to outsiders. Every town has its local beautifier, and so everyone can derive some degree of enjoyment from the humor of recognition at work here. But the song obviously finds its most appreciative audience among the regular readers of Flanagan's column in the *Star*, and these readers would take particular pleasure in seeing their city transformed into a paradigm of America.

By contrast, the baseball tune "Bombo" focused on more arcane local lore, in essence putting local sports news to music. The lyrics not only hailed the arrival of the Twins' new outfielder and clean-up hitter, but also glorified his performance at the season's opener the day before:[31]

> Well we went to the game,
> And we yelled his name,
> And he tipped his hat and smiled.
> The count was three and two,
> And the pitcher threw.
> The crowd about went wild.
> It was a southpaw pitcher, but the ball went nort'
> Up through the hole between third and short.
> Bombo Rivera will carry us to victory.
> . . . .

It takes two to tango and two to mambo
But we can do it all with just one Bombo.
(15 April 1978)

Of course the audience joined in the chorus of this toe-tapper, inspired by its catchy rhythm, but although the pleasures of the singalong enhance the local humor, they don't account for it. Quite the contrary: writing a witty song on the heels of an intercity contest points out the particular satisfactions of local humor. MPR exploited local pride in both the song and *A Prairie Home Companion* by offering a 45-rpm phonograph recording of "Bombo" as a membership premium. In an era of increasing cultural homogenization, if not actual domination by the mega-cities of New York and Los Angeles, Minnesotans could celebrate such local delights as the home team and exclude outsiders.

These two lively and imaginative songs have some elements in common with the musical satire that Tom Lehrer performed and recorded in the 1960s ("The Vatican Rag" and "The Ballad of Werner von Braun" were particularly well known) and that continues today in Mark Russell's stand-up piano performances on college campuses and public television, including his singing lampoon of the 1988 Republican National Convention. In contrast to the sharply pointed political satires of Lehrer and Russell, however, Keillor's lyrics are largely divorced from national events and politics. Keillor occasionally allowed himself a few nonmusical stabs at the Republicans. His songs, however, tended to focus on topics of regional recognition or pride rather than national partisan issues, and therefore many remained local comic property. Minnesotans derived much civic pride from his exploitation of the Matter of Minnesota, as well as a proprietary interest in the show's success. They went so far as to include a tape of it in the state's bicentennial time capsule.[32] Some local fans resented sharing their Companion with a national audience, especially the upscale city dwellers who dominate public radio markets on the East Coast. Just four months after the regular national broadcasts began, a listener from St. Paul wrote to complain about the absence of ads for Jack's Auto Repair, suggesting the possibility that Keillor "canceled Jack because his products have no appeal to the Fancy-Schmantzy Easterners who now listen to the show."[33] Later, local fans would be especially hurt when Keillor decided to leave.

What better way to expand local pleasures than by expanding local boundaries and putting Lake Wobegon on the map? Certainly the category of Minnesota humor could embrace the spot that Keillor originally celebrated as "the little town with no great scenic attractions, such as you'd put on postcards, or print on plates or cups, or salt and pepper shakers and sell in dime stores" (26 Nov. 1976). In 1976 Keillor began to flesh out the various exhortations to shop at Jack's Auto Repair; these were obviously—and therefore, comically—fictional, since public radio has no commercials. So Keillor upped the rhetorical ante by supplementing the ads with imitations of public service announcements, alerting the audience to upcoming events in Lake Wobegon. Thus began the weekly segment that gradually evolved into long narratives of the humorist's mock-autobiographical experiences, "The News from Lake Wobegon."

In its original form, the weekly news exploited the patent fiction that Harold Starr of the *Lake Wobegon Herald-Star* had sent a list of events, which Keillor invited the audience to attend. Never a hoax in the sense of a practical joke on the listeners, the newscasts nonetheless separated the newcomers from the already-initiated, just as western tall tales once did. But even for relative old-timers to the Lake Wobegon joke, the humor hinged on the disproportion between the topics of Keillor's announcements and his elaborate descriptions of them. The "news" featured fictional events of dubious interest in a nonexistent place to which the announcer nonetheless invited real people. At once enhancing the realism of the invitation and calling undue attention to it, Keillor would remind his listeners to behave themselves in Lake Wobegon: "Just remember, if you do drive up to Lake Wobegon—on Sundays, Visitors' Day, to behave yourselves and not stare at anybody and don't point. Cause there's a lot of people in Lake Wobegon who don't care for visitors or Visitors' Day—who refer to it as V.D., as a matter of fact—so be on your best behavior." (22 Oct. 1977)

The events he described did justice to the warning. The pseudo-folklore of the "Columbus Day Booya" and the "Ceremonial Hanging of the Suet," to cite just two examples from the mid-seventies, gave the events a zany realism while characterizing the Wobegonians as hopelessly provincial. For the most part, however, Keillor's comic Minnesota kept one foot in the real landscape. He drew the names for characters Selby Dale and Victoria St. Albans from streets in St. Paul.[34] Ads for Bertha's Kitty Boutique and the Fearmonger's

Shoppe made fun of the various "-dale" shopping malls springing up in the Twin Cities.[35] Jokes about the weather, especially remarks about heavy snow and extreme heat, served much the same purpose: creating and reconfirming a community of shared jokelore.[36]

A related effect arose from the special participation gimmicks. Ranging from the conventional to the zany, the gimmicks built a relationship between the audience and the host. The more traditional efforts included asking listeners to contribute to the Department of Folk Song and sundry Angry Letter campaigns; quirkier ones encompassed such memorable traditions as the Thanksgiving Cantata (an impromptu composition based on phrases submitted by the audience) and the Powdermilk Biscuit Mouth-Off (a spoof of the Pillsbury Bake-Off in which "mouth-musicians" yodeled, tapped their teeth, and thumped on their cheeks).[37] But Keillor also drew on less formal tactics—some of them doubtless invented on the spot—for building rapport with his audience. During the outdoor performance on 28 August 1976, he invited everyone to turn around and wave at the folks in the apartment building across the way. Similarly, in his Second Annual Farewell shows at Radio City, 3–4 June 1988, he trained some five thousand ticket holders to clap only once—and in unison— on cue. But not all his tactics were so elaborate, and indeed many seem spontaneous and instinctive. His most common audience-participation strategy was simple conversation. He would ask questions, and everybody would shout answers. "Who sings that song in the *Wizard of Oz*?" he inquired after a rendition of "If I Only Had a Brain" (12 May 1982); or, on another occasion, "bunch of you here from Lake Wobegon, is that right?" (15 April 1978).

Probably no question ever had more importance over the thirteen-year history of the show than the one he asked near the start of the first live broadcast. "Is there an audience here?" he called out after the opening tag, "coming to you live." More for the benefit of the radio audience than for the twelve folks rattling around in the four hundred seats of Macalester's Janet Wallace Auditorium,[38] the query did not merely prove the existence of the live audience to the folks at home—though it did that, too. More important was its effect in shaping the audience and guiding its responses to the show. The strategy may well have been instinctive rather than premeditated, as Keillor insists that it was,[39] but it was nonetheless ideally adapted to the problem at hand. That is to say, from the very beginning of the live broadcasts of *A Prairie Home Companion*, Keillor demonstrated that he had mastered rhetoric of comic performance.

Following the question, he jumped into his first monologue, using a comic device that received a boost from vaudeville but antedates even Mark Twain. Not unlike Johnny Carson bouncing patter off straight man Ed McMahon or Mark Twain, who early in his writing career invented a "Mr. Brown" for much the same purpose, Keillor proceeded to quibble with Philip Brunelle about his performance of "Hello Love." Keillor's colloquial speech patterns, which lacked the studied dignity conventional to classical music announcers, signaled the different mood of the show. And as the host refused to accept praise for his singing, he worked up to a mock crisis that called attention to the live production:

Why don't you back up the tape; we'll go back and redo part of that; they can do one—you're shaking your head no? I'm just kidding. I know we're on the air live, but ya know it's such a long way from doing this from where I started out in, in radio, uh, at KUOM; used to sit in a little studio, ya know; it was nice in there, little microphones, earphones, eh? And about every hour and a half or so, you'd turn on your mike and say, "You've just heard a recording of the Bach Mass in B-Minor. [pause] For the next 3 hours we'll hear a complete performance of *Parcifal* by Richard Wagner." And then you could turn off the microphone and sit there and eat your lunch in the station, didn't have to worry about the Bayreuth Festival Orchestra coming in late or anything—[everything was] right there on the little disk. Nobody bothered ya and the thing about it is that you didn't have to worry about the audience not liking the music. Ya didn't have people calling up and saying, eh, "Why d'ya play so much Brahms? Brahms is no good." Ya know—people didn't do that. They knew Brahms is good—so is Bach and Beethoven. But in a live show like this, uh, we'd get into a lot of pretty cheesy music like you just heard—uh, ya know country music and folk music and stuff like that, and who knows? Who—I dunno if it's good or not, cause there's no criticism in folk music. There just is not. Like polka music, for example, there's no critic down in New Ulm, who goes around to, uh, wedding and anniversary dances and writes reviews of em. Like Mike Steele and those guys, who writes little reviews like uh, "Walter Grout and his Six Plump Prussians demonstrated uh-eh stunning technical virtuosity along with lyrical sweep and verve—at the twenty-fifth anniversary of Mr. and Mrs. Elmer Shimky in Mankato last night." They don't do it; they're nothing like that, so we donno—we have no idea, how it's, if it's good or not, ya know. I mean it's kinda good, but who knows if it's great music? (6 July 1974)

Even transcribed, Keillor's monologue illustrates the essential values of live radio production. The language demonstrates all the elements of spontaneous speech. No natural paragraph breaks occur. Some sentences have false starts and corrections. Others lack literary precision in grammar and syntax. Nobody reading a script starts a phrase with one grammatical construction, then backs up and restarts with another. Script readers don't say "kinda," and they certainly don't punctuate their sentences with "uh" and "ya know." Communications scholar Erving Goffman has suggested that radio may require such voiced pauses more than conversation or other kinds of talk, if only to assure listeners that the broadcast link remains intact.[40] One mark of the professional radio announcer, however, is fluency, which includes the absence of hesitation markers, at least the most obvious ones, since most announcers rely on time-fillers of one sort or another—very stretched vowels, for instance, or a brief pause.

The absence of a script does not mean the absence of a rhetorical agenda, however. Quite the contrary. The structure of this initial monologue suggests that Keillor knew exactly what he wanted to accomplish with his apparent ramblings. His strategy involves three stages. First, he advises the radio audience that the show is being broadcast live and that any inadequacies in the musicians' performances, his own or anybody else's, should be taken as evidence of the risks involved in the performance process itself. Next, he points to differences between this program and standard public radio fare, in essence warning listeners not to expect the old faithfuls of classical music. These, he says, make the announcer's life too dull and the listener's experience too tame: why should listeners give over to the professional critic their own right to exercise aesthetic judgement? Can only approved music be broadcast over the radio? At the very least, he implies, public radio ought to have room for the music of the public—the folks of folk music. Finally, the possibility of complaints about the format brings the opening gambit to a climax. Although he may have intended the remark about complaints as a subtle reminder to his KSJN colleagues about his resignation in 1971, the comment functions within the structure of the monologue as an announcement to listeners, "This is a musical happening. Don't complain about what you don't understand, but please do get involved with the show." The direct progression from the opening song through these theoretical issues demonstrates that behind Keillor's casual manner stood serious purpose. He wanted to create a new kind of public radio show and train his audience to appreciate it.

Keillor did not need to sound uncertain, however truly uncertain he may have felt about this new endeavor. With all his experience as an announcer in the fourteen years since he wandered into campus radio station WMMR as a freshman in 1960, the host surely could have spoken less colloquially. Or he could have followed the script that he certainly had somewhere; he scripted the show in great detail in the early years and continued to keep scripts with him as late as 1977, though they had become more informal by then.[41] But either way, he would have sacrificed crucial elements of the show's rhetoric. Worse, given the subject of this first monologue—the relative merits of popular and classical music—he would have gained didacticism and pomposity at the expense of at least assumed spontaneity and naturalness.

In July 1974 amateurishness signified integrity and sincerity, among other venerables. A year after the Watergate hearings and amid the Senate Judiciary Committee's evaluation of the evidence for impeaching the president, amateurishness had particular appeal as the antithesis of the Nixon era's slickness and professionalism. The era would end with Nixon's resignation on 9 August 1974, just a few weeks after Keillor's first live broadcast, but at the time animosity in many quarters ran high against such former advertising men as White House aides Robert Haldeman and John Erlichman and the moral relativism they were seen to represent. This political atmosphere entered *A Prairie Home Companion* in Keillor's remarks about the Fourth of July, celebrated two days before. Introducing Wendell Berry's poem "Manifesto," Keillor commented on the truly radical ideas in our Declaration of Independence, and he took a broad swipe at Nixon by pointing out charges against George III—"He has obstructed the Administration of Justice"—before pretending to stop himself short. Though public orations of the sort had a long and honorable history among Independence Day celebrations, Keillor announced, he had decided not to read the Declaration, "which, ya know, might be, uh, kinda controversial; we might get demands from Republicans for equal time" (6 July 1974). The comment suggests that the Old Scout's casual amateurishness, an aspect of his voice manifested in decidedly colloquial speech, had roots in the spirit of the time.

The television programming of the day underscores with what perfect timing *A Prairie Home Companion* was introduced. The influence of sixties-style frenetic comedy typified by *The Beverly Hillbillies* (1962–1971) and *Laugh-In* (1968–1973) had waned, and programming began to turn more sentimental and folksy, although Lawrence Welk had retired in 1971.[42] The television series based on Laura Ingalls Wilder's *Little House on the Prairie* began in September 1974, just two months after Keillor's show and just four months after the failure of *Music Country U.S.A.*, which ran from January 17 to May 17 on NBC. In addition, on CBS from 1972 to 1981, the romanticization of family and self-reliance dominated prime-time drama in *The Waltons*, a paean to intergenerational harmony during the Great Depression. Closer to home, and equally important, Minnesota boosters had already found a source of pride in *The Mary Tyler Moore Show* (1970– 1977),[43] whose success proved that Minneapolis could symbolize centrist politics as well as geography in a forward-looking comedy about a career woman. At a time when many young Americans had already given up on their 1960s dream of dropping out of the rat race and going back to the land, yet had not resigned themselves to the urban marathon that would captivate the yuppies in the 1980s, Minnesota could represent the landscape of contentment.

Contemporary attitudes may also account for the revival of live broadcasting in the early seventies, which saw several notable forays into live production. In this sense, *A Prairie Home Companion* certainly stood at the leading edge of broadcasting, however much of a throwback to the forties its format might seem to have been. In 1971, Norman Lear had led the retreat from filmed entertainment on television by videotaping his innovative situation comedy *All in the Family* (1971–1979) in theatrical-style performance before a studio audience. Lear's example led to other experiments, of course, most significantly *Saturday Night Live*, which from 1975 to 1980 showcased comic talent: Chevy Chase, Steve Martin, John Belushi, Gilda Radner, Jane Curtin, Eddie Murphy. While dramatic programs explored other techniques, especially *cinéma vérité* in such series as *Hill Street Blues* (1981–1987), comic performers found that the spontaneity of live performance generated a free, zany wit.

Although Lear and Keillor brought similar innovations to their different media, Lear's needs (and those of television as a medium) differed from Keillor's. Certainly the two men made different uses of the hallmarks of live performance—bloopers, glitches, and snafus: mispronounced or incorrect words, delayed entrances, and so on. On the radio show, snafus proved the integrity of the host and his program; live programming carries risks, the argument goes, and the brave face up to them. By contrast, radio's integrity is television's artifice. Television requires a tightly scripted performance so the producer can use the most effective camera angles; *All in the Family* was therefore performed and taped before its live audience for later broadcast; the tape could be edited if necessary to maintain precision timing for commercials. Whatever snafus occurred in performance were captured on tape, where they remained as errors. But when Rob Reiner broke character as Mike to laugh at an outrageous bit, the authenticity of live performance did not improve the show. Authenticity sacrificed verisimilitude, unmasking the characters as roles.

But for *All in the Family* as for *A Prairie Home Companion*, the risks proved worthwhile. Whereas radio's intimations of authenticity allowed Keillor to build his myth of Lake Wobegon, Lear needed some relief from the intense realism of the intergenerational and interracial battles he satirized (some said reenacted) on television each week. Divided on the question of whether that consummate bigot Archie Bunker was the hero or the villain of the show, viewers needed reminders that he was in any event an imagined character, and the flaws in live performance provided those reminders. This experience suggests that Keillor also needed to send some fairly explicit signals to his audience. For him, the gaffes helped not only to teach his two audiences how to judge the show but also to distinguish his Saturday show from his more conventional weekday program.

Recalling how his colleagues "used to suffer" over glitches on *A Prairie Home Companion*, Keillor claimed to be puzzled: "I don't know why—everybody knew it was a live show. On a lot of the scripts I wrote, we could have used more mistakes."[44] The remark reveals that he knew very well the role of errors in certifying the show's authenticity, and it hints as well at why amateurishness grew from a rhetorical device to an explicit theme that encompassed his own performances as a singer and host. Presenting himself as an amateur allowed Keillor to exploit the serendipitous opportunities of the live show at diminished risk: he saved face if he failed, and appeared a genius if he succeeded. Still, one danger remained. Unless properly initiated, the audience might very well confuse deliberate or acceptable clumsiness—that is, elements of camp—with genuine ineptitude.

The comic pose offered one solution. Like other successful humorists, Keillor created a variety of comic poses for use both in his writing and in performance. A comic pose expresses the humorist's *implied* attitude toward a particular subject and audience at a particular time. A pose differs from a comic persona, which at least aims to represent a complex and well-developed personality, because a pose serves a limited rhetorical purpose for a limited time and can be abandoned as rapidly as a mask. A humorist of Mark Twain's skill could switch poses three or four times in as many paragraphs, intensifying the liveliness of his humor. Scholar John Gerber has concluded that Twain regularly juggled seven distinct poses: four postures of superiority to be deflated (the Gentleman, the Sentimentalist, the Instructor, the Moralist) and three of inferiority to be ridiculed (the Sufferer, the Simpleton, the Tenderfoot).[45] By alternating his own beliefs with these assumed attitudes, the nineteenth-century master exploited myriad opportunities for comic incongruity and surprise—possibilities that Keillor too recognized early in his career.

Indeed, understanding Keillor's achievement as a humorist involves crediting his ability to invent and exploit suitable comic poses and to subsume them under one persona. Of course, the great abundance of humorous material he composed and performed for *A Prairie Home Companion* deserves respect at the very least, if not downright awe; his comic scripts, spots, and monologues (conservatively estimated at twenty minutes a week) total more than a thousand hours over thirteen years. But all that might have developed into just so much food for the goat had Keillor not found a durable and flexible role for himself. In creating the role that we might call the Companion, probably the crucial element of his achievement on *A Prairie Home Companion*, Keillor could still pose as the Amateur, the Shy Person, the Cracker-Barrel Philosopher/Preacher, the Witness, or the Announcer whenever he saw fit. And he did.

Although his *New Yorker* stories often exploit comically superior narrators, usually variations of Mark Twain's Instructor, characters who give absurd advice, Keillor primarily adopted poses of inferiority on *A Prairie Home Companion*. (In this regard, it's worth noting that Twain himself seems to have largely abandoned poses of superiority after his earliest works.)[46] Keillor's most frequent pose was the Amateur, a broadcaster unworthy to further the noble history of live radio. As the Amateur, he defused various flaws and snafus within the comic parameters of the show while enlisting listeners' sympathies on his behalf. "A person like myself, who has no recognizable talent, you're home free," the Amateur boasted in 1975, explaining the particular advantage in not being a musician or a comedian, " 'cause audiences aren't sure what it is you're doing up there—what you're *supposed* to do. And [so] they're always pulling for you" (8 Nov. 1975). Keillor had already discovered the rhetorical advantages of playing this comic underdog by the time of the first live broadcast, when he used the role to very profitable effect, and he returned to it frequently throughout his career.

In his first monologue on the Saturday show, the Amateur extended the contrast between live-performance radio and its recorded kin by suggesting that his previous radio experience had rendered him unfit for this opportunity. Years of talking into a studio microphone might have made his voice too small to address a studio audience, he worried, or the rarefied devotees of public radio might have warped his instinct for programming. In this context, Keillor's Amateur bears some resemblance to Twain's Simpleton, who speaks with an earnest seriousness in the face of all evidence and logic. And like Twain's Simpleton, the Amateur is a temporary posture. But unlike the Simpleton, the Amateur has an intellectual grasp of the problem at hand.

> The other way, in case you're curious, that doing a live show is different, from doing a record show is that a live stage show like this has gotta work out to some kinda climax, ya know—we can't just stand here and play one tune after another and tell a buncha jokes and do a buncha Jack's commercials, and think that's okay. Because people expect different, when they come out to a stage show; it's gotta build to a climax—do you know what I mean? I mean we gotta get this audience to a point where at the end of the show, they, they're coming up, up these steps, taking pieces of—you know—off the shirts and ties—because that's how show business is. You can't just have ninety minutes of pleasant family entertainment; it's gotta be great or it's nothing. I don't say that this has gotta kill ya, but I say you gotta laugh so hard you get sick.

Some-a you do. I think for this show to succeed, we need a headline in the *Tribune*, you know like "Ten Stricken by Show." Ten? Twelve. (6 July 1974).

Except for the extravagant fantasy that the soft-spoken humorist might achieve a rock star's success, the amateurishness of this passage depends entirely on colloquialisms: *kinda, buncha, gotta, ya-know*. These soften the didactic tone lurking just beneath the surface as the host advises the audience that the Saturday version of *A Prairie Home Companion* would not simply substitute live performers for the records on the weekday morning version of the show. But the seriousness here has a comic purpose, too: it's the setup for a display of just how bad a show the Amateur had in mind. Or so he would have his audience think:

And it's kinda hard for a pretty quiet fella like myself to know just how to go about doin' that. Like, originally, I had planned that the show would start out with a flutist, he'd play for awhile, ya know, solo—flute—whatever came into his head, and then we're gonna have a lecture on macramé, and we were gonna have a short talk on the future of the nuclear family, and we had a Tibetan nose hummer. He's good, but you have to listen to him for half an hour, ya know—he can't come out here in three minutes and make people think he's great—it takes a while for his kinda act to develop, and then as a finale we were gonna have Mayor Al Hofsted come out and talk about the need for charter reform in Minneapolis. I dunno. I thought, I personally I thought it would be a real interesting show, but the chairman of our program committee, Sid Battista, who's had a lot of experience in the carnival business before he went into used cars, he up and canceled all those acts this week—he said it wasn't the sort of thing that people would come to see, and he suggested that as my first guest, I oughta have this fellow, who's been in radio, and who knows how to do this. (6 July 1974)

"This fellow" is none other than Bob DeHaven, a great Twin Cities' announcer who saw the era of live broadcasting come to an end. Consequently, the invidious contrast between Keillor and DeHaven does not really condemn the young disc jockey: few people still in the business rank with DeHaven. The pose of the Amateur does, however, poke great fun at public radio (which originated as *educational* broadcasting), at local politics, and at passing fads, all the while aiming the biggest joke at the Amateur. With the disclosure that he had intended a lesson on decorative knot-tying, the first of many visual jokes exploiting the incongruity of radio in the television era,[47] the Amateur proves that he's hopelessly inept. At the same time, the humorist who created the pose demonstrates that he has the direction of the broadcast firmly in hand.

Keillor posed as the Amateur repeatedly over the years, and the posture led to a series of stock routines into which he drew other performers. Adam Granger, guitarist for the Powdermilk Biscuit Band until May 1978, fell particularly well into the role of the Amateur's more polished sidekick. In October 1977, for instance, in a promotional spot that Keillor wrote for "The Prairie Home Road Show," Granger advanced the pose of the Amateur by suggesting that anyone else—notably himself, of course—could do as well:

> And don't worry about the Powdermilk Biscuit commercials or "Hello Love." . . . I've got your part down cold. . . . What's there to it? Ya know, ya get up and you say it's been a quiet week in Lake Wobegon, and ya do the Lake Wobegon stuff—ya know, uh, Father Emil of our Lady of Perpetual Responsibility, 'n all that. And uh, the Sons of Knute are holding the annual installation of the ancient storm windows 'n you read a letter from Barbara Ann Bunsen and then ya sing "Come Home, Come Home, It's Supper Time," and ya talk about the importance of being a nice person, and then at the end you say, "Good night, everybody, good night," and then you go back to the motel, and you take off your white suit and have a scotch on the rocks. (22 Oct. 1977)

Granger's remarks reveal that within three years *A Prairie Home Companion* had evolved into something very like its mature formula. But the humor of his comments depends on recognizing not only that the program had settled into its formula, but also that, for all its apparent amateurishness, the show succeeded because of Keillor's writing and performance. We can see Keillor making fun of himself here—and taking very wide aim at that, since his targets include the Cracker-Barrel Philosopher and the Announcer as well as the Amateur.

The humorist was still mining the Granger-Amateur vein more than a year later. In May 1978, as the musician prepared to leave the Biscuit Band for a solo career, Keillor wrote a farewell letter to Granger from Jack's Auto Repair, in which the downscale sponsor trashed *A Prairie Home Companion* as the painfully awful product of an untalented amateur. With a stunning mixed metaphor, Jack praised what he saw as Granger's failed efforts to improve the show ("It's like trying to light a fire under the proverbial silk purse") and

expressed his sadness that so skilled a musician had stooped to ac-
company "Hello Love" (an act of self-abasement made worse by
being played in the beginner's key of C) before offering to sponsor
a show of the guitarist's own, "one that is devoted to music and
not to a lot of maudlin meanderin' about mom and apple pie and
the importance of being nice." And lest anyone chalk up the criticism to matters of individual taste, Keillor closed the letter by giving
Jack an unequivocal attack on the Amateur: "Tell Mister Hello Love
to get his beard trimmed. His job is to announce the show, and it's
hard to understand him when he talks when his mouth is full of
hair" (12 May 1978). Well into the eighties, long past the time that
circumstances might justify his claim not to understand live radio
broadcasting, Keillor found ways to continue mining the comic potential of the Amateur.

In fact, Jack's letter to Granger belonged to a series of mock complaints providing a useful variation on Keillor's own pose as the Amateur: other people simply accused him of inadequacy. These accusations maintained the Amateur as a prime target of comic invective
even as Keillor began debunking other aspects of the show besides
live performance. Not surprisingly, he enlisted Jack— embodiment
of everything retrograde—for the job. Jack deflated the show's increasing success with his continual contempt for "Harrison Feeler"
and his "gloomy old gospel song[s]."[48] A revised and edited group
of these letters appeared in the 1987 souvenir program as "The Perils
of Success: Selected Letters from Jack," which fulminated (with
pleasant comic predictability) about how "the show needs a professional emcee."[49] In some of these, the writer widened the range of
Jack's invective to encompass the monologues and their fans:

> Thirty minutes of a man speaking in a flat Midwestern voice about
> guilt, death, the Christian faith, small town life—it isn't what people
> look for in a stage performance, is it. [When] People go to the Ringling
> Brothers circus . . . you don't see them stand up en masse and stamp
> their feet and chant, "share your experiences!"[50]

Jack's accusations allow Keillor the rhetorical equivalent of having his
cake and eating it too. He not only ridicules himself and his critics
but also puts the Amateur at a distance while continuing to exploit
the pose.

But for all that Keillor as the Amateur could coax humor from
a wide range of circumstances—just about every element of the pro-

gram, at least in theory—the original use of the pose remained intact. As late as the tenth anniversary performance, he trotted out the well-worn comic mask, complete with tentative *uhs* and *ya knows*, and gave the audience a familiar display of mock despair that claimed at least comic sympathy:

> Oh, some of our old friends, uh, were a little bit leery when they heard about our show tonight—when they heard that Steve Barnett, and the Night o' Rest Motel Orchestra and Chorus and Dancers were all gonna be on. Thought it was a sign that our show had taken a sharp turn, uh, towards becoming slick, doncha know—not knowing, I guess, that I, that becoming slick is what I'd been trying to *do* for—*years* now! And it makes you feel bad, ya know, that people wouldn't notice—that, uh, you'd strive for years to be smooth and polished, and people would tell you how much they liked the show for that, uh, kinda "homespun quality."
>
> It's kinda like getting dressed up for the dance, and, uh, the lady tells you that, uh, she likes the way your hair sticks up in back, it reminds her of her brother, ya know. It's not what you wanna know at that point. But anyway Steve told us after rehearsal yesterday that—becoming slick was nothing we were in imminent danger of, so, I guess it's all right.[51]

Ten years' experience had taught the humorist a great deal about working a crowd, but the show's playfulness and its interest in authentic folk music continually reinforced the value of the Amateur as the host's primary pose, and he relied upon it all the way down to the Farewell Performance on 13 June 1987, when he bemoaned his inability to tell jokes in Danish. "There's a lot of funnier people around, and a lot of better singers, and you're gonna find another show. But you're my only audience. . . . I don't have any audience in Denmark. I'm not humorous there; I'm a very tall, quiet person who keeps saying the same things over and over again 'cause that's all I know." He proceeded to prove the point by saying something in Danish, and when the audience responded with respectful silence, he chided, "Yeah, see? It gets the same reaction over there. It's not a great joke; it's all I know."[52] The pose served him so well that many people believed that each performance was a 1960s-style Happening falling serendipitously into place.

In addition to demonstrating his keen sense of audience, the success of the Amateur reflects Keillor's ability to turn to advantage the unplanned conversations among performers or last-minute adjustments to skits that every broadcast contained. "The spontaneity that people saw was not false," explains Rosalie Miller, producer of *A Prairie Home Companion* rebroadcast series for MPR; "ask any television production crew who's worked on the show—it makes them crazy, because they want everything planned out exactly in advance. And yet it was not the whole story."[53] Over the course of thirteen years, the context of the Amateur shifted somewhat, and in the yuppie era of the mid-eighties, the pose adopted the voice of the counterprofessional instead of the counterculture, but the very flexibility of the pose argued for its continued use. The purpose of the Amateur, like the purpose of any humorist's pose, was to give personal voice to comic strategies. As he smoothed out the differences between the scripted and spontaneous elements of *A Prairie Home Companion*, polished material and accidents both acquired the appearance of diamonds in the rough.

CHAPTER 3   **It's All I Know**

Prairie Home Postures

Thank the Lord for giving
Us this afternoon again.
And now please pass
the meatballs.
Let's eat. Amen.
—Keillor, "Meatballs"
(17 October 1981)

Over the history of *A Prairie Home Companion*, a variety of poses accommodated the growth of Keillor's comic voice. He never abandoned the Amateur, his first pose, which was particularly suited to the self-consciousness of the early live broadcasts, but it had its greatest utility as a contrast with others, especially the Professional, its opposite. As a posture of superiority, the Professional opened opportunities for the extravagant, even bombastic humor that marked the 1970s, when black humor peaked in American literature and *M*A*S*H* and *All in the Family* led the television comedy ratings. In particular, speaking as the Professional allowed Keillor to lampoon radio rhetoric, from commercials and radio dramas to the news. That strain lost some of its appeal, both to Keillor and to the public at large, in the quieter, more conservative eighties. More to the point, an introspective series of poses assisted the development of the Lake Wobegon story as it shifted from the broad humor of the mock newscast and ironic epistle to the subtler humor of fictionalized autobiography. The development of the Shy Person, the Cracker-Barrel Philosopher/Preacher, the Witness, and the Exile voiced a range of subtleties while giving his stories of life in Lake Wobegon a "becoming midwestern reticence"[1] that no Jack's commercial—or Amateur—could.

As a characterization of the performer, the Shy Person conveyed even greater verisimilitude than the Amateur, probably to its creator's chagrin. If belief in the Amateur amounted to something of an unintentional insult to Keillor's skill at crafting a live show, acceptance of the Shy Person threatened to deliver the *coup de grace*, as fans accused him of fraud for behaving less shyly and more assertively than they expected. A columnist for the *Wisconsin State Journal* exacerbated the problem at the same time that he put his finger on one likely cause of it when he noted, "In the convoluted way that becoming famous hurts the truly shy, Keillor, in becoming extraordinarily successful, became ordinary. Just another *People* magazine feature."[2] One interviewer after another reinforced the humorist's reputation for shyness, usually by confessing to having anticipated a more reticent subject, until in 1985 *Time* declared him Minnesota's (if not America's) Most Famous Shy Person.[3] Long before the national press had even heard of *A Prairie Home Companion*, however, the humorist invited the raised eyebrow by dismissing performers' self-revelation as just so much self-aggrandizement and conceding that any performance involves a public pose. "People who make a show of being open and displaying themselves in entirety, are really fooling themselves—they are simply creating another defense and another screen," he insisted in 1977; "Everybody's a private person."[4] The comment reveals a performer less likely to tell the truth about himself than to feign self-revelation in performance. Natural tendencies toward shyness become largely irrelevant in the process. In the final analysis, Keillor's wide *reputation* for shyness (deserved or not) proves unequivocally how effectively the humorist exploited the pose, which, like any other comic device, he used as needed.

The Shy Person provided an alternative to feigning comic ineptitude as the Amateur. Hints of the Shy Person appear in the first live show in 1974, when Keillor called himself "a pretty quiet fella," and in the very conception of the Powdermilk Biscuit spots, those testimonials and commercial homilies on behalf of the apocryphal brown morsels "made from the whole wheat that gives shy persons the strength to get up and do what needs to be done."[5] The biscuit spots served a variety of purposes on the show, including (Keillor says) a chance to deal with his stage fright. He told a Dallas reporter,

"I really am a shy person. I started out to talk about Powdermilk Biscuits as a way of confessing it—to make myself feel better about the terrors of getting up onstage."[6] Calling attention to shyness in the course of the show may certainly have defused Keillor's anxiety, but making it the subject of weekly narratives shifted it from the realm of emotion to the realm of literature. The biscuit spots, based on the advertising testimonial (itself a form of popular literature), framed and controlled the feelings of shyness and transformed them into art.

This second major pose developed more gradually than the Amateur and came into its own much later in the history of *A Prairie Home Companion*. By 1979, to pick a clear benchmark, when the five-year-old show began addressing a national audience on the occasional broadcast over the National Public Radio network (NPR), Keillor had dropped most of his earlier mannerisms for playing the Amateur, especially the *uh*s and swallowed final *g*'s, and must have needed an alternative pose consistent with the growing reputation of the program. If he wanted to keep the Amateur in his repertoire, he could not suddenly adopt the voice of the Professional Announcer—at least, not seriously (as he indicated on the first live broadcast, when he rejected that pose in his banter with Bob DeHaven)—and the comic counterpart of this role already belonged to his mock commercials and radio-drama parodies. By contrast, the Shy Person offered a second naïve pose with comic potential. A shy radio announcer is even more of an anomaly than an amateur and has commensurately greater capacity to evoke sympathy and sentiment. Emphasizing his insecurity instead of his inexperience would extract proven rhetorical benefits from a different set of circumstances. Better yet, posing as the Shy Person presented opportunities for narration. The Companion could then include confessional storytelling while affirming his integrity as the host.

The Powdermilk Biscuit spots evolved in this context. During the early years of the show, Keillor often called on his guests to testify to the shy-busting qualities of Powdermilk Biscuits. Bill Hinkley and Judy Larson performed a testimonial drama on the first live broadcast, for example. On another occasion a child memorized some banter to recite with the host on a special children's show on 26 August 1976. When Keillor did the biscuit spots himself, however, they increasingly mingled the Amateur and the Shy Person.

A sterling instance occurred in the summer of 1980, four months after regular national broadcasts began:

> Shy people often are afraid to [ask questions] . . . because they are afraid it will make them look ignorant. I think of myself, for example, all the years I've been in radio, and all of the times I have heard engineers talking about equalization, and bass roll-off and things being out of phase, and low impedance and high impedance and the AKG 452s and the SM-5s, and all the rest of it, and I never asked them what they meant by all that, because I wanted to appear knowledgeable, and so I said knowledgeable things, like, "Well, that looks good to me." And as a result, I know nothing about radio—whatsoever. I don't know how any of this works. I have no idea. And when it comes down to the real work of this show, I am about as useful, as—well, you know that old saying—if you don't know ask somebody; I don't know. I guess I won't say that here. (16 Aug. 1980)

This connection between shyness and ineptitude occurs regularly in the Powdermilk Biscuit spots of the 1980s. The link clarifies the utility of the Shy Person as an alternative to the Amateur but at the same time raises questions about just how seriously and for what purpose Keillor posed as shy.

Self-ridicule ranked first among the comic techniques for the biscuit spots; jokes about the imaginary biscuits followed closely behind. Together they deflated the slick, pseudosincerity of commercial rhetoric, which remained a prime target of the segment, whatever its weekly topic. Only the naïve would credit an announcer's comments about himself (or anything else) in a commercial message, much less a mock advertisement for an imaginary product on noncommercial radio—surely as comic a context as one could ever find. Keillor conceded as much in the spring of 1982, two years into his regular national broadcasts and a year after his receipt of the Peabody Award propelled *A Prairie Home Companion* to new levels of popularity and fame. Practically signaling newcomers not to fall for the Shy Person, even if they succumbed to the biscuits, Keillor dropped the pose as he pulled listeners' legs a bit more strenuously than usual:

> Shy persons do not care to be stared at by a whole lot of other people. That's one thing about us. You might keep that in mind the next time you look at a shy person, and that shy person looks kind of odd to

you, kind of queasy in the face, and green around the gills, and saying dumb things, and acting weird. It may be because you're looking at him, see. We're not as good in groups of people you see. We're a lot better by ourselves. I'm a very funny person by myself. I can't cite you, you know, particular funny things I've said to myself; I guess you had to be there at the time. . . .

Many people wonder how a person as shy as that is able to get up and do a live radio show on a stage in front of 850 people in the World Theater every Saturday night. Well I'll tell you. For one thing, we don't have that many people here. We use sound effects. . . . And for another thing, you know that if you're a radio listener, which I assume you are, that when you listen to the radio, you don't sit and stare at it. You go off and you do other things. That's the case with the people who come to our show at the World Theater. We got some people here, studying for final exams down here, people reading newspapers, and kids lying on their bellies with the coloring books and the puzzles, and people with their crosswords, people kind of roaming around, and talking to each other. So it's comfortable here is what I'm saying. (15 May 1982)

The anomaly of a shy performer makes the Shy Person innately comic as a pose. Like the Amateur, the Shy Person succeeds as a comic device because we recognize it as a comic posture, because Keillor connects it to a *feigned* ineptitude. Actually witnessing a shy person suffer the anxieties of public performance would be painful, not amusing. Actually listening to a shy person describe miserable experiences would also lack humor. But Keillor's Shy Person shares his discomfort over events safely in the past, events already survived and therefore defused. Like the Amateur's amateurishness, then, the Shy Person's shyness is funny because it's false. It relies on the artifice of narrative. As in the case of the radio announcer who has become a success even though he can't tell an amplifier from a machine gun, Keillor's Shy Person suffers no truly painful consequences—none whose real pain he exhibits for us, anyway.

Complicating the comic use of shyness are comments that characterize reticence as a virtue in itself or as a manifestation of other virtues, such as integrity or respect. The variations do not so much follow a particular course of development as expand and contract according to the narrative context at hand. A few months after debunking the very idea of the shy performer, for instance, Keillor equated shyness with reverence. "The people at *Reader's Digest* have come out with a new book in their condensed book collection, and it's the *Reader's Digest Bible*," he declared at the beginning of a Powdermilk Biscuit routine, "Which shows that shyness is not a problem everywhere; some people don't suffer from it in the least tiny bit" (18 Sept. 1982). In this instance, an expanded notion of reticence contributes very little to the comic characterization of the Companion, even if the spot does end by joking about a condensed phone book as the next logical step for the series, since "probably 40 percent of the names in your phone book are people you'd never want to talk to, people whose names you wouldn't even be that interested in reading" (18 Sept. 1982). Keillor's explicitly didactic remarks in this spot cannot sustain any comic pose, much less a pose of inferiority such as the Shy Person, but they do reveal the ease with which he could switch from the Shy Person to the Cracker-Barrel Philosopher.

Not that the two poses were entirely separate, at least at the beginning, if only because the Powdermilk Biscuit spots provided the opportunity for homespun wisdom: the rhetoric of the commercial testimonial derives from the parable. Keillor teased humor from both genres in his more philosophical biscuit spots, which became increasingly frequent after 1979, as the show began to reach a wider audience and the humorist needed to develop poses less dependent on local traditions of self-deprecation. The new context made poses of superiority more important. Consequently, the Philosopher grew in importance as time went on. Over the history of *A Prairie Home Companion*, the poses eventually made up something of a rhetorical spectrum, moving from the inferiority of the Amateur to the modest superiority of the Cracker-Barrel Philosopher/Preacher, with the Shy Person standing midway between.

Keillor's Christian faith and his repertoire of Bible verses united into one pose what other humorists might have kept as two distinct elements, homespun philosophy and religious humor. To the discomfort of nonbelievers who, in the apparent need to recreate their hero in their own image, overlook the wide spectrum of religious commitment even among the faithful, Keillor has often affirmed his continuing loyalty to the beliefs of his fundamentalist upbringing even though his religious practices differ from his parents'. The humorist takes plenty of potshots at the excesses of church members, of course, and finds them at least as laughable as laudable; yet for the most part he apportions comic contempt pretty evenly between the

Catholics and the Lutherans of Lake Wobegon (the Lutherans suffer perhaps a trifle more from his greater familiarity with them). Not only does he refrain from calling down a plague on either house, much less both of them, but in fact aims his satire fairly specifically at church members' failures to act according to the highest Christian standards—when they squeezed Pastor Inqvist out of his convention trip to Orlando (12 Jan. 1985; *Gospel Birds*), for instance, or boycotted the interdenominational Thanksgiving service because the preparations didn't include "a signed agreement . . . that there would be no statues" (24 Nov. 1979). Still, the consistency with which Keillor's version of the Cracker-Barrel Philosopher blends the secular and the religious, when he could have kept them separate, provides good reason to take the humorist at his word on his subject, especially since fundamentalist faith can be separated from fundamentalist practice, from which Keillor admits he has departed.

Perhaps the most useful insight into the religious aspect of Keillor's humor comes from a very early monologue in which he abandoned the pose of the Amateur to assure his audience he had the host's job under control. After thanking his listeners for the personal concern evident in reports that "the idea of live radio made them sort of nervous. . . . they were worried for us"—evidence that the Amateur had succeeded a bit too well—he launched into a confession of how as a child he had delighted in making his mother worry. The monologue is notable on several counts: it provides an early example of self-revelation, presents a childhood memory set in his real hometown of Brooklyn Park, and shows the Companion trying his hand at a sustained oral narrative years before he began telling Lake Wobegon tales. But more important to the matter at hand are the actual incidents of the story, which recounts how the boy was required to memorize a Bible verse every Sunday and how he loved to tease his mother by waiting to study his verse in the car on the long ride from Brooklyn Park to South Minneapolis. Keillor exposes the Amateur's artificiality when he reports how he used to pretend not to know his verse very well and how he always kept one verse in reserve:

> The cut-off point was about downtown—downtown, oh, about Tenth and Park. If you didn't have it learned by then, that's when my mother would turn around in the front seat and ask us if we knew our verses. And I would say, "Well—ha, ha—I'm not sure." But I always kept one in

reserve. And, uh, it was, uh, "Whereupon I am called as a preacher and an apostle, and a teacher unto the gentiles, for which cause I suffer these things; nevertheless, I am not ashamed for I know whom I have believed, and am persuaded that he is able to keep that which I have committed unto him against that day. First Timothy, Chapter 1, Verses 11 and 12." (8 Nov. 1975)

The *uhs* preceding the verse recreate the hesitations with which the boy teased his mother, conveying a similar suspense to the storyteller's audience. But the recitation does not so much assure us that boy did finally uphold the family's honor as it reveals a speaker of virtuoso memory. Even if he had rehearsed the verse before the broadcast, and even if he had invented some of the narrative details, the story of his childhood memory training illuminates Keillor's skill at seemingly spontaneous yarn spinning as well as the role of religion in his tales.

Indeed, in extracting the lesson from his little parable, the humorist showed more interest in the comic and narrative uses of religion than in any theological possibilities.

I only used it [the reserve verse] but two or three times. But it was always there when I needed it. *So don't worry.* Don't worry if I ever get in a spot where I need something to say; I have a lot of Bible verses that I know. Because that was the idea behind them, you know. That you'd remember them all of your life, and they would come back to you at critical moments just when you needed them, like right now. (8 Nov. 1975, Keillor's emphasis)

Of all the ways he might have shown off his excellent memory—say, by reciting a Shakespearian sonnet or an obscure article of the Constitution or by performing a parlor game that involved memorizing a chain of names or phrases—Keillor chose to recite a passage from the Bible and use it humorously. That choice is telling about both the depth of his faith and its connection to his humor. Still, we ought to ask what kind of proof relies on a passage so arcane that few listeners would know whether he recited it correctly: only the self-deflating "proof" of the tall tale. A few minor jokes supplement this basic one. The verbosity of the verse renders it nearly meaningless out of context, while Keillor's punch line laughs at the use of Bible verses in a crisis. All told, the humor pokes fun at his religious training, but it nevertheless celebrates those lessons as an element of his professional success and, in the end, for their own sake.

Throughout its history *A Prairie Home Companion* continued to use religious rhetoric primarily for its comic potential, a practice suggesting that Keillor's convictions did not change much between the ages of thirty-three and forty-five. He apparently remained committed to biblical values while skeptical of institutional practices. Consequently, his religious rhetoric does not so much characterize a distinct pose that we might call the Preacher as it contributes a thematically distinct set of comic incongruities to the Cracker-Barrel Philosopher, the Amateur, or the Shy Person.

Not surprisingly, all three poses came together from time to time. As early as the spring of 1979, for example, when the show had irregular national broadcasts, he defended the apocryphal biscuits for their service to the spirit:

> Yessir, we do need something, all of us do, as it says in Scripture: the race is not to the swift, nor the battle to the strong, nor bread to the wise, nor riches to men of understanding, nor favor to men of skill, but time and chance—happen to them all, and even those who are strong and swift and skillful and wise—and that's not me—need something to give them strength to get up and do what needs to be done, and I say, if a simple biscuit can do it, why not! Because it's those simple things that need to be done that are the *hardest* to do. (12 May 1979)

The Philosopher lacks the broad humor of the Amateur, as this example makes clear, though Keillor could have undercut the Philosopher or turned the spot to burlesque if he had chosen. He didn't. With the exception of the Professional Announcer of the radio-drama parodies, none of his poses of superiority serves the broad strokes of farce, as Mark Twain's Instructor did, for example. Compared to the western humor that Twain favored in his early years, Keillor offers a more modest pose of superiority in the homely metaphors and comic diction of the Cracker-Barrel Philosopher. This durable American tradition expresses anecdotal wisdom in a kindly, moderate, and modest voice—in contrast to the sharper, more authoritative voices of the satirist or learned wit, two other didactic comic postures. Familiar cracker-barrel philosophers include Poor Richard and Father Abraham, two of Benjamin Franklin's comic personas, as well as Will Rogers and (some might say) Ronald Reagan.

Keillor's pose of the Philosopher came into its own after 1981, gradually extending beyond the Powdermilk Biscuit spots to the Lake Wobegon monologue as Keillor adapted the weekly news segment to his own voice rather than that of a neutral newscaster. At the time of the first regularly scheduled national broadcast in the spring of 1980, however, the biscuits still enjoyed top billing. The humorist's opening monologue led into a Powdermilk spot, a homespun homily based on the premise that "in softball as in life, you don't have to be perfect to be graceful . . . and to keep some kind of hold on your dignity." The voice of the Cracker-Barrel Philosopher dominated the Shy Person and the Amateur as *A Prairie Home Companion* broadened its appeal to a national audience.

> Now it's not easy for those of us who are shy, because we have a track record and people know it. We have a history of dropping things; we're the last to be picked, when they choose up sides. I've played softball with people who like me, but I'm still picked last, comes down to me and the fat guy. They pick the fat guy to be catcher, I don't even wait, I just pick up my glove, go out to right field. I go to parties, and the hostess looks at me, and I can see her thinking, that man spills, that man is a spiller, and she takes me by the arm, and she—gets me into a long conversation over on the hardwood floor, away from the carpet. But I feel graceful today. I feel—I feel, handsome today, and partly because it's, because we're on radio, and partly because it's live radio, where all your mistakes just go right by; you don't sit and look at em for the rest of your life, and also it's because of Powdermilk Biscuits—I finally got around to them—heavens, they're tasty and expeditious. (3 May 1980)[7]

In contrast to the self-conscious mockery underlying the Amateur and the Shy Person, the Philosopher ridicules the antagonists in his parables. Nonetheless, how seriously can one take *any* parable presented as a testimonial for an imaginary product? Despite the Philosopher's insistence that the difficulty of obtaining Powdermilk Biscuits merely confirms their value ("some people may think it's odd that I stand up and advertise a product that you can't buy in the stores. It makes sense to me. It just means you have to try harder, that's all it means" [18 Sept. 1982]), the humor of fantasy and commercial rhetoric in the biscuit spots could absorb only so much seriousness. More earnest expressions of cracker-barrel philosophy had to wait for the sentimental monologue to supplant his satirical vision of Lake Wobegon.

The process was in motion by the summer of 1977, when Keillor reminisced about his childhood to a mandolin accompaniment between verses of "Supper Time" (1950), Ira F. Stanphill's sentimental song with a hymnlike tune. The pace quickened after 1981, as Keillor adopted Lake Wobegon as "my hometown" and warmed to the possibilities opened by the adoption. Only then did sentimental reminiscence and satiric fantasy merge in the voice of the Cracker-Barrel Philosopher. Only then did the monologue expand from five or six minutes—the average length when regular national broadcasts began. The monologue stretched to eleven or twelve minutes between 1981 and 1983, and after that it began to claim half an hour. As a fully developed pose, that is, the Philosopher appeared rather late in the development of *A Prairie Home Companion*.

The Philosopher appears at both his most explicit and his most polished in Keillor's monologues published in the mid-eighties, both the "butter box" anthology of seasonal pieces, *News from Lake Wobegon* (1983), and *Gospel Birds* (1985). The voice of the Philosopher shapes the comparison between duck hunting and fiction writing at the end of the "Giant Decoys" (18 Sept. 1982), for example, which concludes that standards of utility ought not apply to duck hunting any more than to writing: if writers don't sit around reading their own books, why should hunters eat what they bag? In this case the Philosopher offers disingenuous observation, not sentimentality. "Storm Home" (29 Jan. 1983; *Winter*),[8] an exploration of a child's fantasy life and the importance of the imagination in our lives, looks back at the past with an amused but not wistful smile. Even less romantic is the rueful "Meeting Donny Hart at the Bus Stop" (5 Nov. 1983; *Gospel Birds*), which speculates on childhood and adult perceptions of mental retardation as the narrator recounts his experience of running into, but wanting to avoid, his retarded childhood friend.

The increasing sentimentality of the later monologues suggests that the Philosopher helped Keillor reduce the narrative distance on Lake Wobegon. He had begun this process in the Barbara Ann Bunsen letters of the midseventies, and it intensified as Keillor offered his own first-person tales of life in the town. The courage—or need—to narrow the gap increased as the eighties advanced; by 1985, a very large portion of the monologues offered cracker-barrel philosophy in a sentimental mood. The most successful late examples of such anecdotal wisdom include "Gospel Birds" (27 Oct. 1984) and "The Tolleruds' Korean Baby" (9 Feb. 1985), both recorded on *Gospel Birds*. The earlier story deflates the so-called superiority of the sophisticated while exploring the difference between inner and outer expressions of religious faith. The later tale sums up its meditations on the difference between biological and natural children by suggesting that, metaphorically at least, everyone arrives down a baggage chute to an excited welcoming committee. Telling tales as the Philosopher allowed Keillor to experiment with didactic, yet noncommercial rhetoric without sacrificing humorous language or mood.

In contrast to the ironic point of view in the early monologues, the dominance of cracker-barrel philosophy in the published recordings reflects at least three factors. Matters of production constituted one of them. The published monologues represent a selection of performances meeting a host of criteria unrelated to humorous technique: the length of the monologue or segment, the quality of the master recording, the appropriateness of any given piece to the theme of the collection (with additional considerations of variety and coherence), the effectiveness of the narration, the writer's fondness for the tale—all of which led to the second major factor. Whatever other matters influenced the selections of tales for the collections, none surpassed the effort to address the audience, which grew rapidly after regular national broadcasts of *A Prairie Home Companion* began. With the wider audience came a need for more broadly conceived humor. A national audience (many of them former small-towners) would appreciate sentimental humor universalized by the Philosopher more readily than Minnesota insider jokes about downscale Lake Wobegon; anthologies published for this wider audience would succeed better by nodding toward their tastes. Yet for all their importance, these factors ought not obscure the more immediate fact that Keillor had just perfected the pose of Philosopher as production of the recordings began. Why would he want to publicize points of view that no longer satisfied him instead of newer experiments?

As a result, the published monologues barely hint at how the humorist broke with the retrograde Lake Wobegon of the Jack's commercial and started presenting affectionate portraits of Lake Wobegonians. Still, some evidence of the shift appears in the introduction to "James Lundeen's Christmas," originally performed 12 December 1982 and recorded in its entirety for *Winter* (all the collections mix complete monologues and excerpts). In announcing that the tale illustrates how wrong he used to be in judging Wobegonians stupid, for example, Keillor reveals his changing conception of the town. His ability to finesse the change by attributing it to his more youthful persona demonstrates as much as anything how the Philosopher provided him a pose of superiority, but one whose condescension, if any, involved fondness rather than ridicule.

Historically speaking, the pose of the Philosopher resolved a problem resulting from the failure of the Announcer, a pose that Keillor toyed with throughout the history of *A Prairie Home Companion*. Between the jaundiced first phase of the Lake Wobegon saga (running roughly from 1974 through 1979), defined by the debunking rhetoric of the Jack's commercial, and the sentimental third stage (beginning around 1981 but not fully developed until 1983), defined by the anecdotal wisdom of the Philosopher, lay a long transitional period in which Keillor explored other rhetorical possibilities. The experiments between 1976 and 1982 ranged from the sublime to the ridiculous, including a homespun rendition of the Christmas story (19 Dec. 1981; *Winter*) as well as recitations of doggerel purportedly written by Lake Wobegon Poet Laureate Margaret Haskins Durber, whose editor Harold Starr of the *Lake Wobegon Herald-Star* praised her as "an extremely reliable poet, always neat, always on time."[9] Two routines proved especially fruitful, however, "The News from Lake Wobegon" and the letters from Barbara Ann Bunsen. Both began in 1976, and both depended on the voice of the Announcer, which could switch easily between commercial and narrative rhetoric.

"The News from Lake Wobegon," a feature well established by the fall of 1975, began as yet another parody of radio talk, this time ridiculing the public service announcement. Under the pretense of listing upcoming events in Lake Wobegon, Keillor gradually introduced the town's eccentric citizenry and detailed their customs. Consistent with the characterization of Lake Wobegon in the Jack's commercials, the Announcer created a humor of banality: he extolled in loving detail the eccentricities of Jack's downscale tourist mecca. For example, in the fall of 1976, Keillor's introductory trope, which varied sightly from show to show, deflated the pretensions of conventional tourism: "Every Sunday is Visitors' Day out at Lake Wobegon, of course, the little town with no great scenic attractions, such as you'd put on postcards, or print on plates or cups, or salt and pepper shakers and sell in dime stores, but it does have some wonderful people, and you're all invited to come out there every Sunday and come and meet them and see them—as long as you're nice and you don't point" (26 Nov. 1976).

Sustaining the commercial undertone of the opening, the Announcer of the "News" provided a variation on local-color humor by inflating native customs. He transformed the mundane into the ritualistic. November Rites involved a fairly tame series: the "Ceremonial Hanging of the Suet," the "colorful Cursing of the Squirrels," and the "Coffee Brew-Ha-Ha" (26 Nov. 1976). But the Columbus Day Booya offered a taste of the exotic. Held two weeks after Columbus Day (in the tradition of the inept) because "the soup wasn't quite ready yet," the event derived its full meaning from the Announcer's offhanded remark, "A lot of people in Lake Wobegon claim that a few weeks before the Big Booya, all the stray dogs in town disappear, but—it'll be there anyway, if you want to take advantage of it" (22 Oct. 1977). As a format, the weekly news could encompass a wide variety of material other than local-color humor or pseudo-anthropology, and it continued to do so for the life of *A Prairie Home Companion*. Despite its popularity, however, the focus on eccentric local customs gradually took a back seat to the invented lives of Lake Wobegon's citizens. The expanded narrative elements softened the ridicule of the town as the spots began focusing on the complexities of people's lives instead of simply hawking Jack's products or local events.

The Announcer imbued the spot with the realistic rhetoric of the public service announcement or newscast, which opened the way to telling stories on the air. As he chronicled events in the lives of the Wobegonians, tales of the town acquired an authority unavailable to the incongruous rhetoric of the mock commercial or travelogue. Still, in 1976 and 1977 ridicule of Lake Wobegon remained a high priority in the newscasts. The town's retrograde character shaped its news and the Announcer's delivery. For example, announcing the retirement party for Mary Frances Fisher took a back seat to saluting the service of this omniscient and omnipresent chief operator and treasurer of the Lake Wobegon Telephone Exchange, in whom former *Laugh-In* fans of Lily Tomlin will recognize her nosy operator, Ernestine. "She's been the mediator of a great many family feuds and disputes in Lake Wobegon," the Announcer informed us in a voice not only lacking irony but also evincing admiration, "because she is the person who knows who said what to whom" (26 Nov. 1976). A year later, Keillor had replaced the classic structure of the news story, which leads with its strong points and trails off into insignificance, with a more literary structure based on order of climax. After describing how Shirley and Bob Magendanz triumphantly brought their new car home, the Announcer revealed their decision to trade it back—and pay $450 as well—for their beloved old one (27 Aug. 1977). The superior pose of the Announcer served very well to sustain the jaundiced view of Lake Wobegon that represented the legacy of the Jack's spot, but beginning in 1978, Keillor apparently began to tire of the pose, which required him to sneer at his own increasingly complex, realistic creations.

One sign that the humorist had exhausted the Announcer's superiority occurred on 4 March 1978, when he did not offer a monologue. The show that night marked the troupe's move to the World Theater, and one might have expected the festive occasion to inspire a tale.[10] (It did inspire a song, "World Theater Here We Come.") Another signal came six weeks later. On 15 April, the Announcer's brief description of spring cleaning at Jack's house and the Bunsens' merely introduced the main event: a sentimental rendition of "Supper Time" including an autobiographical recitative about family love. This sentimental impulse would find full expression beginning in 1981, in the third stage of the monologue's development, when Keillor adopted Lake Wobegon as his hometown, but meanwhile he experimented with other formats. In December 1978, after Howard Mohr had reduced an audience to hilarious tears with his pseudo-scholarly analysis of waving, complete with the sociology of who is obliged to wave to whom under what circumstances, Keillor declined to offer a monologue "so as not to invite comparisons" and instead read a poem attributed to Margaret Haskins Durber, who had ostensibly published the doggerel about the Minnesota Vikings in the *Lake Wobegon Herald-Star* (30 Dec. 1978).

During this period, when he apparently struggled to find newsworthy events and a narrative perspective on them, Keillor began commenting on Lake Wobegon's quietness. On 11 Feb. 1979, for instance, a much subdued Announcer conceded, "there isn't a great deal to report this week," before contenting himself to recite the times and themes of Sunday's church services and mention an upcoming Valentine's Day dance. As a preliminary version of the soon-to-be famous "Well, it has been a quiet week in Lake Wobegon," Keillor's remark about the lack of news probably reflected his uncertainty in this transitional period, though he soon seized on its comic potential for a humor based on banal domestic detail. More important, however, the emerging trope demonstrates that as the Lake Wobegon segment of *A Prairie Home Companion* slowly changed over the next several years, the humorist did not so much abandon the idea of anticlimactic news as turn away from the superior pose of the Announcer.

He traded it for a more neutral pose, which he also began tinkering with in 1976. Almost at the same time that he began the more condescending "News from Lake Wobegon," Keillor began to look at the town through the eyes of the insider. In reading letters ostensibly from Barbara Ann Bunsen to her family at home in Lake Wobegon, Keillor solved the major problem of storytelling performance: he could read a prepared text instead of memorizing a script. In this as well as in the rhetorical possibilities of epistolary humor, he had a model in Charlie Weaver (comic persona of Cliff Arquette), whose Mount Idy letters proved how first-person narrative could blend ridicule of eccentricity with affection for the eccentric. When implied by an insider like Barbara Ann Bunsen, instead of advertised by an outsider like the Announcer, ridicule of Wobegonian backwardness would seem less sharp, allowing more of it in the bargain. The letters resolved other dilemmas, too. Combining the Announcer's detachment with Barbara Ann's naïveté allowed Keillor to exploit the comic possibilities of the outsider without sacrificing the ironic potential of first-person narration. Add to this the other advantages of epistolary storytelling, and one can hardly overestimate the importance of the Bunsen letters to the development of the mature Lake Wobegon monologue, which similarly blended literary technique with oral storytelling.

In addition to supplanting the Announcer's superior voice with an insider's, the letters from Barbara Ann contributed four main elements to the later monologue for Keillor's own voice. The realistic sense of ongoing life encompasses three of them. First, narration in real time, rather than the expanded time of the soap opera or the condensed time of conventional drama and fiction, creates the illusion that life in Lake Wobegon runs parallel to life elsewhere. Second, the fragmentary details in the letters imply a full life beyond them: in contrast to the complete fictions that render novels and plays self-contained, Barbara Ann's incomplete information about people and events connotes a life too full for a single letter as well as a shared set of experiences rendering explanations unnecessary.

Third, the blend of intimacy and banality arises quite naturally in correspondence between family members, and both "The News from Lake Wobegon" and Keillor's first-person tales featured the banal matters of daily life; these first found a domestic context in the letters from Barbara Ann. Finally, the letters offered a more moderate comic perspective on Lake Wobegon, presented for the first time as an inside account in the first person. Five years before Keillor began inventing his own life in Lake Wobegon, he had conceived of presenting the town from the viewpoint of the Exile, someone who cherished the family back "in the old hometown" but preferred it from the safe distance of the big city.

Founded on a relentlessly cheerful rhetoric designed to reassure her parents back in Lake Wobegon—"Everything is just fine, I am all right, so don't worry, everything is o.k." (as she always began)—the letters portray Barbara Ann as a dizzy young woman whose tenacity and enthusiasm match her propensity for the oddball and slapstick. The series began in the summer of 1976, after Barbara Ann graduated from high school and moved to Minneapolis from Lake Wobegon, and continued into 1981, when she dropped out of college for the second time, victim of a mysterious flu then in its second month without abating. From the start, Keillor keyed the installments to the passage of real time; in the fall of 1976, for instance, he observed that she had lived in Minneapolis for four months. As a result, the segment soon acquired its quality of ongoing saga, and its combination of the predictable and the inventive (usually outrageous) built listeners' anticipation of the next installment. The writer increased both the realism and the suspense, however, by composing the letters at irregular intervals (just like real correspondence) as Barbara Ann lived her life on a calendar parallel to our own (like the seasonal announcements on "The News from Lake Wobegon").

The realism of the format called for the Announcer to abandon the relative formality of "The News from Lake Wobegon," and substitute a familiar, even amused conversational tone. Introducing a letter in 1979, for example, the Announcer remarked,

> Reminds me for some reason of Barbara Ann Bunsen, that song, don't ask me where I've been, just rolling along. Where she's been, of course is a student at the university and then surprised everybody by getting up and getting married, and moving down with her husband to start an apple and walnut orchard and llama ranch down there in LaCrosse,

Wisconsin. Doesn't have much time to write letters, but we got one from her here this last week. It says. . . . (12 May 1979)

The letters from 1976 through 1978 chronicled her classes and jobs in college, a steady procession of boyfriends and roommates, and the culture shock of a summer in New York City, where she learned that "if you just live in L.W., you might come to think the whole world is Lutheran and everybody mows their lawn and is white and eats lutefish once a year, but come here and you learn differently."[11] Continuing the picaresque saga, the 1979 epistles featured her experiments renovating an old house and running a llama farm after she eloped with someone named Bill. He appears in her letters for the first time when she announces the marriage; the announcement doesn't even mention his surname. Letters after September 1980 chronicle her return to Minneapolis, fed up with quarantined llamas and the hard life of a carpenter, ready to resume student life at the university. "Carpentry is no leisure sport," she conceded in the spring of 1979 from her ramshackle farmhouse. "It's a sport that you learn out of necessity, like long-distance lifeboat rowing."[12] The letters offered Keillor a chance to experiment with narrative continuity in a way that newscasts did not.

Continuity came not only from tracing Barbara Ann's peregrinations over many months and years but also from the emerging portrait of family, friends, and acquaintances. Through the letters Keillor was able to begin inventing a network of characters whose lives appeared to have continuous, independent existence. The epistolary form lends itself particularly well to establishing such an illusion of reality. A letter from anyone presupposes a reader as well as a writer, and even goes so far as to characterize that reader through the subjects and tone of the communication. Thus Keillor had Barbara Ann write about the other people in her life: the former boyfriend now planning to marry her best friend, the brother who had better not dare move into her old bedroom, the new roommate and her child, the committee members at the natural foods co-op. Then he took epistolary narration one step farther by imagining the recipients of her letters, Arlene and Clarence Bunsen, whom he characterized as dedicated and naïve in equal measure—at least judging by the inappropriate food that they continually mailed to her. Acknowledging the care packages became a recurrent theme in Barbara Ann's letters home, and the humorist breathed new life into old jokes about Wobegonians' ineptitude in the process. In the winter of 1977 after bemoaning the tribulations of college life—"My problem is public health. It is an early morning class, and it is very hard to sit there at 8 o'clock and think about gonorrhea"—Barbara Ann added a postscript: "Thanks for the banana bread. It got slightly compressed in shipment, but it is now out on the window ledge to freeze, and if it doesn't turn warm this week, it should be good as new in no time.[13] Over the course of five years, the Bunsens sent their daughter a truckload of unmailables: eggs, squash, asparagus packed in ice. Along with the offhanded bombshell or left-handed postscript, these signs of comic innocence became a regular feature of the letters from Barbara Ann Bunsen, and they helped transform Lake Wobegon from the wholly eccentric town of the Jack's commercial to the affectionately oddball village of the mature monologue. In the absence of aggressive commercial rhetoric, the Announcer could poke affectionate fun at the Wobegonians, who came to appear increasingly real.

A third element of the letters, the assumption that the writer and reader share common ground, also arises from epistolary narration. Unlike a raconteur addressing an audience, a daughter corresponding with her parents does not worry about introducing characters or filling in the gaps of her life story; she can indulge equally in the profound and the banal in a single intimate stream of unrelated anecdotes or observations. Creating a believable Barbara Ann required much more than inventing a character and her modes of self-expression, however. The task also hinged on Keillor's ability to imagine the relationship between the correspondents, to invent their pasts as well as the present, and to determine what Arlene and Clarence in Lake Wobegon knew about the people and events their daughter mentioned. Keillor turned the latter to both serious and comic effect—incomplete details about a Thanksgiving dinner, on the one hand, the casual bombshell about the newest roommate or boyfriend or financial reversal, on the other. Both reveal the humorist's understanding of how less can be more in an epistolary tale. Relying on omissions and fragments to demonstrate the shared knowledge of the correspondents gave the saga a high degree of realism.

Not surprisingly, he transferred the technique from the Bunsen letters to the oral Lake Wobegon tales. Sometimes he gave a character only a first name—as with Gary and Leroy, the town constables, or Bud, who puts up the Christmas lights on Main Street, or Dorothy, who runs the Chatterbox Cafe. Other times he threw in an offhanded assumption of common ground. "I mean, she was a Putnam, after all," our storyteller insisted, trying to explain that Hjalmar Ingqvist's misery over his wife's redecorating project had nothing to do with money (18 Sept. 1982). In this example, the narrator's very syntax suggests that he, his listeners, and the Ingqvists all belong to the same world—even the same community—in which everybody knows about the Putnams. His tone of voice, intimate and casual, even gossipy at times, enhanced the illusion. Telling stories at one remove by reading letters from Barbara Ann put Keillor on the road to this more complex evocation of a real community.

In that sense and in others equally important, the letters represented Keillor's apprenticeship in public storytelling. Letting the young girl speak for herself eased the writer into *oral* yarn spinning and helped distinguish, once and for all, his kind of monologue from the stand-up comic's. He rejected the self-conscious, aggressive, decidedly public aspects of the conventional comic's performance, with its barrage of one-liners, and substituted the self-effacing, voyeuristic pleasures of reading other people's mail. The experience was intimate and, in conjunction with his audience, almost conspiratorial. The performer didn't need to memorize the letters; the writer could enjoy the craftsmanship of composing a first-person narrative of apparent formlessness and spontaneity. The more unstudied and unstructured the letters, the greater their realism—a factor that Keillor would exploit again in the tales of his own Lake Wobegon life. Although the later tales engaged his literary talents much more deeply, even in 1976 Keillor drew on considerable experience writing for the *New Yorker* as he imagined life from Barbara Ann's point of view; his twenty-four pieces in the magazine by 1976 included four particularly sophisticated examples of first-person narration: "The Slim Graves Show" (1973), "Friendly Neighbor" (1973), "My North Dakota Railroad Days" (1975), "WLT (the Edgar Era)" (1976). Typescripts in the Prairie Home Companion Archives reveal that the writer took at least as much pleasure in revealing Barbara Ann's character through her eccentric narrative style as through her curious experiences. His special talent is the non sequitur, as in the letter from New York City in August 1978: "I will have two weeks before classes start. I am having a friend of mine register for me, so I have no idea what courses I'll be taking. Maybe it'll be better that way."[14]

For a writer who enjoys experimenting with first-person narration, writing letters from Lake Wobegon's daughter in exile leads naturally to composing oral accounts by Lake Wobegon's son in exile.

In the rhetoric of the monologue as well as the history of *A Prairie Home Companion*, Barbara Ann Bunsen's first-person narratives stand between the Announcer's third-person "News from Lake Wobegon" and Keillor's first-person tales. The humorist dropped the letters from Barbara Ann after 1981, about the same time that he adopted Lake Wobegon as his hometown and began recounting his childhood there. The coincidence underscores how much narrative invention (if not actual fiction) underlies the apparently autobiographical tales and therefore suggests that their narrator represents yet another of Keillor's poses. We might call this pose the Witness to emphasize the importance of first-person narration to the comic blend of realism and fantasy and also to recognize their encyclopedic range of subjects and styles—everything from adoption to septic tanks, gossip to confession.

As a successor to the Announcer, the Witness proved ideal, for it provided a suitable public role for the insider's point of view and thereby allowed "The News from Lake Wobegon" to expand beyond the newscaster's secondhand reports. Firsthand accounts by the Witness could accommodate Barbara Ann's genuine earnestness as well as the Announcer's mock sincerity, enabling Keillor to offer cracker-barrel philosophy one week and a tall tale the next. So much the better for *A Prairie Home Companion* if the host's featured spot ranged in mood. And it varied enormously, from the confessional and reflective tones of "Storm Home" and "Meeting Donny Hart at the Bus Stop" to the broad comic fantasy of "Babe Ruth Visits Lake Wobegon" (13 July 1985; *Gospel Birds*),[15] a classic tall tale, and the melancholy realism of "The Royal Family," which the humorist liked well enough to reuse twice after its original performance on 13 November 1982.[16]

Many fans zeroed in on what seemed to them, though not to Keillor, elements of nostalgia amid the cracker-barrel philosophy. This point of view was articulated most passionately in an article praising the monologues as the "gospel of the airwaves."[17] But for those willing to see it, Keillor occasionally revived the sardonic point of view. The tale of Roger Hedlund's unforgivable mistakes, for example, concludes with the Witness's jaundiced judgment: "In Lake Wobegon, confession is just corroboration of what they already know about you. . . . That's why I like living down here in the city" (12 March 1983). Additional evidence of small-town small-mindedness appears in "The Royal Family." The comparative infrequency of the more critical tales testifies to Keillor's growing affection for Lake Wobegon and the difficulty of carrying off satire within that framework. The pose of the Witness, however, helps the storyteller reveal the town's dark secrets.

The more pensive narratives involve a variation on the Witness that we might call the Exile, to stress the speaker's ability to see the community from both within and without and to acknowledge his feelings of relief and sadness over his absence from Lake Wobegon. How distinct we hold the Witness and the Exile matters less, however, than the historical fact that the firsthand accounts of life in Lake Wobegon emerged as Keillor gradually abandoned the rhetorical superiority of the Announcer in favor of an insider's view of the town. As poses, the Witness and the Exile are not less fictive than the Amateur or the Shy Person, no matter how realistic the monologues' details, no matter how casual their performance. *A Prairie Home Companion* began with the Amateur's apparent authenticity and artlessness; the monologues from the show's maturity exploit the technique no less.

With a few notable exceptions, such as the evening in Alaska when Keillor couldn't wind up a very involved tale (12 July 1986), he could rely on his carefully worked-out monologue texts.[18] Comparisons of his prepared texts with his performances prove that he did not memorize scripts like an actor, and at least part of his reputation for spontaneous yarn spinning derives from his justifiable insistence on this point. But his performances were hardly unstudied or spontaneous, as the hundreds of monologue texts in the Prairie Home Companion Archives testify.[19] Whether he found at some point in reciting the Barbara Ann Bunsen letters that he no longer needed to read what he'd written, or whether he decided to apply his Bible-study skills to his own compositions, he discovered that the appearance of artless tale-telling takes time to master.

Mark Twain had learned the same lesson a hundred years before. Celebrated as a platform performer, Twain cultivated the art of oral storytelling early in his career, beginning with the publication of his first long narrative, *The Innocents Abroad*, in 1868 and returning periodically through the 1890s. As Twain recalled his experience on the platform, success followed on disaster; at first he'd simply tried to read from his books in the manner of Charles Dickens, whose animated readings in 1867 had captivated American audiences, only to discover (as he put it forty years later) that "written things are not for speech": "Their form is literary; they are stiff, inflexible, and will not lend themselves to happy and effective delivery with the tongue—where their purpose is to merely entertain, not instruct; they have to be limbered up, broken up, colloquialized, and turned into the common forms of unpremeditated talk—otherwise they will bore the house, not entertain it."[20]

Of the several means by which Twain admitted to contriving such "unpremeditated talk," two surface in Keillor's oral tales: posing as an artless raconteur and enacting the tale. Twain's favorite mannerisms for imitating artlessness amount to nothing more than the Amateur's stock-in-trade: "fictitious hesitancies for the right word, fictitious unconscious pauses, fictitious unconscious side remarks, fictitious unconscious embarrassments, fictitious unconscious emphases placed upon the wrong word with a deep intention back of it."[21] The nineteenth-century humorist had less to say about enacting the tale, except to note that a storyteller becomes part of the story and recreates reality by rendering its voices and actions, but he surely considered how such a performance would seem less obviously staged when framed by false ineptitude. Together the two techniques can transform a secondhand anecdote into a genuine experience relayed at firsthand. But, Twain insisted, only a storyteller who has thoroughly internalized a tale can give a believably artless performance.[22]

Keillor might have been paraphrasing Twain's description of the American humorous tale in "How to Tell a Story"—a wandering narrative full of colloquial speech—when he described to Sean Mitchell the storytelling lessons he received at the knees of his uncle Lew Powell and his wife: "I had a great uncle and aunt who were great storytellers. They would come to our house every Saturday night, and all the children would spread out at their feet. Their stories didn't have punchlines or big endings, but they used mimicry and dialogue and we listened carefully."[23] From these childhood experiences and later work on *A Prairie Home Companion* Keillor learned the lessons Twain picked up on the platform, and tapes of the show make it clear that he had mastered Twain's requisites by the summer of 1981, soon after adopting Lake Wobegon as his hometown.

Certainly he could not have recited "Dog Days of August" any more effectively. The monologue, performed 22 August 1981 and later published on *Summer*, recounts the boredom of a Lake Wobegon boy from the child's point of view and with a boy's syntax, thought processes, and voice, too. After his customary "It has been a quiet week in Lake Wobegon," the performer demonstrated virtuoso control over pacing and intonation (as well as word choice and subject) as he shifted from the adult's perspective to the child's, from adult syntax to the child's, from the narrator's measured speech to a boy's whine:

It has been a quiet week in Lake Wobegon, here in the dog days of August, been awfully warm and quiet, except for the noise made by children who are complaining that there is nothing to do. School doesn't start now for a couple weeks, the Tuesday after Labor Day, and there're a lot of these children who've just hit bottom as far as vacation is concerned. They're tired of it; they're bored with it. Of being able to do anything that they wanna do, as if there were something that they wanted to do, which there isn't anything that they wanna do. It's *boring*! Live in a *boring* house with a lot of *boring* people, talking about *boring* stuff that nobody'd ever be interested in. In a *boring* town. It's no fun.

The passage barely hints at the range of Keillor's narrative mimicry. Within the next two phrases, he conveys the children's hyperdramatic demonstrations of misery not only with his pronunciation, which slides into the colloquial "wanna" and offers the onomatopoeic plosives in "Kids just flo*p* on their *b*acks in their *b*eds," but also by singing "I'm bo-o-o-o-red! Bor-ed!" in a loud, sustained falsetto. The series of oral devices suits radio perfectly. It also illustrates Twain's dictum about the need to enact a tale. Instead of telling us about Lake Wobegon kids, in the manner of the Professional Announcer, this storyteller *is* the Lake Wobegon kids. He's also himself as a boy, his mother, and his friend Larry.

The reenactment involves much more than imitating voices, although the whining of children, the terseness of a mother's diminishing patience, and the taunts of a neighborhood tough ("Hey, stupid! Whacha doin, talkin to yerself?") all contribute to the authenticity of the eleven-minute tale. Nonetheless, Keillor's great success in "Dog Days of August" results not so much from rendering tones of voice as from capturing patterns of thought. When the bored boy becomes absorbed by motion in the grass, the storyteller takes up the myth that the earth is really a giant's head, and then devotes the rest of the tale to inversions of this theme. First, he portrays the child as a giant to the ant colony in the grass and then, after the boy has injured the ant he's named Jim, reverses the terms of the fantasy to show the contrite youth imagining giant, mutant ants seeking retribution.

Colloquial narration from the child's point of view makes clear how very carefully Keillor conceived and structured the tale, all the while giving it the appearance of artlessness. It ends on one more inversion of the first image, the world as a giant's head, as the boy's fears lead him to consider the God who may or may not be watching the creatures on earth.

> Some night, while I'm asleep, [there'll be] some kind of radiation or something, and there'll be thirty-foot-tall ants in Lake Wobegon, and Jim'll be thirty feet tall, a big ant with a bad limp. And I'll see a big ant eye in my bedroom window, and a big long ant leg come in—feeling around for me in bed. Big hairy feelers. Maybe I ought to kill him now. Kill all of them. Step on them. Jump up and down on them. Bomb them with rocks. But then all of the other ants would find out, for miles around. And then they'd all come. There'd be millions of them.
>
> God—Our Father who art in heaven, hallowed be your, hallowed be Thy name. Uh, if there are giant ants, God, we—ask that you, we ask that Thou, uh, wouldst, uh, protect-est us from them, and keep them away from our house. And if they're not real, then you can forget about it. And if you're not real, then it doesn't make any difference. (*Summer*)

As the boy questions whether God watches the creatures on earth, Keillor reveals the craft behind his artlessness. What could be more artful than climaxing the boy's train of thought with an inversion of his first image, the world as a giant's head? Like the classic tall tale, this story celebrates the tale-teller's imagination—the boy's and the creator's—by embedding a virtuoso display of fantasy in a narrative so carefully crafted that the artifice is invisible. But like the classic tall tale, this story makes a claim to truth. Speaking as the Witness, Keillor testifies to the historical fact of his experience. As in the best tall tales, however, meticulously realistic testimony is a joke on listeners naïve enough to regard them as fact. In the Lake Wobegon monologues, historical fact is beside the point, not because they are fictitious (though of course they are) but because they are fiction. Historical fact loses all importance in the face of literary truth, a truth of the highest order to a storyteller.

The speed and frequency with which Keillor churned out his monologues may tempt us to discount the craft involved, especially in light of their apparent spontaneity in performance. It's hard to imagine how one person could invent forty-some stories a year for six years, much less polish them into an effective performance week after week, while also writing all the other comic material for *A Prairie Home Companion*—mock commercials for Bob's Bank and the Fearmonger's Shoppe, for instance, and all the parodies of radio drama. The Witness's autobiographical narratives further complicate matters because their rhetoric urges us to attribute a tale's success to happenstance, not imagination, since the daily life of a community seems outside any one person's control. But although "Dog Days of August" probably has origins in the storyteller's autobiography, the story is at most mock autobiography; like other works of fiction, it imitates reality but remains distinct from it both in content and form. Indeed, for all its veracity, "Dog Days of August" takes its structure from a literary form, and subtly literate form at that: the tall tale, that apparently artless narrative contrasting written imitations of speech with more elevated narration all the while concealing the fiction beneath its realism. Keillor's choice of an essentially deceptive literary form underlines how much art went into the construction of "Dog Days of August." With various degrees of success, the same kind of craft also shaped hundreds of other tales about Lake Wobegon and growing up in it. No more than the performances of the Amateur and the Shy Person do these monologues reveal the private Garrison Keillor. At the very least, they fictionalize his experiences, transforming life into a story, an object of artifice; at the other extreme, they are fictions.

An incident that recurred in two monologues illustrates the process of fictionalization and the difficulty and even irrelevance of identifying its limits. In May 1982 and again in March 1983, the Witness told stories about boys who nearly ruined their dads' cars. Each tale features a youth who, smoking illicitly, admired his reflection in the rearview mirror when he should have been keeping his eyes on the road; both stories end without injury to the boys and record key aspects of the scene in almost the same words. But the third-person account of the earlier story becomes an elaborate first-person report in the later one:

[Version 1]

The Diener boy was pulling up the gravel road into the pit when he lit up a cigarette, I think the first of his life, and *he sort of heisted himself up in the seat to see in the rearview mirror how it looked when he exhaled* through his nose, if he was doing it the wrong way. He coughed, *he hit the brake pedal, except it wasn't the brake pedal, it was the gas pedal, the car went down the slope, wound up in the creek*—his father's car. Got out of it, waded into the creek, and noticed all of a sudden that the creek was kind of black and greasy. Transmission. Transmission. Oh, that was ma—That's not bright! That's not intelligent!

Well, he left it there; he left it sitting there, and went off to join his friends on down the road, I don't know, he figured maybe it'd get better. (15 May 1982)

[Version 2]

I remember the first time I had the use of my dad's car was also the first time that I smoked. It was a Saturday afternoon, I took off with my friend Jim, we headed south down the road, and the minute we got out of sight of the water tower, pulled out a couple of cigarillos that he had swiped from his dad. Lit them up cruising down the highway, lit them up, took a deep long drag. And *I heisted myself up in the seat, uh, [to] look in the rearview mirror, see how it looked when I exhaled.* Looked good, smoke coming out of my mouth, boy! I took another real deep drag on it, went up to look at myself again, and then a sort of wave of green passed across my eyes, as *the car drifted off the highway, and it went down the ditch, and it went back up the ditch, and suddenly we were in the middle of the soybeans.* I kept on going because I couldn't see any reason to stop. . . . Both of us got out of the car to see if there was any damage, and also to be sick for awhile. Well, there was no damage except to us, and so we headed back towards town. (12 March 1983)

The common incidents and phrasing testify to some sort of autobiographical origin for the tales, as does the incident's recurrence in at least three other tales.[24] But just what sort of autobiographical origin remains unclear from the tales. What exactly happened to the car? How close was the escape? Had Keillor himself really driven the car, or had one of his friends? Did the event really occur the first time he smoked? Was he smoking cigarettes or cigarillos, and where had they really come from? Who else was involved? Once an event has undergone some degree of fictionalization, its reality begins to matter less than its contribution to fantasy.

Indeed, the facts as Keillor recalls them are something of a disappointment. As a young adult, too respectful of his parents to smoke in their presence, he got into his car after a visit with them eager for a cigarette, admired his reflection in the rearview mirror, and nearly crashed the car as a result. At least as interesting as these details is the writer's belief that what makes them into a good story is the moral, as he sees it, that it's dangerous to be too involved with yourself.[25]

Nonetheless, the absence of any serious consequences keeps the stories humorous, and since comic retribution (or the lucky escape from same) runs through so many of Keillor's Lake Wobegon stories, whether the events actually took place becomes a good deal less important than what the writer makes of them. Two years before the story of the Diener boy's cigarette, Keillor recounted the experience of "the Olson boy," who had just reached for the medallion strategically located below his girlfriend's neck when the grain elevator blew up. The Preacher concluded the tale by advising, "If you're going to sin, you may as well do it boldly," on the premise that God knows anyway, if he exists, and nonbelievers have nothing to lose (16 Aug. 1980). The stories of smoking in dad's car end more equivocally, suggesting that Keillor reworked the incident out of dissatisfaction with the first version. The earlier tale uses the episode as just one of several variations on the theme of adolescent irresponsibility and the conflicts it creates with adults, concluding with the Philosopher's plaintive "Oh, you children! You children, what'll ever become of you, I have no idea"—about the only response to intractable human nature. The later story, by contrast, treats the incident from the more complex perspective of the Exile, which expands the anecdote into an escape from Lake Wobegon's values as well as the father's wrath:

> Every time cigars or soybeans came up in the conversation, I flinched, thinking that it was all going to come out. But it never did. [It] felt wonderful, to know I was out of the woods, felt like a bandit. Confession is good for the soul. Scripture tells us to confess our sins one to the other. But confession is when you get to tell them, it's not when they tell you first, see? In Lake Wobegon, . . . they don't really forgive you,

thinking that it'd just encourage you to do it again. It's hard, hard living among people who are such authorities on you that they don't even have to study you any more, they just take one look and they say, "Yep, dat's Roger, you know Roger, dat's Roger for you." That's why I like living down here in the city. (12 March 1983)

In reviving the image of Lake Wobegon as a place of limited attractions, Keillor transforms the incident from an unexpected opportunity to an almost existential experience of self-realization. And he does so without sacrificing the humor of either his own childhood folly or Roger Hedlund's, which is the primary subject of the monologue. As the Witness, Keillor can switch from self-ridicule to self-aggrandizement or mix his own fond memories with the bitter example of others. The pose demands great skill while minimizing evidence of it.

Like the apparent authenticity of the Amateur, the Shy Person, and the Philosopher, the apparent artlessness of the Witness derives largely from the running contrast between his evidently spontaneous speech and his obviously scripted performances in the parodies of old-time radio melodramas. These segments flaunted their artificiality with the same intensity that the monologues veiled it. To call attention to the comic revival of broadcasting techniques long since abandoned, the players huddled around one or two microphones as they read silly scripts in comically clumsy voices. These parodies, so emphatically dependent on the written text, made the rest of the program seem thoroughly serendipitous—as in fact Keillor's banter with his guests was. And of course the performers could abandon the strict controls of more formal performances and actually risk serendipity, even to the point of failure, because whatever errors and flaws occurred simply reaffirmed that a recording engineering had not tidied up the performance for broadcast. What the audience heard was happening now.

Reading scripts as the Professional Announcer offered many possibilities for playing comic roles instead of assuming comic poses, since the all-too-evident script kept the Professional separate from Keillor's public persona. The usual result was camp. The performers' wooden inflections, mistimed entrances, and plain old goofs, could not have contrasted more emphatically with the Professional's slick—even unctuous—narration. Keillor began lampooning the Professional's booming voice on the first live broadcast in 1974, when he introduced Bill Hinkley and Judy Larson in "The Powdermilk Biscuit Radio Theater," and had not tired of playing with it by the Second and Third Farewell Performances, which featured episodes of "Buster, the Show Dog," a serial that debuted in 1986.[26] The longevity of the Professional reflects the pose's adaptability to formulas ranging from the rhetoric of morality plays to the conventions of cliff-hanger dramas. Comic targets eventually encompassed *A Prairie Home Companion* as well as more distant examples of classic radio. The role of the Professional, with its exaggerated artifice, made fair game of the Amateur's hesitant posturing. The tactic spoke to larger contemporary interest in radio drama as well, since at the same time Keillor's live show began, the St. Paul–based Earplay started to produce old and new radio dramas for American Public Radio and the British Broadcasting Corporation. The Professional's mock superiority allowed the humorist to ridicule his own show along with radio dramas of the past.

The number of targets expanded as the show grew. On the first live broadcast, the humor aimed almost exclusively at the melodramas of advertising—the debased, final vestige of old-time radio programming. With nods to Hansel and Gretel, musicians Judy Larson and Bill Hinkley enacted an urban fable of hapless rustics who find love and happiness in the big city when their trail markers of Powdermilk Biscuit crumbs cross. In this first effort, the Professional simply frames the action of the love story (which briefly threatens an unhappy ending when Judy remarks that she and Bill didn't have "quite enough on which to build a lasting relationship . . . until I pulled a tray of hot, crispy Powdermilk Biscuits out of the oven") and conveys its successful denouement: "What happened after that, I guess, is show business history—Bill and Judy took over the Powdermilk Biscuit Show on WLT and quickly became household words" (6 July 1974). The joke here depends not only on distinguishing radio rhetoric from fact, but also on recognizing that WLT—whose call letters do in fact signify "with lettuce and tomato"—exists only in Keillor's imagination and his 1976 *New Yorker* story. Although the Buster scripts contained many inside jokes, most of the radio parodies on *A Prairie Home Companion* featured widely accessible subjects.

An early knee-slapper called "Dusty Fiddles" (21 Dec. 1974) applied the broad strokes of the initial parody to seasonal material, a Christmas drama about two down-and-out radio musicians played by Hinkley and Larson. Camp seldom comes more broad than this self-conscious performance, billed as "an original drama by an author who's asked to remain anonymous" and narrated in Keillor's most imposing tones. "We find ourselves in a radio script, a dark and mysterious place where many allusions and meanings lie buried," he warned before introducing characters punningly named Linda Hand, Wayne Amanger, and Harold Angel, who traded such memorable lines as "Better close that window because somebody's about to knock on it," before they finally gave up on the script. To the characters' unexpected (but completely justified) lament, "This is terrible. Who wrote it?" Keillor responded with an equally surprising "I did. I wrote all of this," followed by the memorable narration, "It was a tall and strangely attractive stranger, and his obvious way with words made them withhold the bitter criticism they had thought to offer." And so it continued, all the way to the punch line, which the humorist reserved for himself, a remark about hunting that is a punning distortion of "Adeste Fideles": "Even if a Dusty fiddles late he tree 'em fonties."[27] The character of the Professional Announcer gave a parodic edge to "Dusty Fiddles," which has historical interest despite a degree of silliness more appropriate to a high school skit than to a professional show. Such playfulness typified the early years of A Prairie Home Companion, of course, but "Dusty Fiddles" also demonstrates that within six months of beginning the live broadcasts, the writer had begun experimenting with self-reflexive parody, humor that includes itself among its comic targets. The tactic offset the script's sophomoric qualities by conceding and then flaunting them, debunking the Professional and Amateur both.

Send-ups of radio drama continued through innumerable commercial minidramas for imaginary products as well as such longer mock playlets as "The Spillers" (18 Sept. 1982), which borrowed rhetoric from melodramas about alcoholism in order to dramatize the tribulations of adults who spill their food. But whatever the ostensible topic of the playlets, their humor aimed at radio as a profession. In this sense, the radio dramas sustained the rhetoric of amateurism that underlay Keillor's various comic poses, though with a slightly different twist to the self-ridicule as he poked fun at the whole profession. Examples include his public service announcement for MARSH ("The Minnesota Association of Radio Show Hosts..., protecting radio personalities from an ungrateful public for more than fourteen months")[28] and the mock promotional announcement for an apocryphal public radio serial called "The Announcer," "the story of a young man's drive to become a tasteful person" (26 June 1982).

To be sure, Keillor found announcers a staple target even before his live broadcasts began; in 1973 he boasted that he got the job hosting the morning version of *A Prairie Home Companion* because the ad agency for Jack's Auto Repair considered him ideal for their target audience, "a type of person who never fully grew up and who needs a steadying influence in the dim, preconscious hours."[29] His mockery culminated, however, in the parodic serial "Buster, the Show Dog," which ran from 6 December 1986 through the final performance on 13 June 1987 and picked up again a year later at the Second Farewell.

As the Lake Wobegon monologue turned away from announcements of Visitors' Day and grew more sentimental and reflective, *A Prairie Home Companion* lost a main vehicle for caustic humor. "Buster" provided that vehicle, and the opportunity to parody the conventions of serial melodrama seems to have inspired the writer less than having a regular spot for comic sharpshooting on a variety of topics. Writing and reading scripts for the Professional Announcer let Keillor deflate radio across the spectrum—from the most conventional radio rhetoric (on any subject) to elements of *A Prairie Home Companion* itself.

"Buster" most obviously spoofs *Rin-Tin-Tin* and *Lassie*, but it also has debts to "Tippy, the Wonder Dog," a comedy routine by Bob Elliott and Ray Goulding, whose so-called sponsor, Mushies dog cereal, will remind Keillor's fans of Scotty's Cough Syrup for Dogs, sponsor of "Buster." Like Keillor, Bob and Ray lampooned *Lassie* by featuring a boy (Timmy in the last television series, which ended in 1971) who overflows with appreciation for his canine companion: "Didn't I tell you, Gram's? Tippy's the brilliantest, smartest dog in the whole wide world."[30] Keillor alluded to *Lassie* by naming his boy Timmy, but then went far beyond the rhetoric of family melodrama satirized by Bob and Ray. Indeed, the number of targets goes on and on: new reporters ("Timmy the Sad Rich Teenage Boy is——the holidays have been too much for him folks——too many cookies, I think——this ought to be a warning"); serial formulas ("Red ants, vultures, hot sun, no water, burning sand—what else could possibly go wrong?"); university writing programs ("The S.S. Pimento is owned by . . . the English Department of the University of South Dakota . . . as a training ship for writers. Novelists mainly. Writers who want an ocean-going experience as a sailor but they can't afford to spend six months or a year on it"); and after cablecasting began, Disney movie clichés ("[HOWL] Cried the famous Showdog, for as animals often do, he sensed what was about to happen even before it did").[31] As this last example suggests, "Buster" also ridiculed *A Prairie Home Companion*. The serial focused disparate comic impulses in much the same way as the early "News from Lake Wobegon."

The inside jokes of the Buster series developed differently from those of the Matter of Minnesota, however. Many of them, particularly the ones invented in performance, existed solely for the pleasure of the performers and staff.[32] One script misstates the title of the program and tweaks public radio for its continuing lack of funds; the script called for Keillor as the Professional to intone, "A lot has happened to Buster our showdog since last week's show when his friend Little Timmy the Sad Rich Teenage Boy pulled a gun here on the broadcast . . . and demanded more money for Buster and a better contract for performing on the Home of the Prairie Show—for one thing, the check we gave him was no good."[33] On other occasions, the humor had more poignancy. The earliest scripts, which antedate the announcement of his retirement from *A Prairie Home Companion*, make clear that the showdog is Keillor himself. Buster's audiences misunderstand him, at best; at worst, they demean him. The accessible jibes reveal Keillor's waning interest in *A Prairie Home Companion* as he makes fun of the show's success.

Keillor hints at how the pleasures of celebrity had soured in his depictions of overrated announcers and their overimpressed fans. The first installment of the Buster series details how an act of charity instigated by Father Finian leads a radio station to hire Buster as an announcer after discovering that he can neither type nor appear on television. The dog's success at reciting the names of classical composers (as in "Bach!" and "Grrrrrrrrrshwin") draws effusive letters from adoring fans, who write such drivel as "your programs mean so much to us and we sit spellbound, hardly daring to inhale or chew or rustle our clothing, so great is your radio artistry." But while his acclaim mounts, the declining health of plants in the radio station proves that you can't teach a dog new tricks.[34] More direct evidence of how disturbing Keillor found his celebrity appears in a script from 27 December 1986, in which the fictional audience asks, "Could we see your dog degrade himself?" Though the Buster scripts doubtless exaggerate the fatigue and frustrations of a writer whose success has threatened to rob him of the freedom to flirt with failure—the very freedom that had given *A Prairie Home Companion* its vitality—people who faulted his decision to retire from the show likely did not recognize the signals that he had tired of its demands on him.

Like the western, the spy story, the romance, and other types of popular narrative art, the Lake Wobegon monologue appealed to an audience eager for a new twist on the old familiar formula.[35] Eventually, that wish narrowed to the desire for yet another confessional tale of growing up in Lake Wobegon, and eventually, repetition of that formula ceased to provide the kind of literary and rhetorical challenge that had inspired *A Prairie Home Companion* from the start. The predictable elements did contribute to the stock of inside jokes—about the Chatterbox Cafe's hot dish *du jour*, for example, and the current state of the Norwegian bachelor farmers' sheets—but they also began to find their way into book reviews and fan letters, sure signs that the humorist's formulas no longer belonged exclusively to him. And still the goat that is radio kept on eating. Howard Mohr contributed his Raw Bits and Minnesota Language Systems spots until 1986.[36] The staff at Minnesota Public Radio tried to hire writers for the show in an effort to allow Keillor time for other projects, including stories for the *New Yorker* and longer works of fiction, but the search failed to identify anyone perfectly suitable, despite a substantial response to the ads; just returning the sample materials took the staff several months.[37] In the end, Dan Rowles contributed regularly, and the show used pieces from a few outside writers, but the bulk of the comic material continued to come from Keillor himself.[38]

The humorist's Valentine's Day announcement that weekly performances would end on 13 June 1987 saddened staff members but did not surprise them. Although they had just a few weeks' advance warning, most had seen the end coming since 1984, when they celebrated the tenth anniversary of the live broadcasts with a gala performance whose hundred-dollar tickets would have sounded like a pretty tall story to the autoharp player and his twelve ticket holders in 1974. Hindsight also lets us discern messages of doom through the *Ten Years* performance and its souvenir program. During the show, however, Keillor seemed only to be offering the audience one more twist on his comic poses of inferiority when he mentioned "sponsors who have stuck with us through those early thin hard years of our show and who are still with us now as we enter the years of our gradual decline,"[39] and the same humor infused the last few entries of "A Prairie Home Almanac." Though the anniversary show took place in July, the chronicle for 1984 ran through the fall, concluding with reports of one debacle after the next: "From Sept.–Nov., nearly 200 stations drop show in favor of BBC Science Magazine," "Record number of non-shows. Popcorn sales drop," "World Theater accidentally razed [during performance]. . . . Audience applauds."[40]

Nothing of the sort occurred, of course, and far from the fate he foresaw for his history of Lake Wobegon—"GK completes years-in-progress book . . . & discovers that faulty word processor has eaten all 400 pages and compressed them into one small burst of static"—Keillor reached even greater popularity with the publication of *Lake Wobegon Days*, which gave the oral humor of *A Prairie Home Companion* a new and different life.

CHAPTER 4   *Lake Wobegon Days*
Doubling and Division

*I'm more comfortable
put into the third person.*
—Keillor, quoted by John
Bordsen (1983)

*Books must be read as de-
liberately and reservedly
as they were written.*
—Thoreau, Walden (1854)
In a symbolic scene near the end of
Lake Wobegon Days (1985), a high
school senior indulges his fantasies of
fame by turning on the phonograph and
mouthing the words to the anthem,
"Minnesota, Hail to Thee." In his imagination, the tenor voice that drew
snickers from the sopranos during
choir practice earlier in the day has now
become a magnificent baritone capti-
vating an audience of sixty thousand at a Memorial Day service.
Before the enormous crowd, which includes the governor, assorted
dignitaries, "and five thousand Boy Scouts in formation holding
American Flags"—the whole lot of them represented by the blank
bedroom wall—the youth pretends to sing, "Thy sons and daughters
true will proclaim thee near and far." The exalted moment promises
all the rewards an injured adolescent could ask: the crowd's admiration, indicated by rapt silence, and parental pride, expressed by sir-
loin steak and french fries. But the fantasy fizzles when his mother
enters the room, her arms loaded not with laurels but with laundry.

She walks between me and the chorus to the dresser and puts the socks
in the top drawer. The governor, the sixty thousand fade away—the song

goes on.

    "What are you doing?" she asks.

    "I'm practicing," I say. "For choir."[1]

The incident exemplifies Keillor's highly complex and highly ambivalent attitude toward the Matter of Minnesota in *Lake Wobegon Days*. The humorist's only extended narrative overflows with familiar icons of childhood and small-town American life—daydreams and disappointments, baseball and Boy Scouts, lawn ornaments and storm windows, Main Street and Founder's Square. But Keillor works his local-color material so that it debunks the same sentimentality and nostalgia that it evokes. As abruptly and comically as the presence of mother and socks punctures the boy's dreams of glory, so Keillor ridicules rosy views of childhood and small-town America. The novel has indeed proclaimed Minnesota near and far, but in the final analysis the narrator's praise for small-town America is about as trustworthy as the boy's booming baritone.

Our sentimental smile at the injured kid changes into a kind of wry smirk at the failure of fantasy when reality intrudes in the banal forms of laundry, choir practice, and phonograph records, and it brings the incident to an anticlimactic end. The tricky rhetorical tactics underlying the shift hint at Keillor's very complex—but equally ambitious—use of his homespun material. On the one hand, the Matter of Minnesota provides him access to the most honored and affectionate traditions of American humor: the town booster's brags, vivid regional portraits, poignant reminiscences of childhood, realistic deflation of fantasy, anticlimactic ridicule of sentiment—that is, the stuff of *Tom Sawyer*—all rendered by a vernacular voice of surprising range (the third-person narrator of *Tom Sawyer* is an amused, literate adult). But on the other hand, the Matter of Minnesota also allows Keillor, particularly in his role as Lake Wobegon's mock historian, to ridicule and, on occasion, even savage the Wobegonians without sacrificing the presumed good nature of his own voice. This essentially subversive use of sentimentality allows Keillor and his audience to pay lip service to old American rural verities while insisting on the superiority of contemporary urban life.

Such nuances would get lost in oral storytelling. They require the reflective, self-conscious narration of print, and this factor explains the book's unusual reliance on visual humor. Comic typography is most obvious in the early and closing chapters of *Lake Wobegon*

Days, but visual jokes appear throughout. Lengthy footnotes, doggerel verse, italicized and capitalized phrases contribute relatively accessible jokes to the novel's fairly sophisticated literary humor. The most elaborate visual humor involves pseudoscholarly footnotes, whose typographical humor enhances more subtle incongruities. Beginning on the first page and recurring sporadically throughout the novel, earnest citations of apocryphal documents and sources interrupt the main narrative and imply an overeager, slightly inept writer behind it. Descended from Keillor's radio pose of the Amateur, such narration debunks both the narrator and his tale.[2]

The first footnote, for instance, gets *Lake Wobegon Days* off to a playful start. The first page has two different openings, neither of them fully appropriate, and in a reversal of normal procedure, the footnote provides more information than the text. Introducing Lake Wobegon more formally and completely than the opening paragraph, the note makes fun of the conventional, objective description typical of guidebooks:

> right 1.2 m to LAKE WOBEGON (1418 alt., 942 pop.), named for the body of water that it borders. Bleakly typical of the prairie, Lake Wobegon has its origins in the utopian vision of nineteenth-century New England Transcendentalists but now is populated mainly by Norwegians and Germans. (1)

It also mocks the narrator's more subjective report, which preceded it:

> A breeze off the lake brings a sweet air of mud and rotting wood, a slight fishy smell, and picks up the sweetness of old grease, a sharp whiff of gasoline, fresh tires, spring dust, and, from across the street, the faint essence of tuna hotdish at the Chatterbox Cafe. (2)

Keillor piles other incongruities onto this basic contrast, between what we might expect of a book about small-town life and what we'll get from this one. The asterisk for the footnote appears four words into the opening sentence, in the middle of the first clause. As a result, reading the long note requires us to turn to page 2 even before we've reached the verb of the first sentence on page 1. Still more jokes are embedded in the content of the note, with its deadpan recitation of mileposts and local landmarks attributed to a *second*—nonexistent—1939 edition of the Minnesota history from the Federal Writers' Project. This bibliographical detail, so appropriate to a footnote, signals ever so subtly that this narrative, far from being a scholarly or even a personal history, belongs to the narrative traditions of the tall tale, whose meticulously rendered false details lead to a great lie. Equally to the point, the visual humor as a whole—including spurious documents, chapter-long footnotes, parodies of outline form and old-style spelling—declares that, despite its own mock-oral narration and its origin in the oral tales of *A Prairie Home Companion, Lake Wobegon Days* was meant to be read. *Caveat lector*: let the reader beware.

Indeed, although the author diffidently described the book as "a collection of pieces which are trying to make themselves into a novel,"[3] *Lake Wobegon Days* presents plenty of evidence of the novelist's concern for form and theme. The book relies on several familiar literary structures, and although the episodic center of the volume might suggest otherwise, Keillor has carefully ordered and woven together the various strands of the narrative. The narrator's childhood reminiscences form the most obvious strand, a mock autobiography beginning with his ancestors and concluding with his high school graduation. A second strand doubles this structure; the story of Johnny Tollefson, a young writer, follows the general outlines of the *Bildungsroman*, debunked in this case as the portrait of the artist as a young misfit. As the third strand, the chronicle of the town's founding and development by New England transcendentalists borrows formulas of (mock) history at the same time that it piles realistic details into a tall tale. Recent events in Lake Wobegon history belong to a fourth structure, made up of the novel's seasonal tales. These anecdotes appear to be linked only by their time of year, but their casual, mock-oral narration conceals a serious aesthetic. Behind the send-up of *Bildungsroman*, American utopianism, and small-town life lies a structure borrowed from *Walden*. Like Thoreau's personal narrative about New England utopianism by the shore, Keillor's book begins in summer, follows the seasons in a year that compresses several years' experiences, and culminates with the spring and "Revival." The comic spirit of the novel obscures its ambitions—quite a common problem in humorous fiction[4]—but they suit a comic novel whose targets range from Martin Luther's *Ninety-Five Theses* to high school football rousers.

They also cast some seriousness on Keillor's ridicule of both transcendentalism and small-town institutions. Why not look to the master of marching to one's own drummer when debunking utopianism and social rituals? Keillor sustains the borrowed structure through the end, where he finally ties all the strands neatly together. Through a narrative montage that merges the lives of the narrator, Johnny Tollefson, and Clarence Bunsen, the ending fulfills Bunsen's faith in the transcendental principle that "anything that ever happened to me is happening to other people" (334). Unfortunately, the ending wraps up the story at the expense of its coherence. Since the narrator himself has not grown older or wiser over the course of his tale, the affectionate sentimentality of the ending coexists uneasily with the exuberant lies, parodies, and ridicule of the start. More troubling, the novel ends by affirming the transcendentalism that it began by lampooning. The conflict may explain why the aesthetic ambitions of *Lake Wobegon Days* went unnoticed by the dozens of reviewers who discussed the volume; certainly it accounts for why many readers abandoned the book in the middle, unable to find the thread linking the seasonal stories and unable to determine the author's attitude toward Lake Wobegon.[5] But whatever else it means, the conflict worked against Keillor's apparent goals for the book. Given the extent of his aspirations—not to mention the novel's rich comic achievements—we should not be too surprised that the writer's ambivalence toward the Matter of Minnesota finally interfered with the coherence of *Lake Wobegon Days*.

The divided feelings are at their most graphic in the footnotes, which heckle the main text and split the book into two narratives, to be read one at a time. In contrast to the fairly conventional footnotes at the beginning of the novel, later notes run for pages. Keillor makes fun of his own method in his longest note, which extends the length of an entire chapter, nearly twenty-five pages, and which he claims may be "the longest footnote in American literature."[6] Divided by the customary hairline, "News," the tenth chapter (250–74), contains two contrasting narratives. The main text ridicules the irrelevant pabulum that owner and publisher Harold Starr printed in the *Herald-Star* and contrasts it with the text of the note: the unsentimental, occasionally mean-spirited, but true (or at least truer) copy that Starr didn't or wouldn't set—a Lake Wobegonian's equivalent of Luther's *Ninety-five Theses*, his condemnation of the town and its people. Over the length of the chapter, the humor of these theses wears thin. Still, Keillor had several purposes in mind for the technique, one of them quite serious. As he saw it, footnotes provide both writer and reader greater control over the sequence and content of the narrative, a marked difference from live storytelling, which moves in only one direction—and quickly. "There is supporting material which can be read in sequence or earlier or just glanced at or eliminated entirely, and that can go into footnotes," he told a reporter for *Publishers Weekly*. "It really allows a person freedom of digression that you want in a book."[7]

As the comment suggests, the digressions are hardly aimless, nor are the mixed feelings accidental. On the contrary, ambivalence about Lake Wobegon is very often the whole point. With a didactic undercurrent that Thoreau would approve,[8] the two texts of "News" joke individually about the irrelevance of what newspapers call news, but even jointly they don't provide news—at least not recognizably. The chapter plays with one of the standard anomalies of the Lake Wobegon monologue, originally billed as the retrograde "News from Lake Wobegon," which never related *events* of any real consequence but usually conveyed some important insights anyway. The main narrative of the chapter borrows that formula, which uses a humor of negation:

> It wasn't news that Ruthie and Bob got married, marriage was more or less inevitable under the circumstances; the *news* was the miracle of architecture Mrs. Mueller worked on Ruthie's dress, making it look flat in front. . . . "The bridal suite featured violet satin bedsheets and a quilted spread with ironed-on bride & groom appliqués, . . . a bouquet of funereal red roses, and her husband sick in the john," the *Herald-Star* did not report. "The bride felt queasy herself." (256–57)

For all the promise of its title, "News" finally settles for an anticlimactic, deconstructionist view of the news as a series of highly idiosyncratic readings of events by various Wobegonians, every reading as incomplete as the last. In this context, *news* is as good a name as any for the writer's explanation of how he found his calling: he loved the pencil given to him when he was left as a newborn on the Keillor doorstep by the cotton candy man from the circus, who had misunderstood the intentions of the infant's real mother, a fat lady tightrope walker who gave birth to the boy while crossing the high wire and handed him to the candy man while she returned to her act. If such news raises as many silly questions as it resolves theoretical ones, not least about whether no news really is good news, it also insists that news lies everywhere for the skilled interpreter. Like the narrator himself, for instance. To "the careful reader," Aunt Flo's apparently simple announcement overflows with information: "she still dotes on her wayward nephew, pointing out his gainful and glamorous employment and suggesting that he is no slouch on a bean row, either, giving a little plug for family longevity and complimenting the guests with a good lunch" (273). Equally important, the chapter demonstrates that even when Keillor himself seems to be aiming for the quick and easy joke, *Lake Wobegon Days* warrants close and serious reading.

Still, the spirit of the book remains firmly comic, and "News" provides the most extended example of the basic incongruity of *Lake Wobegon Days*, a device that we might call *comic paradox* because it focuses on what isn't (the news that isn't news, for example) and then proceeds to make it so. Certainly comic paradox shapes the most successful portion of the book, roughly the first half, from "Home" and "New Albion" through "Summer," with their exceptionally coherent and sustained comic rendering of ambivalence. In these six chapters, Keillor sets banal details about Lake Wobegon against an idealized image, often literary in origin. Regardless of the narrative type he considers—sentimental, didactic, historical, oratorical, poetic, epistolary, or journalistic—Lake Wobegon comes up short in comparison, with the additional fillip that so much talk about an imaginary place is utterly absurd.

Debunking guidebook sentimentality for starters, the opening chapter, "Home," quickly establishes Lake Wobegon as a retrograde place with "few scenic wonders such as towering pines or high mountains but . . . some fine people of whom some are over six feet tall" (9). Always Keillor plays with the idea that a crucial element is absent. The sun on the lake "would make quite a picture," he notes, "if you had the right lens, which nobody in this town has got" (3). A similar incongruity extends to the town itself, which has inspired visitors from 1836 to the present to look at Lake Wobegon and conclude, "*It doesn't start here!*" (3). Comic paradox provides a metaphor as well as a strategy for relating the history of an apocryphal town.

As a result, the chapters titled "New Albion" and "Forebears" not only parody American historical writing and mythmaking but ridicule Keillor's own pseudohistorical writing and mythmaking as well—if anyone remains inclined to take it straight. Regardless of why the various settlers came or what they called the town, it didn't fulfill either their original expectations or their subsequent fantasies.

More to the point of this tall history, every last one of the founding fathers and mothers was a fraud. A somewhat dim guiding light, Henry Francis Watt, wrote the town's first poem, "Phileopolis: A Western Rhapsody"—648 deservedly unpublished lines of iambic tetrameter couplets—before renaming himself "Dr. Henry Watt, Ph.D., Litt. D., D.D." and accepting an appointment as the first president of New Albion College in 1852. (The college represents the town's first institution if we don't count the real-estate boosterism—leaning heavily toward hucksterism—that led to its founding.) Fifteen years later, in 1867, Katherine Schroeder, the town's matriarch, misrepresented herself as Norwegian-speaking when responding to Magnus Oleson's ad for a mail-order bride. Oleson, for his part, had reached the town in 1863 on a horse stolen from General George McClellan's regiment, which he had deserted after President Lincoln failed to respond to his letter explaining why this "was no war for a Norwegian" (67). Other countrymen arrived by accident and stayed by default. So did the local railroad spur. What more appropriate history than this comedy of errors and wrongs for an imaginary place apparently left off the map by drunken and dishonest surveyors?

Perhaps the best example of Keillor's strategy in the early chapters of the novel occurs in "Sumus Quod Sumus," ostensibly devoted to explaining the official Lake Wobegon motto (translated into Latin ineptly, of course): "We Are What We Are." (The error may reflect a local joke, since the motto of the Great Seal of Minnesota has a similar error, "Quo Sursum Velo Videre" instead of "Quo Sursum Volo Videre.")[9] Near the beginning of the chapter, structured as a series of answers to questions about Lake Wobegon, the narrator responds to the question *"What's special about this town, it's pretty much like a lot of towns, isn't it?"* with the reply "There is a perfectly good answer to that question, it only takes a moment to think of it" (92). He then allows nonanswers to dominate the chapter. He begins well enough by asserting that Lake Wobegon differs from other towns because it has the Statue of the Unknown Norwegian, but what he has to say about the statue undermines his point. The unsuccessful work of a second-rate sculptor, the statue has uncertain, worried eyes that capture the ineptitude of the town, which for lack of funds never provided a proper pedestal for its landmark. Adding insult to injury (and comic euphemism and anticlimax to irony), the tornado of 1947 "blew a stalk of quackgrass about six inches into . . . an unusual place, a place where you've been told to insert nothing bigger than your finger in a washcloth" (93); there it continues growing, so that Lake Wobegon's sole municipal employee must reach up to the statue's right ear and clip the new growth every time he mows the grass. But the joke goes full circle, since, despite everything, the Statue of the Unknown Norwegian does furnish an appropriate landmark for the town. A genuine emblem of "Sumus Quod Sumus," it unquestionably symbolizes Lake Wobegon's ineptitude.

The rest of the chapter gives readers a firsthand demonstration of that backwardness. In the digressive, anticlimatic manner of a typical western yarn spinner—Jim Blaine, for example, telling the story of "My Grandfather's Old Ram" in Mark Twain's *Roughing It* (1872)—Keillor almost but never quite gets around to the story he promised to tell.[10] Returning to the question of his town's special virtues, the narrator elaborates on what the town is not: "What's so special about this town is not the food" (94), and it's "not smarts either" (97). The digressive anecdotes following each proposition explain in convincing detail why neither food nor intelligence accounts for Lake Wobegon's specialness, but they explicitly avoid saying what does. Unless, of course, *special* means "uniquely weird," in which case there's evidence aplenty. The shopping is so bad in Lake Wobegon that the economy has taken on peculiar adaptations best described as "voluntary socialism with elements of Deism, fatalism, and nepotism" (95). Like the people of Sholom Aleichem's Chelm stories, who try to capture the moon in a bucket of water, the Lake Wobegonians put on red, white, and blue baseball caps to form a living flag and then lose it as they look up at their reflection in a mirror. But considering the town motto's echoes of both the sublime and ridiculous—Yahweh's "I am that I am" and Popeye's "I yam what I yam"—we should expect nothing less.

In these early chapters, the chief beneficiary of the conflicting feelings about Lake Wobegon is, of course, the tall tale. So much historical and rhetorical nonevidence in support of a nonexistent town! Like a classic western liar, Keillor piles up one realistic detail after another in support of his great lie: that central Minnesota really has a Mist County containing Lake Wobegon, which took its name from the Ojibway "Wa-be-gan-tan-han," meaning either "the place where we waited all day in the rain" (39) or "Here we are!" (8). The early chapters of *Lake Wobegon Days* stand so firmly in the classic traditions of the tall tale that they even contain a bear story. Obviously indebted to Thomas Bangs Thorpe's "Big Bear of Arkansas," with which it shares a scatological joke,[11] and somewhat less to William Faulkner's story "The Bear," Keillor's tale grants the Minnesota beast the customary characteristics of the species: epic dimensions, elusiveness, ferocity, and social symbolism, to boot. The New Albion bear sends several students to the grave, another to an insane asylum, and still others to the safety of their families; it seems intent on destroying Albion College. But the conclusion of the anecdote, an example of narrative one-upmanship, is entirely appropriate to a tall tale that also parodies the genre. When a townsman slays the bear, he doesn't bring the story to a climax; he merely sets up the remaining faculty and students for attack by a second critter.

It is hardly surprising, given this inauspicious beginning, that the hunting in Lake Wobegon does not improve as the years and the book go on. The patience of the duck hunters in the Pete Peterson Memorial Blind fizzles out early in the day. Carl Krebsbach, moreover, cannot really claim success in bagging a doe: as tame as a pet, she wouldn't leave him alone and he feared being shot by his companions in the woods. Like the other members of his community, Lake Wobegon's official chronicler heads "straight for the small potatoes" (7) when he borrows the heroic narrative traditions of the braggart.

In addition to the yarn-spinning traditions of western tall talk, *Lake Wobegon Days* also adopts the burlesque traditions of nineteenth-century literary comedy, which found American history an irresistible target. The double debt follows quite logically from Keillor's experiments in his short fiction, which plays with literary forms as well as mock-oral narration, as his mock history does here. In lampooning the characters and incidents of American history, such as the New England transcendentalist who set off for Minnesota to convert the Indians through interpretative dance, he not only peppers his descriptions with ridiculous details but also allows his fools to unmask themselves through a series of mock-historical documents.

These reveal the characters' pretensions as writers while parodying their chosen forms. The diary of Prudence Alcott (distantly related to Bronson, et al.) chronicles her gradual acculturation to the wilderness: her prose style shifts from its original eastern stiffness ("Henry & George snort . . . & disgust me [with] their gross sensuality & brute appetites" [26; Keillor's brackets]) to a softer sentimentality ("Base metals may to pure gold chang̀ed be" [27]) before she finally decides to marry a swarthy French trapper ("my petticoats were so cumbersome I dispensed with them &c" [28]). At least one reader found these passages realistic enough to take offense at them as a distortion of American history, a response that attests to the accuracy of the imitations.[12] Equally inspired as parodies are the various literary exercises of Albion College President Henry Watt, particularly the epic "Phileopolis" (rejected by James Russell Lowell at the *Atlantic*) and the Founder's Day speech of 1855, immortalized in a student's notes: "Gratitude. Much accmp. Much rmns" (47). Reminiscent of the comic misspellings perpetrated by nineteenth-century Phunny Phellows, who similarly debunked their narrators' writings, Keillor's cacography here also serves another purpose.[13] Excerpts from newspapers, family correspondence, song books, and other documents provide the mock authenticity of clippings in the family album.

The anecdotal second half of *Lake Wobegon Days* fits more clearly with these early chapters if we think of it in similar terms, as anecdotes from the town album. Still, the mock ethnohistory of the first six chapters doesn't blend easily with the Waldenesque anecdotes of the last six, not least because the two parts have different narrative styles. The first half uses chronology, parody, and allusion to give literary shape to colloquial, mock-oral narration; the process conceals the oral origins of the material, much of which first appeared in the monologues of *A Prairie Home Companion*. More important than strict chronological organization (which in any case concerns only the second and third chapters, since "Sumus Quod Sumus" and "Protestant," the next two, jump from the distant past to recent years), the early chapters boast a consistent narrative voice and point of view: Garrison Keillor, native son in self-imposed, grateful exile, smiles at the formative influences of his town. As elements in an obviously literary structure, the settlers' writing remains subordinate to Keillor's narrative voice, which shapes our interpretation of such historical "evidence" as Prudence Alcott's diary and Gunter Muus's letters to Norway. Keillor might have provided structures for the last six chapters comparable to those of the first, but he apparently chose not to, or rather, chose instead to rely on the more oratorical structure of *Walden*. The narrator's voice remains a presence in the last six chapters, to be sure, but it diminishes in importance as other voices of Lake Wobegon offer other points of view. In the last six chapters, we jump from Keillor's highly particularized first-person narration to many different third-person stories, ranging from the limited viewpoint of Lyle's thoughts to omniscient reports on town council meetings. As a result, the second half of the book comes to seem more anecdotal and oral than the first, not because the first half relates any fewer unusual incidents but because the second relies on oral rather than literary forms.

This is not to say that *Lake Wobegon Days* carries over into print the symmetrical structures of the oral monologues, which, like traditional oral stories, build a long yarn from a series of distinct but parallel incidents.[14] In contrast to the live monologues, whose duration Keillor controlled while his voice kept listeners rapt, the anecdotes in the second half of the novel seem shapeless and fragmentary. Tales of Clarence Bunsen or Norwegian bachelor farmers have no clear relationship to one of the larger structures—autobiography, *Bildungsroman*, or town history—though they always enhance our understanding of the townspeople and their values. Still, every new anecdote shifts the point of view; the degree of the change varies from the slight differences among omniscient third-person stories to the substantial shifts between first person and third. Since the individual narrators do not have their own chapters (as they do in Faulkner's *As I Lay Dying*, for instance), and since the typography seldom sets off sections within a chapter, the individual anecdotes lack the boundaries that might call attention to the craft within them. The resulting mosaic lacks a discernible shape, and so the anecdote and the incident—not the chapter and the themes—remain the units of narration in the second half of the novel. The series of anecdotes in a chapter comes to seem representative, even arbitrary, instead of well made.

Following "Sumus Quod Sumus," the chapters "Protestant" and "Summer" serve as the turning points between the literary, historical structures of the first half of *Lake Wobegon Days* and the oral, autobiographical structures of the second. Although the narrator confesses his autobiographical bent in the introduction to the town's landmarks and citizenry, the first chapter also confides his mixed feelings about leaving Lake Wobegon and making his own life elsewhere. Not until "Protestant" and "Summer" does he actually talk about his Lake Wobegon childhood. "Protestant," the fifth chapter, shifts the focus from the public life of Lake Wobegon past to the private life of the narrator's youth. Recounting the eccentricities of both the town and his family nonetheless makes a bridge with the mock-historical chapters. Every element of Lake Wobegon lacks something. The landscape lacks impressiveness; its history lacks respectability; the townspeople, urbanity; the Keillors, worldliness.

As young Gary sees it, his life lacks ceremony. He feels the loss most keenly when he compares his family's religious practices to those of more liberal Christians—which means just about everybody else ("We were Sanctified Brethren, a sect so tiny that nobody but us and God knew about it" [101]). But his yearnings also extend to more secular rituals such as funerals and Queen Elizabeth II's coronation, as well. The anecdotes in "Protestant" include such insights into Lake Wobegon life as the principle that "car ownership is a matter of faith. Lutherans drive Fords. . . . Catholics drive Chevies" (112). But the narrator's childhood memories dominate. As a result, "Protestant" has a much more coherent point of view than "Summer," the next chapter, which punctuates Keillor's mock memoir with a variety of independent tales: Lake Wobegon's "all-time biggest tomato ever raised," Father Emil's annual vacation tour to the battlefields of the Civil War, lunchtime conversations in the booths at the Chatterbox Cafe, the fish-cleaning policies of Art's Bait & Night O'Rest Motel, the churlishness of Johnny Tollefson and other college kids, and Fred Krebsbach's disappearance. These anecdotes, like their counterparts in the six chapters that follow, substitute thematic development for sequence or progression; like *Walden*, *Lake Wobegon Days* limits chronology to the cycle of the seasons. In "the little town that time forgot and the decades cannot improve," one summer blends easily into another, and the anecdotes within a seasonal chapter need not follow one another in any sequence of causality. The anecdotes of "Summer" shift gradually from the satisfactions of childhood to the unhappiness of adult life and the need to leave Lake Wobegon, but this structure hides amid two others. The first is the appearance of stasis in Lake Wobegon, and the second, the illusion of progress as young Keillor and his peers grow older. In their ambiguous relationship to one another, these structures fit uneasily with the comic certainty of the opening sections.

Within this triple structure of seasons, constancy, and growth, stretching the mock autobiography over seven chapters makes perfect sense. So does the doubled structure, which matches the narrator's *Bildungsroman* with Johnny Tollefson's. If the seasonal anecdotes lack the narrative depth and duration we count on in a novel, especially when their prose style seems more familiar than experimental, they need some overarching structure to offset their variety and brevity, and they especially need a literary structure to offset their orality. And considering the number of anecdotes needing control, two stories are twice as good as one.

Even by itself, however, the mock autobiography contains the most powerful writing in *Lake Wobegon Days*. The reason lies partly in Keillor's eye for detail but more particularly in his vision of childhood. By recalling thought processes as well as people and events, he represents children's mental lives with breathtaking authenticity. His personal narrative resurrects the whole range of children's superstitions, not only the folklore of fear (as when big kids taunt little ones with tales of child-hungry dogs or tongue-freezing handles on the pump) but also their strivings to unravel the mysteries of the universe:

> When I was a child, I figured out that I was
> 1 person, the son of
> 2 parents and was the
> 3rd child, born
> 4 years after my sister and
> 5 years after my brother, in
> 1942 (four and two are 6), on the
> 7th day of the
> 8th month, and the year before
> had been 9 years old and
> was now 10.
> To me, it spelled Destiny. (14–15)

The narrative revives readers' memories of their own childhood experiences, which—however different from Keillor's in specific details—share with his a blending of the sublime and ridiculous. Consider, for example, Gary's musings on why he and his "more sophisticated" friends lack an interest in football, after learning that the coach had taunted them as homosexuals:

> We hear about it later, and far from being sophisticated, we are filled with terror. All those afternoons we went skinny-dipping, the curiosity about what each other looked like—is something terrible going on? Are we that way? Perhaps we are, otherwise why are we so uncertain about girls? We don't talk about this. But each of us knows that he

is not quite right. Once, at the river, Jim made his pecker talk, moving its tiny lips as he said, "Hi, my name's Pete. I live in my pants." Now it doesn't seem funny at all. (186)

Keillor zeroes in on the feelings we all remember with chagrin, recognizing that no matter how minor they seem in comparison to adult difficulties, we still wouldn't willingly undergo them again. Present-tense verbs suggest his enduring discomfort. Instead of a sentimental fondness for the good old days or such subdued emotions as nostalgia, he offers intense recollections: glee, pain, curiosity, adventure, mischievousness, jealousy, injury, outrage, disappointment. Not surprisingly, his sharpest memories involve secrets. With the exception of his death-defying nighttime ride up to the top of the Norge Co-op grain elevator, few of these secrets border on the cosmic. Most are quite minor, like the antics of "Booger Day," when Darla Ingqvist picked up "a giant gob" from the classroom doorknob (171–72). But all of them, to one degree or another, evoke guilt. Vivid representations of pleasure and pain leave little room for nostalgic musings about the town where they occurred.

As the narrator sees it, Lake Wobegon kids suffer at the hands of the various adults (and adultlike goody-goodies) around them. Portraying children's feelings of powerlessness in the first person gives *Lake Wobegon Days* an emotional validity, justifying Gary's sense of victimization. The less comic aspects of this theme, however, belong to the third-person anecdotes, which make short shrift of adult dignity. Small-town comraderie disintegrates amid such controversies as whether to buy new street lamps ("It was the late Leo Mueller who suggested that with a little more inner light . . . , fewer people would need assistance in walking home. He hinted that it was Lutherans who were walking into trees" [211]). Battles and feuds are commonplace. Cold war breaks out over plans to welcome the king of Norway, and the animosity endures for two generations beyond his canceled visit. Loyalties of various sorts influence every aspect of daily life. People shop at Ralph's Pretty Good Grocery, despite his higher prices and inferior quality (fresh fish at Ralph's means a new case of cod in the freezer) for the same reason that they buy ugly glasses at Clifford's variety store instead of designer eyewear at the suburban mall. The official justification is predictable: "Calvin Klein isn't going to come with the Rescue Squad and he isn't going to teach your children about redemption by grace. You couldn't find Calvin Klein to save your life" (96). The narrator explains it differently: "This is socialism, and it runs on loyalty" (95). But an outsider, bewildered by the private language and obscure politics of his Wobegonian wife and her family, offers a less comforting analysis. "The whole town is like this," he marvels, "A cult" (215).

Gary's complaints about the town and his parents lead to old and durable comic routines in the mock autobiography. Much as Mark Twain portrayed Huck Finn squirming under Miss Watson's "sivilizing" or the Connecticut Yankee struggling in his medieval armor to scratch his nose, Keillor characterizes himself as the Sufferer, one of Mark Twain's favorite comic poses.[15] The Sufferer pops up frequently in *Lake Wobegon Days*, as in the scene where the boy's mother discovers him mouthing words along with the baritone on the phonograph record.

For the most part, comic suffering in *Lake Wobegon Days* recalls the near-universal indignities of youth. Speaking in his adult voice, the narrator laughs as much at himself as at his mother when he recalls her scrupulous, even proprietary inspection of her son in his first rented tuxedo:

> She stood up and fixed a few stray hairs, adjusted the black bow tie, shot the cuffs, flexed the lapels, and walked around the back and pinched off a loose thread. . . . An invisible microscopic speck of dust appeared on one shoulder, and she brushed it away with the hanky, and then, noticing something above my left eyebrow—unconsciously, out of habit, she spat a little *ptui* in the hanky and rubbed my forehead. *Mother spit.* Our holy water, the world's most powerful cleansing agent.
> The spot burned all night. (292)

Keillor's portrait of adolescent misery pits the young man's pleasure in having his grooming admired against his embarrassment at still being treated like a little boy. But the punch line keeps the tale good-natured: the episode climaxes with a silly symbol of universality shared with his readers: "*our* holy water." In addition, as viewed from the calm distance of adulthood, the indignity seems almost charming, appropriately relegated to the past tense. By contrast, Keillor uses present tense to convey the greater embarrassment of getting caught singing "Minnesota, Hail to Thee" to his blank bedroom wall.

Still other portraits of the comic sufferer exemplify, much as Tom Sawyer's transcendence of Aunt Polly's fence-painting punishment, the imagination and triumph of the hero. These vignettes celebrate the irresponsibility that is a child's privilege, and their intense feeling also shifts the narration from past to present tense. "On this morning in August when I am thirteen," the narrator recalls, inviting readers to share his retreat into reverie, "it's hot by ten o'clock" (135). His family has moral objections to air conditioning (it's decadent and violates the idea of summer) and, worse still, has developed an oversupply of tomatoes, the product of forty plants so prolific that even his mother joined him in sneaking over to their next-door neighbor to deposit half a bushel, like some illegitimate child, on the back step. The stage is set:

> my mother sent me out to pick tomatoes. . . . I picked one and threw it at a crab apple tree. It made a good *splat*. The tree was full of little crab apples we'd have to deal with eventually, and a few of them fell. My brother and sister stood up and looked: what did you *do*? we're gonna tell. . . .
>
> I picked up a tomato so big it sat on the ground. It looked like it had sat there for a week. The underside was brown. Small white worms lived in it. It was very juicy. . . .
>
> A rotten Big Boy hitting the target is a memorable sound. Like a fat man doing a belly flop, and followed by a whoop and a yell from the tomatoee. (135)

As the narrative moves back and forth between past and present tense, it also shifts between the adult's and the child's perspectives, between present understanding and past memory. Keillor skillfully modulates the grown-up voice of the boy, still enjoying the old mischief and rebellion, still smarting from the old insults and pains as well: the heat of the day, the burden of chores, the rivalry among siblings. In this case, and in others, past and present, adult and child merge. Juvenile monosyllables and tactile terms invite us to join the young Keillor in his act of comic vengeance against his always-responsible sister, vengeance so tempting and sweet we can just about taste it, too.

Like the celebration of stolen pleasures, recounting guilty and negative feelings gives the novel a strong flavor of psychological realism. These feelings also carry over the image of a retrograde Lake Wobegon from the mock history of the first half to the mock autobiography of the second. A conventional autobiography would attempt to explain how the town helped make our man, but this story (Keillor announces early in the book) does just the opposite. Appropriately enough, considering that in this case our man quite literally made the town, *Lake Wobegon Days* reveals how "most of Lake Wobegon's children leave, as I did, to realize themselves as finer persons than they were allowed to be at home" (3). That is, the autobiography looks at Lake Wobegon and concludes, like the town history, "*It doesn't start here!!*" (3)—except insofar as the town is a great place to leave behind. In the convoluted logic of the tall tale, however, Keillor's characterization of himself as a long-suffering Wobegonian still ends up crediting the town with his success. After all, the opening chapter implies, if he hadn't left it, he never would have come to understand Lake Wobegon, which ultimately made him successful. But taken together, the anecdotes refuse to come down unequivocally on the side of either sentiment or smirk. Pseudosentimental memories of puppy love ("I think of her lovingly every time I use Clorox" [16]) lead to sardonic recollections of adolescent angst, implying that Lake Wobegon is best loved from afar—whether in memory or imagination doesn't matter. On the one hand, he takes an old adage to absurd lengths: if absence makes the heart grow fonder, the nonexistence ought to inspire adoration. On the other, his quotation from Shakespeare's Sonnet 73 sincerely considers the relation between love and loss. When he rues, "This thou perceive'st, which makes thy love more strong, / To love that well which thou must leave ere long" (23), Keillor clearly refers not to the town, but to his youth and the innocence he enjoyed as a boy.[16]

With such a climax to the opening of the novel, Keillor quite logically ends the mock autobiography at his high school graduation, the last time (he reports with self-indulgent misery) he and his friends still "felt successful and shining in *some* way": "Once graduated we would disappear into the crowd of faceless adults and be like everyone else, old, a little tired, disappointed, and things not work out. College would be too hard and flunk us; the Army would unmask us as cowards; marriage would turn sour and love would die. One way or another, we would find disgrace, as others had" (295). As in a vaudeville farce, however, the next chapter rescues youth from premature demise. "Revival" shows that Johnny Tollefson, at least, has survived his freshman year of college "something of a success" (303). As this example indicates, the two *Bildungsroman* plots give the second half of *Lake Wobegon Days* its chronology, theme, and endpoint. Perhaps more important, the doubled *Bildungsroman* plot allows Keillor to maintain an attitude of bittersweet recollection toward his Lake Wobegon childhood without denying those elements more bitter than sweet and without settling for a single point of view. Years before the publication of *Lake Wobegon Days*, Keillor confessed to distributing his feelings and experiences among many Lake Wobegon characters: "I'm more comfortable put into the third person," Keillor told John Bordsen in 1982, nearly three years before the novel's publication. "There are a lot of characters to whom I ascribe what happened to me.[17] Considering that Keillor had already invented young Gary as fictional persona, blatant similarities between the Gary and Johnny raise the question of why the double was necessary in the first place.

Part of the answer lies in Keillor's experimentation with avatars of himself. Even though the book stops with the two young artists teetering on the brink of maturity, our awareness of the author's own success helps us fill in the missing details.[18] The procedure encourages a certain comic confusion between the author and his fictional embodiment, both Garrison (once Gary) Keillor, and such confusion is obviously the point. Keillor plays around with it from the very beginning of the novel, most broadly when he professes relief that his parents did not move from Lake Wobegon to Brooklyn Park in 1938. "Otherwise I'd have been a Brooklyn Park kid where I didn't know a soul" (13), he declared, offering the cognoscenti a joke: John and Grace Keillor did in fact build a home for their family in Brooklyn Park in 1947, when Gary was five, and Keillor lived there until he went to college.[19] Comic or not, such deliberate confusion between fact and fiction has become something of a minor tradition in contemporary American writing, figuring in works as different as the historical fiction of E. L. Doctorow and Truman Capote, the comic fantasies of Philip Roth and Thomas Pynchon, and the narrative experiments of Joan Didion and John Barth.[20] The trend involves what Jonathan Wilson calls "counterlives," characters who bear their authors' names and experiences. Although Wilson's discussion does not mention *Lake Wobegon Days*, it has some relevance nonetheless. In an era when deconstruction has attacked the very idea of the individual personality, he observes, a counterlife takes a tale in two directions at once. On the one hand, the narrative enacts "the disintegration of the self into a series of fictional selves"; on the other, the reader's interpretation (re)constructs the whole person.[21]

Wilson's analysis helps point to the contradictory impulses underlying the second half of *Lake Wobegon Days*. Ultimately Keillor seems uncertain about how much narrative distance to put on his experiences. He compounds the comic confusion of the counterlife with the doubled—and intensified—narrative of Johnny Tollefson. As Keillor divides things up in *Lake Wobegon Days*, the *Bildungsroman* plots conflict with the counterlife. At the same time that the doubled *Bildungsroman* gives the novel emotional credibility, it also makes the mock autobiography seem disingenuous rather than playful.

Even if Keillor had not narrated the Johnny Tollefson sections more extensively, sympathetically, and consistently than those of any other Wobegonian, the details of the boy's life would indicate his role as the genial narrator's darker brother. The moody, unhappy kid who won the Sons of Knute Shining Star Award (a college scholarship) has some of the same wishes, discomforts, and fights with his parents that the narrator reports having had himself, and like the narrator, Johnny aims to turn his adolescent agonies into great literature. Keillor debunks Johnny's literary ambitions along with the boy's mortification at having to register for his freshman year in college in the company of his mother, grandmother, Aunt Mary, and Uncle Senator K. Thorvaldson.

> How do you tell your mother that there's something funny about your old relatives? They talk funny, and they look funny. It's less noticeable in Lake Wobegon, but put them in a big city like St. Cloud and *everybody sees it*, like they have signs around their necks that say "Hick."(153)
> ... Why couldn't his family be more like the Flambeaus? Emile and Eileen Flambeau in the Flambeau Family mystery series he has read every one of which twice. Emile is a Nobel laureate microbiologist whose travels around the world in search of elusive viruses seem to put him time after time in the vicinity of violent crimes committed by rings of dope smugglers, whom Emile brings to justice with the use of his superior intelligence, his own and that of his wife, the former screen star, and his teenage son, Tony Flambeau. (154)
> And Uncle Senator K. Thorvaldson—who else has a great-uncle named Senator? ... If he was normal, it might be okay, but he's even battier than the others. (155)

Keillor's sympathy for Johnny shows not only in the point of view here, with its narrative mimicry, but also in the characterization of the boy's family. Johnny apparently has some reason to be embarrassed, since his mother can't cope with the one-way streets in St. Cloud, and they cause a traffic jam by driving the wrong way, only to decide that the university is too big for them to want even to get out of the car, anyway. Johnny's dream of growing up in the Flambeau family belittles his plight—this is still a kid, after all, one young enough in spirit to get lost in his fantasy while sneaking an illicit smoke on his way to the registrar's office, while his proud and patient relatives wait in the car.

This gentle ridicule of Tollefson and family falls flat just a few pages later, however, when Keillor's persona, miffed at his parents' faith in self-denial, also finds his family a poor second to the Flambeaus:

> *You'll appreciate it the most if you never get it,* I thought.
> That wasn't how the Flambeaus lived in The Flambeau Family Series: scarcity wasn't the guiding light in their lives. Emile and Eileen and son Tony, when they were in the Congo in *The Case of The Strange Safari* and the Land Rover went over a cliff and the native guide M'Bulu ran jabbering into the underbrush when he saw the skull on the rock and the three Flambeaus' [*sic*] were sleeping on the dirt and eating nuts and berries, they did this because they had to, not out of some misguided notion that it was good for their character, and you knew that when they solved the case and went home to Manhattan, they'd have themselves a night on the town and drop fifty or sixty bucks without blinking. (163)

With its juvenile syntax representing the kid's muttering, the passage succeeds in debunking both his own persona and Johnny, but at a high price. If the two boys barely differ, Gary Keillor comes to appear not only less heroic but also less appealing. Turning an author/narrator into an antihero has potential for a comic pseudo-autobiography. Turning him into a kvetch does not.

The repetition cannot be accidental: it links the doubled comic plots to the novel's most serious themes. The reference to the spurious literary family recurs in the final chapter, "Revival," where it serves as proof that "our lives are being lived over and over by others" (334). But Keillor seems unwilling to attribute any significance beyond repetition itself. First he has the narrator evade the issue with a fence-straddling "If that is true . . . I don't know if I should laugh or cry" (334). Next comes an anecdote—apparently a projected vision rather than a past incident—about an unnamed boy (like Keillor and

Tollefson, "a good reader" who has made his parents proud), who is portrayed eating his bran flakes while fuming to himself over his parents' banal conversation, *"Why can't we be more like the Flambeaus?"* (335). The repetition is disturbing. Two pages from the end of the book, a townful of eccentrics does not easily or convincingly devolve into a series of universal types. Nor does acceptance of the status quo ring true after the narrator has conceded that Lake Wobegon, in essence, evicted him.

Moreover, Johnny Tollefson's complaint might pass for a crankier portion of Keillor's mock-oral tale, except for the occasional *he* thrown in to remind us that Keillor has switched from first to third-person narration. Tollefson's role as the bearer of Keillor's bad news becomes uncomfortably clear when we look at the very different renderings of Johnny's and Gary's very similar wishes (also related to someone named Johnny—or at least *Chonny*) about growing up in a more glamorous family:

> Sometimes I imagined that we weren't really from Minnesota, we were only using it as a cover, disguising ourselves as quiet modest people until we could reveal our true identify as Italians. One day, my mother would put the wieners on the table and suddenly my father would jump and say, "Hey! I'ma sicka this stuffa!" She'd yell, "No! No! Chonny! Please-a! The children!" But the cat was out of the bag. We weren't who we thought we were, we were the Keillorinis! *Presto! Prestone!* My father rushed to the closest and hauled out giant oil paintings of fat ladies, statues of saints, bottles of wine. . . .Then we would dance, hands over our heads. . . . —*Mama mia!* Now that's *amore!* (20)

When presented as the idea of his own persona, the fantasy is isolated from any context other than his insecurities as a college freshman and the brilliance of his comic imagination. The self-mockery and comic extravagance in this passage contrast with the criticism of Lake Wobegonians in the passage about Johnny Tollefson and his family. Because Tollefson's experiences in the story barely differ from what Keillor exuberantly claims as his own, Johnny's story diminishes the novel's good humor.

Despite its limitations, the use of Johnny as a double seems benign and even somewhat conventional. With *95 Theses 95*, a former Wobegonian's epic complaint, on the other hand, Keillor takes narrative doubling a step further. At the same time that he adds yet another comic sufferer only superficially distinct from his fictional persona, Keillor splits the chapter in half and runs the anonymous manuscript as a footnote extending the entire length of the chapter "News." As part of the joking and serious exploration of what news is, the division of the chapter succeeds admirably—all the more so because the numbered points in the aging, yet-unpublished complaint give the footnote a definite progression lacking in the episodic nonnews above the hairline divider. But the material works less well as the testament of yet another unhappy Lake Wobegon youth. Although its almost cosmic angst provides a rather universalized portrait of the adolescent comic sufferer, the particulars come a bit a too close for comfort to Keillor's own remarks.

The basic situation exemplifies the humorist's inventiveness. Several years earlier, a disaffected Wobegonian young man (now residing on the cheerful-sounding Terpsichore Terrace after some years of moving around the country) brought 95 *Theses* 95 to Lake Wobegon when he came to introduce his parents to his wife. Intending to nail his "neatly typed manifesto" to the door of Lake Wobegon Lutheran, in the manner of Martin Luther himself, he lost courage when he got there. Instead, he offered the manuscript to Harold Starr, daring him to print it in the *Herald-Star*. Though he has occasionally considered publishing it, Harold plans to return the manuscript in one of the many self-addressed, stamped envelopes that the writer has sent him over the years—that is, he'll return it as soon as he cleans his desk and finds the three missing pages. Consequently, the "unabridged . . . document" reproduced in "News" (where a barely sympathetic Keillor has published it in Starr's place) is incomplete. It lacks not only theses 42–55, from the missing pages, but also numbers 63–67, which narrator Keillor punctiliously reports as "[Obliterated by beverage stain]" (267).

But even with these little jokes, the humor of ninety-five variations on a single complaint runs low long before the twentieth page. The homespun hostility gradually becomes not-so-comic suffering:

> 11. You taught me, "When the going gets tough, the tough get going," teaching me to plod forward in the face of certain doom. (256)

> 15. You taught me an indecent fear of sexuality. . . . For years I worried because my penis hangs slightly to the left, and finally read in a book that this is within the realm of the normal, but then wondered, What sort of person would read books like that? (257)

Lake Wobegon Days   113

78. . . . Your mindless monogamy made me vacillate in love, your compulsive industry made me a prisoner of sloth, your tidiness made me sloppy, your materialism made me wasteful. (269)

Worse still, many of the charges repeat gripes made by Keillor's own comic persona. Early in *Lake Wobegon Days*, for example, Keillor complains about his father's friend Bob, whose nostalgic reminiscences of heroism and patriotism during World War II point to one conclusion: "Clearly I was a sign of how far the country had gone downhill: an eighteen-year-old kid with no future" (18); more than two hundred pages later, thesis number 18 reads: "You instilled in me a paralyzing nostalgia for a time before I was born, a time when men were men and women were saintly, and children were obedient, industrious, asked no luxuries, entertained themselves, and knew right from wrong. I, on the other hand, was a symptom of everything going to hell in a handbasket. I was left to wonder why I bothered to be born" (257–58). Keillor's stylistic care means that we cannot discount these coincidences, here doubtless aimed at reinforcing the idea that conflict between the generations represents the way of the world. But however one interprets the thematic effect of such doubling, the narrative strategy remains a problem: an understandable but disappointing and unsuccessful attempt to put severe criticism of Lake Wobegon at arm's length.

Moreover, the strategy raises unpleasant questions about Keillor and his persona, the dominant narrative voice. At some point in the composition, Keillor decided to attribute 95 *Theses* 95 to an anonymous author so inhibited that when he reached the door of Lake Wobegon Lutheran he was "afraid to pound holes in a good piece of wood" (251). That narrative decision contains a good joke all by itself, but it undercuts the sincere affection in *Lake Wobegon Days* by implying that the author remains a child too cowardly to admit what he thinks. At the very least, the doubling represents a serious division about the Matter of Minnesota and its connection to childhood memory.

So does the heartwarming ending to the novel. The final vignette offers one last projection of the principle that other people reenact our experiences. In contrast to the invidious comparison between an anonymous boy's parents and the Flambeau Family, just two pages earlier, the closing scene depicts love and acceptance. Having gone out in the car for a carton of cigarettes in the middle of a blinding

These photographs of the entrance to Prairie Home Cemetery (in Moorhead, Minnesota) and Bob's Bank of Belleview were among the many photographs sent in to Keillor by listeners as comic proof in the reality of Lake Wobegon. A Prairie Home Companion was named for the cemetery. Courtesy of Prairie Home Companion Archives.

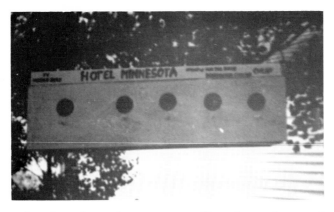

Like the other gifts sent to Keillor, these photos of the Chatterbox Cafe and Hotel Minnesota testify to the pleasure that fans took in his comic stories. Courtesy of Prairie Home Companion Archives.

Fans' comic proof of the reality behind the Lake Wobegon tales took many different forms. This sign designating the Woe-Be-Gone Forest exploits the same ambiguity between woebegone and "be gone, woe!" that Keillor used on A Prairie Home Companion. Courtesy of Prairie Home Companion Archives.

The listener who sent Keillor this full-sized drawing saw Lake Wobegon as the only spot worthy of mention by name between the Berkshires and the Pacific Ocean. Courtesy of Prairie Home Companion Archives.

THE
BOSTONIAN
VIEW OF THE WORLD

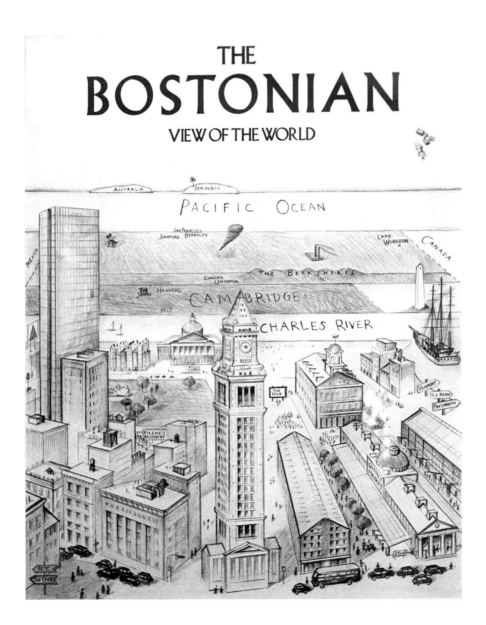

Gifts to Keillor in the spirit of A Prairie Home Companion *included needlework and a "real" box of Raw Bits cereal. Courtesy of Prairie Home Companion Archives.*

A few of the many public testimonials to Keillor for A Prairie Home Companion. *Courtesy of Prairie Home Companion Archives.*

The Lake Wobegon bumper sticker in this collage went into orbit on the space shuttle Columbia for seven days, 12–18 January 1986. The caption below the aerial photograph of Minnesota reads, "Presented to Garrison Keillor with Appreciation from the National Aeronautics and Space Administration. Unfortunately Lake Wobegon is just off the picture." Courtesy of Prairie Home Companion Archives.

blizzard, despite the justifiable objections of his wife and child, an unnamed man discovers on his return—after driving for miles hanging out the door to guide the car along the tire tracks—that he left his Pall Malls on the counter of the Sidetrack Tap. Close behind his feelings of chagrin, however, comes an epiphany:

> But what a lucky man. Some luck lies not in getting what you thought you wanted but getting what you have, which once you have it you may be smart enough to see is what you would have wanted had you known. He takes deep breaths and the cold air goes to his brain and makes him more sensible. He starts out on the short walk to the house where people love him and will be happy to see his face. (337)

The convoluted syntax undercuts the sentimentality somewhat, maintaining the homespun, comic touch by portraying revelation in a roundabout, tentative voice. Still, such warm family feelings emerge as something of a surprise this late in the novel, which has tended to portray family affection in more metaphorical terms— Barbara Ann Bunsen's decision to try to improve Clarence's diet, "to steer him away from bacon and toward yogurt" (216), for instance, or Gary's pleasure in finally getting his boomerang, a homemade gift from his dad, to work. Furthermore, given the number of avatars that Keillor has invented for himself (not to mention his many references on *A Prairie Home Companion* to having quit smoking), the episode invites us to see the narrator as its unnamed hero. Reassurances that Keillor's adult life offers satisfactions unavailable to the child, or that his complaints add up to a lot of sound and fury over nothing, or even that life is sweet, especially when you've cheated death—all these implications bring the novel to a mellower end than its themes have led us to expect.

Still, any disappointment with *Lake Wobegon Days* deserves to stand in proportion to the writer's obvious goals for it. Certainly other ambitious comic novels have suffered similar problems. For that matter, a survey of Twain's struggles between his artistic program and his desire to appeal to what he called "the belly and the members" suggests that humor may be the most difficult mode in which to realize aesthetic aspirations. In this sense, *Lake Wobegon Days* has much in common with *Roughing It* (1872), Twain's second book, a best-seller that capitalized on the humorist's popularity through door-to-door subscription sales. Both books rely on previously composed material (newspaper articles, in Twain's case) that the author organized more successfully in the first half than in the second, where in fact *Roughing It* also abandons its *Bildungsroman* plot in favor of anecdotes and mock-oral tales. Similarly, problems with form in what scholars call "the evasion sequence" nearly derail the ending of *Huckleberry Finn* (1885), perhaps America's greatest humorous novel, when Twain follows the profundity of Huck's decision to go to hell with the tomfoolery of Tom Sawyer's romantic game of rescuing the already-free Jim. Still more aesthetically destructive conflicts emerge in *Connecticut Yankee in King Arthur's Court* (1889), the last long work of fiction Twain completed; its slapstick medieval romp turns first into a political satire and then into an apocalyptic nightmare.

The related difficulties of contemporary American humorists suggest that the novel itself is less congenial to humorous narration than the short story or sketch. Thomas Pynchon's novels *The Crying of Lot 49* (1966) and *Gravity's Rainbow* (1973) stand as rare exceptions of complete success. Philip Roth's *Great American Novel* (1973), Erica Jong's *Fear of Flying* (1973), John Irving's *World According to Garp* (1978), and Anne Tyler's *Accidental Tourist* (1985) all fall short of the mark despite valiant efforts to put real humor of character and situation—not just verbal wit—into long fiction of thematic and formal seriousness. All in all, *Lake Wobegon Days* stands in good company. If Keillor has reached the *Roughing It* stage of his career, we yet await his masterpiece.

More problematic in some ways is how Keillor's sophisticated audience has tried to gloss over the hostilities and subversions in favor of the sentimentality and nostalgia. Few reviewers followed the lead of J. D. Reed, who insisted that "far from an ideal of Norman Rockwell hominess, Lake Wobegon reverberates with terror and finalities."[22] Most readers, by contrast, considered the portrait of Lake Wobegon quite affectionate, and one reviewer went so far as to call the book "a love poem to small towns."[23] Barney Cooney, recognizing that such a viewpoint requires overlooking "some of Keillor's most astute observations" about small-town life, nevertheless saw the evocation of childhood in *Lake Wobegon Days* as "the romanticized past of midwestern small-town America."[24] Regardless of the suggestions of the reviewers, many fans of *A Prairie Home Companion* quickly sided with J. Alan Youngren, who claimed the book was a "listener's dream: a Saturday night monologue that goes on and on."[25]

The desire to see the novel in the sentimental terms of the oral tales testifies to the chord that Keillor touched in the Matter of Minnesota. One element involves local-color humor, which has a tradition of sentiment for bygone times. The narrator of *Lake Wobegon Days* sounds almost homesick when he introduces Lake Wobegon—a small town where the elm trees have miraculously survived Dutch elm disease and a person can walk down the middle of Main Street. It is no accident that the so-called baby boomers in general and the so-called yuppies in particular have entered so willingly into Keillor's fantasy of childhood.[26] This postwar generation, now well into adulthood, is remarkable not only for causing a large bulge in population statistics but also for being the first generation forced to lower its expectations in a country where for three hundred years people have taken for granted that children would have better lives than their parents.[27] The evocation of youth in *Lake Wobegon Days*—in loving, though not always lovely, detail—signals how irrevocably over are the halcyon days of childhood, as justifiably represented by midwestern innocence as by anything else. Whatever else he thinks of them, they're gone with the elms.

But it is perhaps more sensitive to the complexity of *Lake Wobegon Days* and our own times to remember that there are only two villains in the book: the town itself and parents. With apologies to William Butler Yeats, we might say of Lake Wobegon, "That is no country for *young* men." The attitude suggests that the highly critical—even hostile—use of the Matter of Minnesota resolves the problem of rural nostalgia for a highly literate, largely urban audience approaching middle age. For this audience, and for Keillor, too, I would say, the ambivalence of the Matter of Minnesota means, "You can't go home again—that's true—but then, who really wants to?"

CHAPTER 5   **The Short Stories**

In (and against)

the American Grain

I love my fans, but they   Garrison Keillor published nearly fifty
don't understand me.   short stories in the *New Yorker* before
—Keillor,   his forty-fifth birthday, but they stand in
"On the Road, Almost"   the shadows of his Lake Wobegon tales.
(1972)   The diluted impact of magazine fiction
(especially in comparison to the power
of radio) partly explains why such a distinguished record has gone
largely unappreciated, although Keillor suffers in this no more than
other comic writers. Indeed, he probably manages better than most,
considering the popularity of *A Prairie Home Companion*. Such
New Yorker colleagues as James Stevenson and George S. Trow, for
example, lack Keillor's visibility despite their many followers among
the magazine's regular readers. In the Minnesotan's case, however,
fame has been part of the problem. His renown as the host of a
popular radio show has eclipsed even his role as its chief writer
(indeed, its *only* writer for most of its thirteen-year history), and
his short fiction has come to seem somehow extracurricular, as a
result.

The two volumes based on his radio monologues bolster rather
than dispel this impression. Highly promotable as the work of a
media celebrity (albeit from public radio), Lake Wobegon books such
as *Lake Wobegon Days* and *Leaving Home* easily become marketable tie-ins to *A Prairie Home Companion* because public radio lis-

teners are readers. Similarly, *Prairie Home Companion* audio cassettes can be sold in bookstores in the trade category known as "spoken books." And of course, Keillor's collection of short stories, *Happy to Be Here*, capitalized on this phenomenon—nearly 600,000 paperback copies were in print in four editions by 1990.

The relatively low status of Keillor's comic magazine writing is a reminder that patterns of literary reputation and mass-market appeal have changed very little since the nineteenth century. The inclusion of popular culture studies in universities has not substantially increased respect among the literati for humorous writing, just as the direct-mail marketing of books and tapes has not significantly improved on the door-to-door subscription sales of Mark Twain's day.[1] In this respect, the careers of earlier American humorists offer convenient comparisons with Keillor's. Despite the celebrity that Mark Twain earned from "The Celebrated Jumping Frog of Calaveras County" (1865), for example, or his newspaper reports from on board the *Quaker City* (to cite the most obvious examples), his reputation rests on his books—and more particularly on literary volumes such as *Huckleberry Finn* (1885) rather than travel books such as *The Innocents Abroad* (1868). Had he written mainly short stories and comic sketches, like his contemporaries Petroleum V. Nasby and Dan De Quille, Twain's fame might not have outlasted theirs. It might have faded like that of Will Rogers, whose waning reputation illustrates the same principle in a modern form. Much of Rogers's radio audience has died, and books figure very little in his public image. The scratchy radio performances of the cowboy philosopher, recently issued on audio cassette by Caedmon, have an authenticity that will surely interest nostalgia buffs and scholars but will probably not attract a new audience to monologues on the New Deal.

In the final analysis, Garrison Keillor's reputation will almost certainly rest more on his books than on either *A Prairie Home Companion* or his short fiction, but it is the short fiction that reveals the dimensions of his literary imagination. Moreover, the short fiction locates his work within the contexts and traditions of American literary humor, whose primary genre from colonial days on has been the sketch, not the novel or long narrative. As it has dominated American humor, so it dominates Keillor's fiction, and the short stories therefore offer important insights into his comic imagination.

The supremacy of the sketch as a humorous genre emphasizes an important link between written humor and oral yarn-spinning, since the anecdote remains the unit of humorous narration in both print and speech. (Both *Tom Sawyer* and *Lake Wobegon Days*, for instance, structure their larger narratives around anecdotal episodes.) Nonetheless, Keillor uses first-person narrators differently in his written stories from the way he uses them in his radio tales. The written stories, for example, lack the sentimentality and consistent point of view that became hallmarks of the monologues. The host of *A Prairie Home Companion* juggled a repertoire of poses, all of them purportedly facets of a single persona that we might call the Companion: the genial, shy, sentimental, homespun philosopher who served as Keillor's public voice. The author of the short stories, on the other hand, has created dozens of voices, only two of which pretend to represent (much less expose) the writer behind the speaker. Though many of the voices come from small-town Minnesota, only a few are genial, and those he debunks.

Such skepticism toward his apparently beloved Matter of Minnesota is not too surprising when we note that most of the stories originally appeared in the *New Yorker*, a magazine almost as famous for its sophisticated sense of humor as for its condescension toward the little old lady from Dubuque and other Americans living west of the Hudson River. Keillor's *New Yorker* stories feature local-color characters as authentic as alfalfa, and they pose family and small-town dilemmas as corny as Kansas, but the sketches themselves are burlesques. The self-conscious ridicule that results calls for an urbane (perhaps even urban) reader—one who enjoys not only the traditional vernacular humor of Mark Twain but also the modern literary wit of E. B. White. Specifically, Keillor's short stories exploit a blend of techniques from three major traditions of American humor: local-color narration, literary comedy, and *New Yorker* humor. Not that the Minnesotan has simply dug into a bag of old tricks. He writes mock-oral yarns, tall tales, parodies, and local-color sketches in the best tradition of the nineteenth century, all the while (like his predecessors) debunking sentimental ideals and parodying the rhetoric of his time. But *his* time is the last quarter of the twentieth century, and in the tradition of *New Yorker* humorists, Keillor portrays the madness of modern life in prose of exquisite, even finicky, precision. In short, he mixes the comic conventions of the past with voices and values of the present to create a distinctly contemporary humor in the American grain. Through their link to these traditions, the short stories clarify, in ways that the Lake Wobegon monologues and *Lake Wobegon Days* do not, just what Garrison Keillor has borrowed from and contributed to American humor.

His affinities with the traditions of mock-oral, vernacular humor—what Walter Blair called "a man's voice, speaking" in an article of the same title—are most obvious. Keillor writes in a contemporary vernacular instead of regional dialect, but the cadences, circumlocutions, slang, and eccentricities of oral talk interest him as much as they interested his nineteenth-century predecessors. Like them, Keillor finds colloquial speech amusing, and his vernacular tales reveal their speakers' personalities through their language and phrasing in much the same way as do T. B. Thorpe's "Big Bear of Arkansas" (1841) and Frances Whicher's *Widow Bedott Papers* (1856).

The very title of "How Can I Be Happy When I Can't Play Hockey Like I Wanna?" (1967) indicates that as a college senior Keillor already enjoyed playing with oral talk and trying to represent its nuances, even when writing a journalistic feature rather than fiction.[2] Certainly his vernacular characters speak a wide variety of comic jargons. These range from the baseball player's "Hey babe hey babe c'mon babe good stick now hey babe long tater take him downtown babe" (116) in "Attitude" (1979) to the adolescent's pompous credo in "Who We Were and What We Meant By it" (1984): "If ever a movement resisted celebration, it was us Momentists. That was why I went back to St. Paul—to repeat the message that the world has misunderstood: Not Us but Yourself, Not That but This, Not Then but Now, The Answer Is Not on My Face. The moment is gone, now is the moment. We are gone, we will come back in a moment."[3]

As one might expect, however, the broadest use of vernacular humor occurs in sketches written early in Keillor's career. In "On the Road, Almost" (1972), for example, a mock-oral tale loosely based on Bob Dylan's song "On the Road Again" (1965), a successful but dissatisfied disc jockey laments his lot in rhymed country-and-western style couplets. His fans misunderstand him, the job leaves his deepest ambitions unfulfilled, and he feels like a fraud: "Just a clown sitting around and earning lots of money trying to make the whole town think it's funny, but in my heart I know it's only a show and I'm playing the part of the Fool on the Radio."[4] The narrator's vernacular voice defines the form and the genre of this sketch, but cliches like "They say we're too young to be in love" combine with such lyrical phrases as "we're going, someplace far away where the dewy grasses touch our minds with wonder and the dawn comes up like thunder" to portray a speaker imprisoned in the world of the conventional music he plays.

A more ambitious use of country-western lyrics and mock-oral narration followed a year later in "The Slim Graves Show" (1973), which recounts how Slim Graves and his wife Billie Ann Twyman, the musician-hosts of a rural wake-up show, give up show business to save their marriage after Billie's fling with lead guitarist Courteous Carl Harper. The story not only sounds like it came from a country-and-western ballad but, in fact, emerges in the narrative from the various songs that the musicians choose to sing for their listeners. The fans first learn of the love triangle from Carl's lyrical confession, "Forgive me for I know she's yours but loyalty don't open many doors" (48), and it seems all the more startling to the fan who is telling the tale because Carl had never before sung a solo. Over the next few months Slim's songs bemoan his injury and Billie Ann's rue her quandary, yet the conflict reaches its greatest intensity (in true American fashion?) over a question of commerce: "It seemed like Carl renewed his pledge of love to Billie every morning now, replacing Slim in the big duet spot, but while Billie sang with Carl, she was still in the SunRise commercials with Slim, fixing the golden-brown waffles for him as if nothing was wrong with their marriage. You knew it couldn't go on." (49). The solution takes from Halloween to mid-January to develop, but in the end neatly dispatches both the sponsor's and Billie Ann's dilemma—which the reader, though not the narrator, begins to suspect may have been commercially motivated all along. Pictures of the each of the two suitors will appear on different boxes of SunRise Waffles, and the audience can vote through their purchases. Unwilling to decide after just one week, and then two, Billie Ann extends the contest until the vote declares Slim the unequivocal winner by a margin of more than 50 percent. At the end, the couple leaves show business to protect their marriage; so the SunRise company replaces "The Slim Graves Show" with "Courteous Carl Harper with the Pierce Sisters and the Riders of the Sky." The new scenario offers even greater possibilities for romantic and commercial exploitation—or, as the narrator sees it, "it's pretty clear he has his eye on both of them . . . but they go on hoping for the best and not realizing that big trouble lies ahead" (52). The cycle will continue.

From the narrator's viewpoint, the problem has nothing to do with blurred distinctions between art and life, though the end of the story establishes their importance. In the narrator's mind, the words of a song, the context of its performance, an advertising campaign, the disc jockey's persona, and the listener's own life all merge seamlessly into a special kind of reality.[5] His willingness to buy thirteen boxes of SunRise Waffle mix (four for Carl, nine for Slim) in batches of three and four over the course of thirteen days, apparently without opening any of them, testifies to the effects of radio. The medium weaves advertisements and musical and conversational programming together so they are no longer separable; the medium is indeed the message. Not surprisingly, then, "The Slim Graves Show" is both the show that the narrator listens to and the story that he tells. And he does not seem to understand either of them.

A countrified version of Keillor's own morning version of *A Prairie Home Companion*, complete with livestock and weather reports and letters from the listeners, "The Slim Graves Show" testifies to the importance of commercial rhetoric in Keillor's vision of radio, explaining in part why he invented Jack's Auto Repair and other Lake Wobegon enterprises as "sponsors" for his broadcasts over noncommercial radio. But even though the country-and-western rhetoric of Slim and the unnamed DJ of "On the Road, Almost" implies that Keillor considers radio a psychological environment, the two narrators do not serve as mouthpieces for the author. Graves had already figured in the weekday *Prairie Home Companion* before "The Slim Graves Show" appeared in the *New Yorker*, and in MER's *Preview* for February 1973 Keillor used the character for yet another of his inside jokes about the huge imaginary staff of his radio show:

> The musical director is the well known Slim Graves. A star in the country & western music field before his retirement due to a broken heart caused by the cheatin' ways of his wife Billie Ann, Slim now selects the records used on the show in addition to carrying them into the studio. Though he was personally hurt by the listeners' adverse reaction to Gene Autry's music, he took the criticism to heart and is now programming much more Lester Flatt and Merle Haggard.[6]

As the Companion characterizes him here, without mentioning the imminent publication of the *New Yorker* story, Slim Graves belongs more to the apocryphal world of Lake Wobegon, where imaginary characters live full lives, than to the invented world of fiction, complete in itself. For the most part, Keillor has maintained the division between these two worlds.

"The Slim Graves Show" reflects the writer's early interest in and ambivalence toward the naïve tale-teller, the conventional frame narrator of a tall yarn (a classic example is the gullible Mark Twain who passes on Simon Wheeler's story in "The Celebrated Jumping Frog of Calaveras County"). One of Keillor's favorite voices, the wide-eyed innocent represents a strong link with the nineteenth-century traditions of literary comedy. But unlike such nineteenth-century predecessors as Twain, Artemus Ward, and Petroleum V. Nasby—to mention just three contemporary Phunny Phellows renowned as both writers and platform comedians—Keillor seldom ascribes such innocence to his own narrative persona, although he has written newspaper opinion pieces and journalistic sketches in his own voice since 1974 (since 1972, if his commentary on *A Prairie Home Companion* for MER publications is included). Nor does he limit comic undercutting to first-person narration. Two of his sketches take the form of memoirs, to be sure; the tall performer recounts his embarrassment in "After a Fall" (1982), and the reminiscing father recalls "Drowning 1954" (1976). But nearly all his other fifty-odd tales have a well-defined speaker, emphatically *not* Garrison Keillor himself, who serves as the butt as well as the vehicle of the tale's jokes.

Like the diarist of "The Slim Graves Show" and the newsletter writer of "Friendly Neighbor," most of these narrators are writers, not mock-oral speakers. But as amateur writers, they make the same sorts of self-exposing errors that have tended to characterize so-called vernacular "speakers." Through these tales purportedly written by incompetent authors, Keillor (like a good many other American writers since Faulkner) explores the limits of narrative reliability. Such stories drive humor to the edge as they play with the reader's ability to distinguish between fond and scornful mimicry, but his modern narrative acrobatics also continue an old, familiar nineteenth-century tradition of exploiting the incongruity between the plot and its context. In this variation on a classic technique of the Old Southwestern frame tale, Keillor's rural innocents adopt the role filled by gentleman narrators from A. B. Longstreet to Mark Twain, who consistently misunderstood the odd characters whose rough and tumble stories they retold. In Keillor's case, a different self-deprecating or unconsciously ironic voice stands at the center of every tale, and even the third-person narratives expose the characters of the voices behind them.

Keillor's midwestern stories follow the example of nineteenth-century local-color fiction: they detail the customs of the region (many of them rapidly disappearing) and the comically colloquial speech of its inhabitants (including a retired railroad worker, the loyal fans of a call-in radio show, and a host of remarkably ordinary midwesterners). But unlike Harriet Beecher Stowe or Joel Chandler Harris—or the narrator of his own Lake Wobegon monologues for radio—Keillor undercuts whatever sentimentality he evokes in these stories. For all their self-conscious old-fashionedness, these tales of local color treat emphatically modern topics with unsentimental mockery. The voice is familiar, but the song and its meaning have changed.

Not that Keillor has neglected the classic vernacular story, the tall tale. Two recent examples express lively interest in the genre: "If Robert Frost Had an Apple . . ." (1983), a report on the imagined struggles of earlier writers with their word processors, and "What Did We Do Wrong?" (1985), the apocryphal story of the first woman major league baseball player.[7] But the contemporary topics of these examples illustrate Keillor's affinities for the traditions of *New Yorker* humor while they exemplify his apparent determination to reshape old comic traditions for a modern sensibility. So do the tales set in the rural Midwest, a distinct group of ten.

An early *New Yorker* story, "Plainfolks," (1974) debunks the good old days twice over. This sketch pokes fun at teenage fads of the 1950s and 1960s by characterizing customized cars, smoke rings, and boards-and-bricks bookshelves as folk arts of an older generation, a comic aggrandizement made funnier by a touch of realism: the narrative purports to be a twelfth-grade project in oral history. As a result, the tale can ridicule informant Don Wojcak's seriousness about maintaining a model railroad ("You have to put in a regular shift, otherwise it gets dull" [193]) and at the same time make fun of the narrators' own adolescent hyperseriousness, as when a student writer reports, "One problem for model-railroad builders has always been grass" (193). In the end, the tale limits its admiration of the good old days to the nearly universal nostalgia for one's own youth—but not anybody else's.

A similar jaundice infects "WLT (the Edgar Era)" (1976) and "Who We Were and What We Meant by It" (1984). The titles' allusions to the bacon sandwich and *Walden*, respectively, suggest the tone of the self-conscious narration that follows, and although eight years and a good many comic experiments separate "wlt" from "Who We Were," the two tales have a comic convention in common: both allow the vernacular narrator to speak for and debunk himself. Keillor has used this device with increasing complexity over the years, but even his early local-color tales—including "Friendly Neighbor" (1973), "The Slim Graves Show" (1973), and "My North Dakota Railroad Days" (1975)—stand, like "Plainfolks," at comic distance from nostalgia.

"My North Dakota Railroad Days" (1975) illustrates how fully Keillor can exploit self-debunking narration. The story goes through several twists simply on the question of its genre as the narrator offers one misleading hint after another about the kind of story he is telling—beginning with the title and opening epigraph, which imply a nostalgic journey into the past. His colloquialisms character- ize the story as a mock-oral tale in the classic vernacular tradition, but the many visual devices from numbered arguments to unneces- sary capital letters call attention to its literariness. The narrator himself is hardly a typical mock-oral yarn spinner. Neither a genial cracker-barrel philosopher, a tall talker, nor a homespun guide to a little town that time forgot, he speaks a colorful language that includes both vulgarities and homely comparisons. He describes his pension, for instance, as "an annuity hardly big enough to plug your nose" (96) and considers the state's response to the railroad bosses like that of "an old maid asked to dance. . . . [it] bought the deal on sight alone and overlooked the smell" (98). And not surprisingly, in a twist on these twists, the tale that purports to explain why "our Brotherhood of North Dakota State Railroad Employees is broke, flat busted, beat down, and a *sorrier* mess than can be imag- ined" (95) ultimately becomes a tall yarn about the disappearance of the Prairie Queen and "her mighty whistle" (95).

The early memories of a slightly crotchety old timer imbue the tale with local color. As he describes it, for example, the whistle-stop celebration for Theodore Roosevelt in 1912 has elements of both a county fair and a political rally, with races and dancing and speeches; Keillor pokes only the gentlest fun at the townspeople for starting the party in the early evening even though the President's train wasn't expected until 3:30 A.M. Like Jonson Ingqvist, who en- tertained the king of Norway in *Lake Wobegon Days* by offering him a nap, the citizens of Lakota, North Dakota, worried that a hearty welcome might disturb Roosevelt as he slept, and they therefore decided not to risk waking him:

> As a courtesy to the sleeping President we would delay the shout until the train had gone through. With a burst of steam and a shower of sparks and a mighty roar that shook the earth President Roosevelt's train came into town highballing west. I grabbed on to my Dad's leg and watched the swinging red lanterns on the last car disappear into the dark. Then up went the shout, "Welcome to Lakota! All Aboard with Roosevelt" and they fired a shotgun and went home to bed. (96–97)

Mild ridicule of the North Dakotans' innocence provides rhetorical distraction from the increasingly tall details describing the wonders of the Prairie Queen and her equally extravagant management. But even the most nostalgic details evoke the real, political world of the past. A reference to the Socialist leader Eugene Debs finds its way into a celebration of the Queen's unsurpassed suspension system; she rode so smoothly that passengers could enjoy a fine game of billiards on board "except one curve north of the Forks named the 'Debs Transit' for its tendency to redistribute the balls" (99).

Darkness lurks beneath the glamour, however. The train often ran as a charter, making stops at the whim of its passengers, and the combination of its high speed and irregular schedule caused it to kill a fairly high number of people. Not surprisingly, the narrator treats this detail extravagantly as well. "The Prairie Queen killed more people in her twelve years than floods and blizzards put together," he brags. "She must have wiped out half a county" (102). But even disaster could not tarnish the train's reputation, he tells us, since survivors of a crash tended to appear "sort of awe-struck, *proud* even, to have been hit by the Queen" (102).

Considering that the story reaches a climax over a fire on the Queen and her ultimate demise at the Debs Transit (both subsequently blamed on the employees' union), it is probably not coincidental that Debs himself (1855–1926) was a midwesterner who became a locomotive fireman in 1871, secretary of the Brotherhood of Locomotive Firemen in 1880, and president of the American Railway Union (which he organized) in 1893. This political theme stands second, however, to the rhetoric of the tall tale that emerges near the end. The narrative becomes increasingly colloquial and increasingly hyperbolic when the time comes to explain just why the Prairie Queen no longer rules the rails. "It was that bone-cracking rail east of Williston . . . that busted the eggs in Houtek's basket," the narrator insists defensively, but his absence from the scene while "off fishing . . . with my good fiend Ramon Kilgore" (106) would make his explanation suspect, even if Keillor weren't winking at us with an allusion to Richard Brautigan's *Trout Fishing in America* (1967). Even more suspect is the disappearance of all the evidence. When the train hits the bad rail, spilling vast numbers of papers implicating the railroad management in graft and fraud, the papers suffer the same fate as most evidence in tales told by vernacular liars: "All was released and flew away and scattered itself over thousands of square miles of North Dakota to be plowed under as compost, and so poisonous was the ink that crops were thin for years thereafter" (107). And like the paper evidence, so the Queen herself disappears, with all the extravagance of Mark Twain's Good Little Boy being blown to bits and strewn across several counties:

> They say she hit the curve at 80—some say 100—and her wheels screamed as she jumped the track. She dug a double furrow three feet deep in the ground, and flew from the high bank of the Red River. They say she was airborne for only four seconds but it seemed like a week. They say a million birds rose from the valley and all was suddenly silent but for the rush of wings and the cry of a child in the crowd, and then she hit water. Hit so hard, they say, she sent a three-foot wave two miles upstream and four down, and the steam was so thick the eastern shore could not be seen until noon the next day. There, they say, rests the Prairie Queen today, and they say on a quiet day if you put your head underwater you can still hear the slow tolling of her bell rocked by the current and the groaning of her joints as she sinks ever deeper in the mud. (109)

But like all tall-tale-tellers, the narrator must concede that he has not seen or heard the evidence himself, and like all tall yarns, the story leaves us with the narrator's vivid imagination and colorful language as the only sureties of the tale.

In the dozen years since "My North Dakota Railroad Days," Keillor has continued to deflate the voice of rural innocence and sentimentality in his short fiction. Close attention to the sounds of words underscores the subtlety with which he can fashion comic contempt. Sometimes a well-chosen rhyme conveys the ridicule— in calling a town Lakota, North Dakota, for instance, or in the country-and-western song whose title sums up the theme of "The Slim Graves Show": "A-D-U-L-T-E-R-Y (Don't Say That Word, It Makes Me Cry)" (49).[8]

Often, however, Keillor undercuts his homespun characters by giving them unfashionable, uneuphonious names, as with the three sadsacks named Earl: a musician in "The Slim Graves Show" (1973), Don's father in "Don: The True Story of a Young Person" (1977), and the narrator of "We Are Still Married" (1984). Keillor's radio monologues and the unpublished materials in the Prairie Home Companion Archives at MPR show him continuing to poke fun at the flat sound of the name Earl. An unlabeled radio script probably dating from 1976 features thoughts on Jimmy Carter by Earle Miller, "owner and operator of Earle's 'As You Like It' Barber Shop in St. Paul": "Whaddaya think of this election? Pretty pitiful, huh? I donno. I mean, you take Carter: this guy don't even talk right—I figure, a politician oughta at least sound good sometimes, but this guy looks like he's got a mouthful of Novocaine."[9] This wisecrack about the colorless contest between Jimmy Carter and Gerald Ford places Earle among America's vernacular oracles, the class of colloquial philosophers that includes Seba Smith's nineteenth-century pundit Jack Downing as well as the better-known Huck Finn and Jim. The script's deliberate misspellings reflect the literary convention, though Keillor did not intend them for print. Like his fellows in this antebellum humorous tradition, Earle has a truth to impart, but the joke here also redounds upon him; faulting Carter's speech while committing a grammatical error himself amounts to the pot calling the kettle black.

Still other Earls from *A Prairie Home Companion* include the namesakes of two dubious commercial operations. "Earl and His Buddies Driving School" (1983) teaches "Driver Assertiveness . . . [including] basic skills like the left-hand turn against heavy oncoming traffic." Similarly, "Earle's House of Accents" (1986) recommends buying accented English instead of learning a foreign language. In the typescript of a monologue dated 8 March 1986, Bill the janitor becomes Earl the janitor. And finally, Keillor wrote a routine punning on the World Theater and the "Earl Theater." In the spot, Stevie Beck learns that she has mistakenly assumed that an agent, Mr. Earl, had promised her a chance to perform: "You mean——there *is* no Mister Earl?" she asks. And Keillor responds, "I'm sure that somewhere there is a Mr. Earl. Everybody has their Mr. Earl."[10]

This quip amounts to a private joke, but it also suggests that any Keillor character named Earl serves as the target as well as a vehicle of homespun humor.

By contrast, a more recent story presents a much less ambiguous sneer at cracker-barrel philosophy. "The Tip-Top Club" (1981), first published in the *Atlantic Monthly*, extends the burlesque of sentimentality to include both older and younger generations.

In its original format as a relentlessly cheerful call-in radio show, "The Tip-Top Club" appealed primarily to oldsters, who promoted homespun remedies of all sorts. With deadpan neutrality, the third-person narrative smirks at all the listeners' ideas for bettering themselves and their world: "the idea of pouring warm soapy water into overshoes and wearing them around the house to give yourself a relaxing footbath while you work . . . the idea that if you're depressed you should sit down and write a letter to yourself praising all of your good qualities, and the idea of puffing cigarette smoke at violets to prevent aphids" (59). But as the tale chronicles the radio program's successive formats, younger folks emerge as no less sentimental than their elders, and the ridicule broadens to encompass the two generations' similar rigidity:

> Wayne had little interest in the old Tip-Top topics. He was divorced and lived in an efficiency apartment (no lawn to keep up, no maintenance responsibilities) and had no pets or children. His major interest was psychology. "People fascinate me," he said. (You don't fascinate me," someone said.) He read psychology books and talked about them on the air. He said that he was undergoing therapy, and it had helped him to understand himself better. ("What's to understand?"). (72–73)

"The Tip-Top Club" characterizes pop psychology and folk wisdom as equivalent, and equally foolish, varieties of cracker-barrel philosophy, and its appearance at a crucial time in Keillor's career suggests that the humorist had a few qualms about the direction that the new audiences and broader focus were taking the Saturday night show. "The Tip-Top Club" appeared in August 1981, between the beginning of regular national broadcasts of *A Prairie Home Companion* and his retirement from the morning version of the show. The tale doubtless has more than a few private jokes about the differences between his own and his listeners' expectations for *A Prairie Home Companion*, not to mention MPR's. Speculation aside, it is worth noting that at just about the same time that Keillor vigorously debunked sentimentality, self-revelation, and rural nostalgia in his fiction, he had begun employing these same elements affectionately in his oral Lake Wobegon tales.

"The Tip-Top Club" loses some of its humor at the end in a didactic announcement of the program's latest incarnation as "'a modified middle-of-the-road pop-rock format' with a disc jockey who never talk[s] except to give time, temperature, and commercials" (75), but the conclusion demonstrates that nostalgia in Keillor's tales depends less on sentimental themes than on familiar voices. These voices flaunt their creator's gifts as a mimic, but they do not speak for him. Quite the contrary. Keillor's vernacular characters consistently fail as cracker-barrel philosophers, no matter where their voices originate—whether they hail from small-town Minnesota or more worldly parts of the nation, from the pages of other writers or the studios of imaginary radio shows. For all their reliance on techniques of nineteenth-century vernacular and local-color humor, Keillor's tales look askance at rural innocence. Ignorance may be bliss to a rural narrator or an amateur writer, but it is always a bubble off center, moving toward burlesque. In a familiar subversion of borrowed traditions, the tales use homespun style to lampoon homespun values, one of the favorite tactics of the nineteenth-century literary comedians.

Keillor's fondness for burlesques and his diverse comic masks locate his short fiction in this second American humorous tradition. The tradition embraces a very large group of pseudonymous humorists including Artemus ward (Charles F. Browne), John Phoenix, Esq. (George Horatio Derby), Mark Twain (Samuel L. Clemens), and more recently, Garrison (Gary Edward) Keillor. Flourishing mainly between 1860 and 1900, these writers, known variously as literary comedians or Phunny Phellows, alternated poses of superiority and inferiority depending on the subject at hand; their pseudonyms stood as comic signatures, not coherent literary personas. They wrote fewer tall tales and mock-oral yarns, devices of an earlier humor or character, and more verbal and literary jokes instead. Infamous as misspellers, the Phunny Phellows played with language, tone, and theme as they ridiculed sentimentality and traditional values through burlesques of literary and oratorical forms. Their humor often had an ethical dimension. Among their favorite devices were misquotation and illogic; they adored deadpan narration by an "amiable idiot."[11] Although many literary comedians took to the lecture platform, their pleasure in typographical humor and parody made their sketches particularly literate and literary.

From the beginning of his career to the present, Keillor has demonstrated a literary comedian's interest in all kinds of verbal play, from the weird word and strange sentence to parodies of familiar literature and rhetoric. The nub of his second published story—"Snack Firm Maps New Chip Push" (1970), a parody of business reporting that describes the marketing strategy for a new product—depends entirely on a single pun: that buffalo chips are not only dung but also a "breakthrough into food areas heretofore untouched."[12] Another early piece, "Sex Tips" (1971), offers advice with a punning, pompous vacuity that Artemus Ward would have been proud to claim. Keillor's version of the perfect dimwit, "Harley Peters, U.S. Department of Agriculture Extension Sex Agent," receives a stupid question and responds in kind. The expert is asked, "I hear so much said against sex education in the schools. Is sex educational?" And Peters replies, "Today, most educators agree that sex should be taught. In fact, sex *is* learning."[13]

Keillor's use of traditional techniques probably does not reflect deliberate debt but rather the tendency of comic minds to think alike. Still, there are a few loud echoes. With the tale of how Dad Benson got lost in the prairie just outside his door during a blizzard, for instance, "Friendly Neighbor" repeats one of the literary comedians' stock stories, which Mark Twain included in *Roughing It*. The fractured grammar at the beginning of "The People's Shopper" (1973), a parody of the neighborhood advertising circular, recalls Artemus Ward's linguistic offenses: "Shop the Co-op Way and Save! These Fine Peoples Are Happy to Serve You" (198). The chart of irrelevant baseball statistics in "How Are the Legs, Sam?" (1971) provides visual humor of the sort that Phoenix sprinkled throughout his work, most notably in "Illustrated Newspapers."[14]

As the dates of these examples suggest, the broadest literary comedy appears in Keillor's earliest work, from the early 1970s, but nearly all his tales illustrate the Phunny Phellows' hallmark: burlesque. Equally important, his burlesques sort themselves into groups not too different from those of his nineteenth-century kin.[15] Whereas they debunked sentimental fiction, history, and oratory, Keillor ridicules formulaic literature (both high and low), professional writing (especially by scholars and other jargon lovers), and the mass media (mainly newspapers and radio).

Common to all these burlesques—some twenty-five tales—is the ridicule of the narrative voice as well as the generic formula. Keillor had already mastered the voice of the amiable idiot in his first published story, "Local Family Keeps Son Happy" (1970), the chatty report of how two creative parents saved their son from a "reckless" adolescence of smoking and drinking by providing him with a live-in prostitute. Conveying the same wide-eyed innocence usually associated with first-person narration, the writer reveals an inability to understand any of the subjects of the piece, including the fancy girl's recipe for "Fancy Eggs" (itself a fancy name for huevos rancheros). After this running start, Keillor continued exploring the voice of innocence. The burlesques as a group, like his mock-oral and local-color tales, argue that innocence may succeed as a narrative device but fails as an ethical stance.

Not surprisingly, his literary parodies, a very large class of burlesques, show Keillor at his least inventive, unable to throw off entirely the tired, often sophomoric enthusiasms of the genre. But the pieces still take very accurate aim at their targets. "Ten Stories for Mr. Richard Brautigan, and Other Stories" (1972) zips through the job in a single page of the *New Yorker*, complete with a structural joke: "Ten Stories" contains only *nine*. But then brevity suits the send-up of a writer who, our narrator tells us, writes 110 stories every day before lunchtime. "Of these," continues the damningly faint praise, "more than forty are quite good and some are amazing in the way they create a mood or depict a paragraph in just a few words" (243)—as in the opening "story," which reads in its entirety, title and all:

BELIEVE IT OR NOT

Some of his stories are no longer than this. (243).

Such burlesques as "Ten Stories" are slight but very funny, especially in their original *New Yorker* contexts, where they command most of the 8½-by-11-inch page and benefit from the serendipity of the magazine, which surrounds the burlesque with other comic fiction, cartoons, poetry, "Talk of the Town" sketches, and nonfictional features.

A more imaginative literary parody takes on a genre rather than an individual author. "Nana Hami Ba Reba" (1980) establishes its travesty of science fiction in the opening sentence: "I had just motored the night shield over the dome and coordinated into the body pod to initiate sleep mode when the Chief Exec's audible crackled over the talk circuit embedded in my third upper-left molar" (175). The story concerns the day that the narrator lost his job with the government (or fantasized that he did), but not surprisingly, considering Keillor's interest in comic diction, the prime target of the parody is language itself. The comic attack zeroes in on Metro, the post-1984 version of Newspeak, representing the verbal component of America's total conversion to the metric system. But it also encompasses bureaucratese, cliches, folk expressions, puns, and nonsense—sometimes all in a single passage:

> "Nubi gana, bwana. Weeni lala," I stammered. ("I am not impacted by that which you have spoken. The number you have reached is not a working number." At least, that's what I meant, although I was oc-curred to that I might have said that the elk were upwind of the river.) . . .
> "Is it safe to go back?" I asked." ("Olli olli infree?"). (178-79)

With the burlesque writer's typical unconcern for the details of plot, Keillor ends a tale of political intrigue and linguistic confusion with all the anticlimactic sentimentality of Dorothy finding herself in Kansas, after all. Having stepped on the ray pad and closed his eyes, he returns from the future to his kitchen where the mundane reigns: meat and potatoes for dinner and stereotypical conversations between parent and child. "'What'd you learn in school today?' 'Nu-thin'" (180).

Unlike the amateur writer in "Friendly Neighbor" or the crusty yarn spinner of "My North Dakota Railroad Days"—stories at least four years older than "Nana Hami Ba Reba"—this narrator barely reveals himself through his tale, except to suggest that he finds the future (especially the metric future) incomprehensible and the pres-ent comfortingly banal. This implication, however minor an ele-ment in the story's burlesque of language, nonetheless has some biographical significance, considering that "Nana Hami Ba Reba" appeared in the *New Yorker* just as Keillor's monologues on *A Prairie Home Companion* were delving more deeply into the Lake Wobegon past and just three months before the weekly radio show entered upon the uncertain future of regular national broadcasts.

More successful still are three less narrowly conceived burlesques.

"Found Paradise" (1971) and the two Jack Schmidt, arts administrator, stories combine literary parody and contemporary satire. A takeoff on *Walden* and Brautigan (with sideswipes at Proust and others), "Found Paradise" appeared in the *New Yorker* with the subtitle "(A Midwestern Writer Nobody Knows and How He Found Peace of Mind)," before being revised as the title story of *Happy to Be Here*. The story makes fun of the romantic back-to-the-land movement of the early seventies, particularly its self-conscious mythmaking. Carefully measured understatement and an anticlimactic ending lampoon the intense 1970s-style quest for nirvana: "Found paradise. I said I would and by God I have. Here it is, and it is just what I knew was here all along. Well, I guess that is about it. I'm happy to be here, is all" (270).

In contrast to such deadpan narration, literary humor seldom comes broader than the Jack Schmidt tales, "Jack Schmidt, Arts Administrator" (1979) and "Jack Schmidt on the Burning Sands: A 'Jack Schmidt, Arts Administrator' Adventure" (1982), both takeoffs of the hard-boiled detective formula. The earlier story shows the parodist at his most inventive. From the opening scene, "one of those sweltering days when Minneapolis smells of melting asphalt and foundation money is as tight as a rusted nut" (3), Keillor ridicules one hard-boiled convention after the next—all the way up to the final comic climax, which (in the true tradition of Sam Spade) promises a corresponding sexual climax, as Schmidt and his secretary celebrate the unexpected arrival of the (predictable) *deus ex machina*, here in the literal form of a telepone call resolving their insolvency. Capping the zaniness is the title character, Jack Schmidt. Although he complains, conventionally enough, that "the private-eye business was getting thinner than sliced beef at the deli" (5), he contributes less to the tale's literary parody than to its culture satire. In the spirit of '76, he tells us, Schmidt's Arts Mall had brought together seventeen artisans, including a spatter painter and a dulcimer maker, taking advantage of federal funding "when Bicentennial money was wandering around like helpless buffalo" (4). The end of the story finds him infatuated with the jargon of the pseudoaesthete as he imagines "The ArtsTrip": "The median as medium! Eight-lane environmental art! . . . Wayside dance areas! . . . A drive-in film series! The customized car as American genre! . . . People can have an arts experience without even pulling over onto the shoulder. They can get quality enrichment and still make good time!" (13). Keillor's talent for parody not only emphasizes his affinities with the Phunny Phellows of the nineteenth-century but also underlines the artifice and skill behind his mimicry of vernacular speakers.

The pleasure of ridiculing the arts administrator's jargon recurs in a second group of Keillor's burlesques, the travesties of professional writing. Comic attacks on individual genres and their writers, these pieces display a virtuoso range of voices. In addition to the government agent who dispenses sex tips are the sociologist who analyzes the game in "The New Baseball" (1971), the historian who contributes the encyclopedia article titled "Bangor Man" (1972), the anthropologist of "Oya Life These Days" (1975), the wedding consultant who offers advice in "Your Wedding and You" (1975), the public-relations officer who speaks on behalf of his agency in "Your Transit Commission" (1981), and the social worker who outlines the dimensions of a new social problem in "The Current Crisis in Remorse" (1983). As this chronological list shows, Keillor has gradually abandoned parodies of academic writing for more public targets, although the mock history in *Lake Wobegon Days* demonstrates his continued willingness to exploit the genre's potential for comic understatement and deadpan.

Burlesques in a third category, aimed at the press and radio, also have taken on broader subjects over the years. Most of Keillor's burlesques fall into this class, undoubtedly because he adores radio as a medium but perhaps also because radio offers so many distinctive voices and because newspapers and magazines present so many comic incongruities.[16] (In a similar vein more than a century ago, Artemus Ward posed as a showman and John Phoenix temporarily played newspaper editor.) Keillor's earliest pieces parodied newspaper rhetoric, and within a few years he had hit nearly every journalistic target from sports and business reporting to political commentary, book reviews, and the women's page.[17] His more recent sketches, mainly mock magazine articles, show more narrative complexity. "How It Was In America A Week Ago Tuesday" (1975), for example, a travesty of national surveys, purports to be written by amateur authors (one of Keillor's favorite variations on the amiable idiot) who catalogue a day in the life of the American people, complete with statistics: "already, the first of 125 million beds, 160 million cigarettes, and 40 million quarts of orange juice were creaking, smoking, and being poured" (158). A later sketch, "Be Careful" (1979), overlays a guilt-inspiring voice on the ubiquitous health feature article. Instead of the usual didactic tone, this narrator offers material scolding. The advice on avoiding accidents: "Chances are you will have read this article in very poor light. You knew it was wrong but you went right ahead and did it anyway. What can I tell you that hasn't been said a thousand times before?" (242). More recently, "My Stepmother, Myself" (1982) lampooned the confessional article of the women's magazine. The title alludes to Nancy Friday's popular memoir *My Mother, Myself*, and the article itself exonerates "the evil stepmother" (183) with testimony from three experts: Snow White, Gretel, and Cinderella. These sketches offer slight, topical humor, but they rise above their specific targets because Keillor defines their narrative voices so clearly.

The best of this lot, "Don: The True Story of a Young Person" (1977), puts the literary comedians' burlesque to very sophisticated, very modern effect. Purportedly written by a novice journalist, "Don" is a mock magazine story tracing the rise of a punk-rock group called Trash from its humble origins, a small band performing at the President's Day [*sic*] County 4-H Poultry Show dance, to "some sort of stars" (32), whose lyrics and performance style merit a feature story in the music tabloid *Fallen Rocks*, a blatant send-up of *Rolling Stone*.

The comic genius of the story lies in the multiplicity of its targets. The list barely begins with Don, the adolescent whose moral dilemma shapes the story: does a proper punk performance require him to bite a live chicken? The hyper-dramatic narrator poses the problem: "Don knew he must decide whether to stay in Trash and risk banishment from home and the permanent hatred of a community (and perhaps a nation) united in outrage at the senseless injury (or even death) of a barnyard fowl, or not" (24). The group's lyrics—truly inspired bombast—include references to Little Red Riding Hood and lawn mowers. Don's morally concerned but ineffectual parents, Mavis and Earl, hope the crisis "will just bring us closer together" (23); these upstanding citizens support their son the first time he succumbs to peer pressure and bites the bullet (that is, the chicken) but not the second. And the list of comic targets goes on. In contrast to the rural community's horror at cruelty to chickens is the music community's admiration. The group's big chance as a warm-up act fizzles into a paltry three songs followed by fifteen minutes of chicken routine.

Debunking all—and punctuating both Don's small-town talk and the amiable idiocy of his biographer—is the inflated, pseudoscholarly rhetoric of the *Fallen Rocks* story itself:

> Perhaps no bird [the sophomoric author quotes], not even the eagle, bluebird, or robin, has entered so deeply the folk consciousness of the race as has the common chicken (*Gallus gallus*). . . . the chicken, from Plymouth Rock to lowly Leghorn, has come to stand for industry, patience, and fecundity. . . . And yet, even as the chicken rides high as symbol of the Right Life in the pastoral dreams of the post-agrarian bourgeoisie, its name has attracted other connotations. . . . It is the peculiar genius of Trash to exploit this dichotomy to its fullest resolution, and thus to release in an audience such revulsion as can only indicate that profound depths have been reached. (29)

It is possible that Keillor took inspiration from Page Smith and Charles Daniel's comic-scholarly compendium *The Chicken Book* (1975, two years before "Don"), since the humor of his story balances pseudoscholarship and burlesque journalese with carefully modulated scorn. But contemporary influences on Keillor's burlesques, including the postmodern writer's pleasure in elaborate narration, do not diminish his affinities with the nineteenth-century traditions of American literary comedy.

The melodramatic tableau at the end of the tale sustains the burlesque: Don stands (chicken-hearted?) in the wings, wondering once again what to do about that chicken. But the youth's deceit and corruption show in the language of his indecision, with its comic contrast between low style and high purpose. "Perhaps by doing it and feeling sick about doing it he would do some good," he thinks, trying to persuade himself "that maybe it would be an example to them about violence." Even in third-person burlesque narration Keillor controls his style so well that he can unmask his character with alliteration and low diction: "And besides, . . . they were some sort of stars" (32). Rendering a character's voice with such exquisite precision is Keillor's particular gift. It takes "Don: The True Story of a Young Person" beyond parody and nearly obscures the tale's complexity by making the difficult look easy.

Certainly no nineteenth-century literary comedian mimicked the voices of the mass media more accurately. In addition to experiments with various voices of the press, however, Keillor has also burlesqued the voices of radio. Examples range across a decade, from "On the

Road, Almost" (1972) and "WLT (the Edgar Era)" (1976) to "The Tip-Top Club" (1981). Among the best of his early pieces, "The Slim Graves Show" (1973) and "Friendly Neighbor" (1973) explore radio's ability to blur fantasy and reality. Not surprisingly, the year after publishing these tales, Keillor exploited much the same blurring on *A Prairie Home Companion*, with its parodies of old-time radio dramas like *The Shadow* and commercials for apocryphal Lake Wobegon enterprises like Bob's Bank and Ralph's Pretty Good Grocery. Within the tight focus of the short story, however, Keillor could take these issues a step farther. If the mock-oral narrator of "The Slim Graves Show" cannot find the line between the performers' real lives and their roles on the air, much less fathom the deliberately fuzzy distinction between the program and commercials, it's no wonder: the country-western musical hour contains a series of commercials in the form of country-western melodramas that inspire the songs in the main part of the show. Keillor surely intended the confusion not only as a reflection of the narrator's involvement with the show, but also as a joke on the reader and a comment on radio, as well. "I can't think of anything I don't enjoy about radio," he told an interviewer in 1985, "It's a magical country."[18] Though he staked out the boundaries with devices derived from the traditions of literary comedy, he also made the territory his own—as he also did with the traditions of *New Yorker* humor.

Debunking both old-time values and contemporary life—especially while exploring the power of mass media—puts Keillor's fiction quite squarely in a third American comic tradition, the modern humor of the *New Yorker*. *New Yorker* writers' passionate interest in the mass media and their self-conscious interest in language reflect, to be sure, their own kinship with the literary comedians,[19] but *New Yorker* humor has become most clearly identified with aesthetically finicky portraits of modernity at its zaniest. In contrast to the conventions of vernacular humor and literary comedy, which he seems to have picked up indirectly, Keillor quite explicitly modeled his writing on the prose of *New Yorker* writers. He has made no secret of his admiration for E. B. White, S. J. Perelman, and Robert Benchley, whose work he discovered, along with the magazine, as a fifteen-year-old aspiring intellectual.[20] Not surprisingly, then, at least two of Keillor's stories—and sometimes as many as seven—have appeared in the *New Yorker* nearly every year since 1970, when he made his debut.

Most of the fifty signed *New Yorker* sketches listed in the Bibliography appeared while Keillor was still hosting *A Prairie Home Companion*, that is, before he joined the *New Yorker* staff in October 1987. Yet not one of them indulges the trademark sentimentality of his Lake Wobegon monologues. Its absence stems from the humorist's apparently deliberate decision to keep his written and radio stories distinct from one another. But the decision did not, as one might expect, involve a determination to subdue sentimentality in favor of more urbane satire. On the contrary, as the chronological development of his short tales suggests and the author himself has confessed, Keillor began writing the sentimental monologues as an alternative to his *New Yorker* humor. Compared with the ease of writing the satirical sketch, he claimed, the sentimental oral story offers more challenge.[21] Still, despite the clamoring of his fans for a constant stream of Lake Wobegon tales, he has not abandoned the satiric *New Yorker* piece.

In its classic form, *New Yorker* humor focuses on some little man driven insane by some element of daily life. For S. J. Perelman in "Insert Flat 'A' and Throw Away" it was the do-it-yourself project. For E. B. White in "Dusk in Fierce Pajamas" it was fashion reporting. For Robert Benchley in "Back in Line" it was the post office. For Ring Lardner in "Large Coffee," it was room service. For James Thurber in "The Secret Life of Walter Mitty" and a dozen other stories, it was the nagging wife. More generally, hallmarks of the *New Yorker* tradition include an obsession with the mass media (particularly the rhetoric of advertising), empathy for the overwhelmed little man, and practically legendary scorn for the little old lady in Dubuque—all rendered in prose of finicky precision. A few of Keillor's advertising burlesques—for example, "The People's Shopper" (1973), "Your Transit Commission" (1981), "Maybe You Can Too" (1983)—convey a comic intensity similar to classic *New Yorker* humor, but from its very earliest days the magazine also published a comparatively quiet humor of passing values.[22] In this style, perhaps the most relevant here are Clarence Day's sketches of his family, eventually collected in book form as the *Life with Father* series. Like Day, Keillor combines cracker-barrel caricature and mild criticism, suggesting that his vernacular characters are out of step with their time.[23] Still, the more consciously literary tales of Thurber and White have left a stronger mark on Keillor's prose.

The decision to cast White as the protagonist of "If Robert Frost

Had an Apple" (1983) provides only a small indication of the enormous regard in which Keillor holds him. A few months before the story appeared in the *New York Times Magazine*, the younger humorist paid homage to his hero's birthday in a rap song performed on *A Prairie Home Companion*. The rap declared White's work "elegant, simple, and right" before concluding:

> Happy birthday to a writer on the Maine seacoast.
> Some writers wrote more, but mister, he wrote the most.
> Happy is the tree torn limb from limb
> To make pulp for the paper of a book by him.

E. B. White, E. B. White, E. B. White, E. B. White, yeah! (9 July 1983)

The rap raises the possibility that Keillor may have considered "If Robert Frost Had an Apple" to be yet another birthday present for White, but the birthday seems to have provided the opportunity, not the motivation, for expressing his admiration. Two years later, in an interview about *Lake Wobegon Days*, Keillor continued to insist, E. B. White is still my hero in the writing biz."[24]

A tall tale rather than a *New Yorker*–style personal-experience narrative, "If Robert Frost Had an Apple" purports to chronicle the word-processing disasters that have destroyed some of America's most important fiction. During a visit to White, the narrator tells us, he learned how many great American novels were gone with the static as the result of the primitive word-processing technologies in use before the development of his own beloved CPR-66. Its name suggesting an ability to resuscitate a lifeless text, the CPR-66 boasts a "fiction function that can . . . adjust a full-length work from indicative to subjunctive in one second" (80). Using the typical frame-tale structure of the tall story, Keillor describes his own word processor to introduce a story about days gone by, when great writers took in stride the possibility of losing their work to a power surge. The list encompasses great works, indeed: Hemingway's comic Oak Park novel (known to his friends as "the big one [that] got away" [84]), Robert Frost's science-fiction thriller, *Fire and Ice*, F. Scott Fitzgerald's perfected version of *The Last Tycoon* (accidentally destroyed by the cleaning lady who was writing her own novel on his Reo WP23), Faulkner's novel *The Planet Yoknapatawpha*, and (of course) E. B. White's "big" novel for adults. The crude technology of his machine—a homemade LST using no. 4 barbed wire instead of floppy disks and requiring the command "ROPAY-RAMGAY" (80) (that's *program* in pig latin)—forever limited White's reputation.

Not surprisingly, considering his admiration for the *New Yorker* author, Keillor dwells on the sad fate of White's lost masterpiece, which, he testifies (moving the story along toward its verbal climax), presented "a far different White than the world had seen, even during his playing days as 'Winger' White with the Bangor Bombers—a raw, primitive, *darker* White" (80). These jokes don't show Keillor at his most inventive—which may explain why this sketch appeared in the *New York Times Magazine* instead of the *New Yorker*, which has had first right of refusal on his short fiction since the early seventies—but in any case, the story publicly claims the company that the Minnesota writer wants to keep. And this story is no sillier than some of the *New Yorker* sketches that White and others wrote for the "Talk of the Town" section, especially in the twenties. The tale ends with the narrator's explanation of what happened to his own great novel. Like White, apparently, he has yet to produce a big book, and he looks forward to astonishing those who have hinted that he isn't really capable of writing a novel. And like White, he has a strange tale to tell: during a game of Space Invaders, an alien ship "captured a whole bunch of stuff I had written" (84). Funny enough as a lame excuse for the absence of the promised draft-in-progress, the story seems even funnier in retrospect: Keillor had acquired a word processor for his work on *Lake Wobegon Days*, his own long-awaited big book, and must have been at work on it at the time. More important from a generic standpoint, this story about a *New Yorker* writer, like only two other tales published before his retirement from *A Prairie Home Companion* ("Drowning 1954" and "After a Fall"), features Keillor's own narrative voice, in the familiar manner of Benchley and White.

Although Keillor's deliberate prose has doubtless benefitted from White's essays on the pleasures of farming (originally published in *Harper's Magazine*) and the wit of his "Talk of the Town" pieces, the unacknowledged influence of Thurber seems even stronger. Keillor's characters have the same comic conflict between inner and outer reality that characterizes Thurber's most famous tales, from the frenzied false alarm of "The Day the Dam Broke" (1933) to the studied calm of "The Unicorn in the Garden" (1940). One of Thurber's least characteristic stories seems to have provided the most direct influence, however. A very tall mock-oral tale, Thurber's

"You Could Look It Up" (1941) pokes fun at baseball fans' delight in maintaining and disputing the record—and quite unexpectedly set one of its own; the fantasy tale of a midget ball player with an impossibly small strike zone led to the actual hiring of the St. Louis Browns' Eddie Gaedel.[25] Keillor's five baseball stories testify to his interest in the game, which has also inspired several contemporary novels, including Robert Coover's *Universal Baseball Association, Inc.* (1968) and Philip Roth's *Great American Novel* (1973), as well as Bernard Malamud's *The Natural* (1952). Keillor's "What Did We Do Wrong?" (1985) borrows Thurber's premises.

Like a lot of baseball fiction, "You Could Look It Up" and "What Did We Do Wrong?" exploit the sport's reputation as a game of records. They poke fun at the fans' delight in mastering and disputing the official record, all the while describing how an unusual (indeed, apocryphal) character changes the history of baseball before conveniently vanishing from the scene. As the title suggests, Thurber's vernacular narrator protests too much when he insists that his anecdote about America's first midget baseball player is all there in the record of "thirty, thirty-one year [*sic*] ago; you could look it up."[26] By contrast, Keillor's narrator claims only the fans' disappointment as evidence for his tale about America's first woman ballplayer. Both writers strayed from their normal storytelling patterns to tell a tall baseball yarn—Thurber did not ordinarily write mock-oral tall tales, nor does Keillor—but Keillor's tale provides some interesting variations on the classic themes of *New Yorker* humor. Keillor does not remember reading "You Could Look It Up," although it has often been reprinted in anthologies of sports literature and modern short stories, but he does recall reading *The Great American Novel*, which quite explicitly reworks Thurber's tale.[27] Regardless of the line of influence, "What Did We Do Wrong?" parallels "You Could Look It Up" in ways that illuminate both the similarities and the differences between two *New Yorker* humorists of different temperaments and generations.

The most important difference involves narration. Keillor substitutes a third-person narrator for Thurber's unreliable mock-oral speaker, Doc, a semiliterate misspeller borrowed wholesale from Southwestern humor. The change in the recent story not only shifts the focus from the teller to the tale itself but also removes the story from the mock-oral tradition of the tall tale to the literary tradition of verbal wit. Still, even without a first-person narrator, Keillor's story has plenty of comic vernacular, just like Thurber's. But whereas Thurber focused on the veracity of the record—the baseball record and the historical record—Keillor, in typical *New Yorker* fashion, takes on the issues of his own day. Instead of debunking the tall-talking vernacular narrator, he targets machismo and feminism, and no one escapes his wit. First comes Annie Szemanski, the main character. Her name implies Annie-is-a-man-ski, and every sentence shows just how tough she is. "That's when I started chewing tobacco," she explains early on, discussing her years in the minor leagues, "—because no matter how bad anybody treats you, it's not as bad as this" (32); later on, she responds to criticism of her behavior with a euphemistic "If they don't like it, then Ritz, they can go Pepsi their Hostess Twinkies" (35). The rest of the characters—less vulgar but almost as colorful—are shown responding to her. There are the grudgingly respectful male sportswriters, one of whom exclaims, "You've been chewing this for two years? God, I had no idea it was so hard to be a woman" (32). Then there is the still-grudging woman sportswriter who ultimately causes Annie's fall, explaining, "Sports is my way out of the gynecology ghetto, so don't ask me to eat this story" (33). And finally, there is the representative narrator of baseball games, who reports, "The home-plate ump hauled her off a guy she was pounding the cookies out of" (32). But in this burlesque, even the fans get lampooned:

> One man in Section 31 said, "Hey, what's the beef? She can chew if she wants to. This is 1987. Grow up."
> "I guess you're right," his next-seat neighbor said. "My first reaction was nausea, but I think you're right."
> "Absolutely. She's woman, but more than that, she's a *person.*" (32)

With its ridicule of 1970s-style feminist rhetoric, here defused by being attributed to men, this passage shows Keillor at his best. The story presents the nearly perfect mimicry of conventional speech, the gentle debunking of a political agenda, and a satire elevated by literary aspirations.

With its focus on appropriate women's behavior, the story revives in contemporary terms the obsession of earlier *New Yorker* humorists with the war between the sexes. The theme was a staple of Dorothy Parker's poems as well as Thurber's and Perelman's stories and (in the magazine's early years) Clarence Day's *Life with Father* series. But Keillor's characters are different from Thurber's henpecked yet superior little men or from Day's smart yet outwitted father. The male victims in classic *New Yorker* humor always deserve to win. The men and women of "What Did We Do Wrong?" on the other hand, are about equally foolish and, as the guilt-ridden title implies, about equally victimized. In this comic fable from 1985, a tale claiming to predict life in the near future of 1987, men and women both lose.

So, in a modern variation on the old theme, the story of a woman too macho and too hard-hearted to appreciate her fans' love for her ends as a tale of *masculine* heartbreak. Not even love of baseball, much less the pleas of her fans, the advice of the press, or the fines of the commissioners—nothing, in short, can persuade Annie to apologize for making an obscene gesture at an umpire. So it is the men who suffer, as she does not, when Annie leaves baseball rather than apologize. In her perfect integrity, the woman ballplayer enacts their saddest fantasy: "The woman of their dreams, the love of their lives, carrying a red gym bag, running easily away from them" (35).

Keillor could have ended the story by vilifying Annie instead of allowing her some admiration, just as he might have taken some quick shots at co-ed locker rooms, maternity leave, and other tropes of the equal rights debate. But refusing to write strong social satire is crucial to the success of Keillor's humor, just as it was crucial to earlier *New Yorker* humor. *New Yorker* writers typically take on the topical without extracting from it any redeeming social value except the pleasure of watching a virtuoso prose stylist and wit in action. In this sense, despite the many differences between their tall tales, Keillor and Thurber belong to the same *New Yorker* tradition.

Like his predecessors, Keillor turns his back on the little old lady from Dubuque as he exercises a penchant for parody, an obsession with the mass media, and a vision of the little man in a mad, mad world—all amid a mastery of what his hero called *The Elements of Style*. Over the last two dozen years, Keillor's short fiction has lampooned punk rock, the canonized 1960s, life-style weddings, the health food crazes of the 1970s, the pressure to quit smoking, and a vast range of voices from the mass media. As tall tales rather than burlesques, neither "If Robert Frost Had an Apple" nor "What Did We Do Wrong?" typifies the *form* of Keillor's *New Yorker* fiction, but neither do they typify the rhetoric of western and Southwestern tall yarns, which conventionally involve a humor of character or situation rather than parody. The humor of Keillor's tales is a verbal wit, and reaps enormous comic capital from his skill as a literary mimic. He nearly always finds exactly the right word, phrase, and cadence for his distinctive blend of old-fashioned voices and contemporary concerns.

Indeed, Keillor's ability to mimic so many different voices obscures how thoroughly his vernacular tales, though standing in the most durable narrative tradition of American humor, reflect a modern sensibility. In short, he likes humor that keeps to the edge. The narrative convolutions of "Slim Graves," the tonal modulations of "Don: The True Story of a Young Person," and the satiric targets of "What Did We Do Wrong?"—all Keillor's best fiction uses sophisticated narrative techniques to undermine apparently simple, familiar voices. Subversion of the sentimental so pervades his humor that on this point, at least, the attitudes of the short fiction and *A Prairie Home Companion* converge. The teasing ambiguity of calling Lake Wobegon "the little town that time forgot and the decades cannot improve" is of a piece with the strategy of his self-deflating comic fiction. As in "Slim Graves," "Don," and other sketches, the irony suggests that Keillor numbers among the targets of his humor those readers and listeners too naïve to identify his tales as burlesques. Though it has roots in the comic hoax and the tall tale, such combative storytelling has become a hallmark of contemporary writing.

Certainly it is fitting, considering Keillor's fondness for the techniques of nineteenth-century humor, that his reputation has spread like Mark Twain's—first by short fiction in the weekly press, then by public performances, and only later by full-length fiction. Like the short stories of many other writers, Keillor's have stood in the shadow of the more predictable (and therefore more easily promoted) *Lake Wobegon Days* and *A Prairie Home Companion*, from which the tales differ so markedly that the radio audience has treated them as extracurricular.[28] The author of an otherwise perceptive article titled "The Short and Tall Tales of Garrison Keillor," for instance, barely mentioned the *New Yorker* fiction.[29] One loyal listener, who praised the monologues as "the gospel of the air waves," found the stories collected in *Happy to Be Here* entirely unfamiliar: "[These] are not Lake Wobegon stories,—fans of the radio show should be forewarned."[30] But in fact, the volume contains several yarns of undeniable kinship with the Lake Wobegon monologues, midwestern local-color tales that belong to the Matter of Minnesota. With his error, the critic unwittingly proves E. B. White's point that a humorist needs a trademark image—some marketable "handle"—to succeed with the public.[31] Huckleberry Finn was such a trademark; so are Lake Wobegon and, as its official chronicler, the Prairie Home Companion, whose real name was never announced on the show. The short stories cannot benefit from the trademark, however, without losing the uniqueness that they were written to express.

Indeed, differences between the Lake Wobegon monologues and the short fiction emphasize how the humorist at his best matches narrative voice to the medium and subject at hand. The short stories in print demonstrate that Garrison Keillor is no old-fashioned humorist, no matter how authentic his small-town folk or how genuine his nostalgia for the good old days of youth. He is, rather, a virtuoso modern stylist who has learned the lessons of America's comic masters and may yet outdo them all.

CHAPTER 6

**If I Forget Thee,
O Lake Wobegon**
Exiles and Defectors
in *Leaving Home*

*This job is like being
married to Arlen . . .
thirteen years later, she's
right where she started
from.*
—*Keillor, "Darlene
Makes a Move" (1987)*

With *Leaving Home*, fans of *A Prairie
Home Companion* finally got the book
they had longed for, a series of Lake Wobegon stories. *Leaving Home* contains
thirty-six pieces, including about two-
thirds of all Keillor's monologues from
February 1986 to March 1987, when
work on the book began. (The show ran

forty live broadcasts a year, and the book has twenty-eight tales from
these thirteen months.) Keillor introduces the pieces as "written for
performance," implying that he did not revise them for print, but
in fact all differ in some degree from the radio versions.[1] These texts
were produced not from transcripts of the oral tales but from the
written texts—not exactly scripts—that Keillor produced before-
hand. Instead of memorizing or reading these texts on the air, he
used them as proofs and prompts. In these drafts, he worked out
the overall structure, key phrasings, incidents, and digressions. Written on a word processor (after 1983) and then printed, the pre-performance texts usually have a few handwritten emendations on them,
but electronic texts do not, of course, leave an extensive trail of
revisions. Although all the stories were revised for publication in
Leaving Home, most underwent fairly modest alterations: a paragraph dropped here, some changes in wording there, and the conver-

sion of three hyphens (the favored punctuation mark in the monologue texts) to conventional commas, dashes, and periods.[2] Just a
few stories combine material from two or more monologues (see
Appendix); only "The Royal Family," broadcast on 13 November
1982, dates from before 1984. As a result of its genesis, *Leaving
Home* has something of the coherence of Sherwood Anderson's
Winesburg, Ohio (1919) or James Joyce's *Dubliners* (1914), while the
tales retain much of their oral quality.

Although *Leaving Home* surely offered consolation to aficionados
of *A Prairie Home Companion* saddened by the farewell broadcast
on 13 June 1987, three months before the book appeared, it also
sends numerous signals, beginning with its title, that change has
finally caught up with "the little town that time forgot." Every
sketch opens with the monologues' comforting trope—the reassur-
ance that "it has been a quiet week in Lake Wobegon," as always—
but Keillor no longer claims it as "my hometown," nor does he close
each anticlimactic tale with the tag that summed up the essence
of the good life: "That's the news from Lake Wobegon, where all
the women are strong, all the men are good looking, and all the
children are above average." The absence of these familiar formulas
hints, indeed, that *Leaving Home* constitutes Keillor's farewell not
only to his listeners but to his myth, as well.

Literal expressions of farewell frame the volume. They dominate
the introductory "Letter from Copenhagen," which characterizes
the Companion's removal to Denmark as a reverse migration from
America back to Scandinavia as well as an escape from sundry post-
industrial threats to the rural landscape he loves. In this introduction, Keillor speaks defensively in his own voice of his reasons for
leaving St. Paul, although in the last story, "Goodbye to the Lake,"
he speaks lyrically as the Witness on his way to becoming the Exile.
Reminding us that Lake Wobegon belongs to the landscape of his
mind, he looks at the lake in the rain and insists, "through that
mist I can sail to anywhere" (244). A more symbolic farewell
emerges, however, from the stories themselves. In contrast to the
explicit comments of the narrative voices, the tales chronicle the
exodus of rural Minnesotans even more loyal than Keillor, who (after
all) left Anoka years earlier for the brighter lights of St. Paul. The
main point of *Leaving Home*, as well as its thematic unity, comes
from these fictional departures, which claim representatives of
nearly every generation and family in Lake Wobegon. Some escapees,

such as Corinne Ingqvist, are temporary exiles who return like pilgrims at Christmas or to borrow money, but others can only be considered defectors. Leading the latter category is Father Emil, whose retirement from Our Lady of Perpetual Responsibility sums up in an ironic image one undeniable fact: the good old days of Lake Wobegon are gone.

Signs of the changing times begin in the opening sketch, "Trip to Grand Rapids," when Roger Hedlund suddenly agrees to take his wife away for the weekend. To leave before planting his corn is plenty odd for a farmer; to leave after discovering his teenage daughters' party (which Roger and his wife detect on their way to the highway) is unthinkable for a father. But back in the car after spying briefly on the young people, Roger reveals that his life has reached a turning point: having been a parent long enough, he now retires from the job. Other Wobegonians have also reached their limits, and in every case leaving home means escape. Darlene wants to retire from the Chatterbox Cafe and divorce her husband. In one episode, "Truckstop," Florian Krebsbach, hard pressed to articulate an answer when his wife Myrtle demands to know just how much he loves her, absentmindedly leaves her at a truckstop; in another, "High Rise," Myrtle advocates mosquito-free life in a St. Cloud apartment building for senior citizens. Dale Uecker is joining the Navy, even though he can't swim. Nor is the exodus a recent phenomenon. Val Tollefson's father, David, left Lake Wobegon in 1946, when he and Agnes Hedder abandoned their mates and children and ran away together. The list goes on and on, including Grace Tollefson, who has left the town twice. The first time, in 1938, she ran away with Alex Campbell (he deserted her in 1948, and she returned home in shame). The second time occurred just a few years ago, when she found Lake Wobegon an unsuitable place to await the Campbell family's restoration to the throne of Scotland. This move was prompted by letters sent anonymously to her and her children by the long-lost Alex before his indictment for mail fraud.

Not surprisingly, a few tales allude to their creator's own departure. Although the book is not for the most part autobiographical, or even mock autobiographical in the manner of *Lake Wobegon Days*, *Leaving Home* does make a variety of connections, some more explicit than others, between Keillor's decision to leave and his characters'. The few direct allusions reveal just how painful the host of *A Prairie Home Companion* found that decision to be, and they demonstrate that the sense of frustration and loss expressed in "A Letter from Copenhagen" is neither hyperbole nor churlishness. "Darlene Makes a Move," based on the monologue from 6 December 1986, nearly two months before he announced his retirement, contains hints that the show had become like a disappointing marriage. Darlene's thoughts about leaving the Chatterbox Cafe, getting a divorce from Arlen, and starting a new life for herself suggest Keillor's own relationship to *A Prairie Home Companion* and MPR:

> She's been married to him for thirteen years, as long as she's had this job. This job is like being married to Arlen: you wait for something that isn't going to come. It's taken her too long to find this out. Fifteen years ago she got up the courage to go to Minneapolis and try to find something for herself, and what did she find? Arlen. . . . and now, thirteen years later, she's right where she started from. (168)

Although the comparison with the burdensome Arlen probably exaggerates Keillor's relief at leaving the show, the dates match Darlene's closely enough to convey at the very least the finality he felt: he had left Collegeville for St. Paul in 1971, fifteen years earlier; his Saturday-night show, begun in 1974, had reached its thirteenth season. The word choices are also telling: Darlene intends to "wind up her *business* with him and start something with somebody else" (171, my italics). The time had clearly come to move on.

A less veiled message figures in "Post Office," which originally aired three weeks earlier, 15 November 1986. The story takes up the problems of maintaining one's privacy in a small town. In the yarn, an early, unexpectedly severe cold snap causes Bud's car radiator to crack, a great embarrassment to the mechanic, who fears that everyone will figure out that he hadn't put in his antifreeze in time, and the rest of the tale shows that Bud has good reason to worry. A broken furnace leaves the Lake Wobegon post office too cold for the postmaster to sort the mail, so he has dumped it on a table and left people—including our storyteller—to fend for themselves. An intriguing letter from a Houston attorney to Mr. Berge inspires wild fantasies in our narrator, who wonders whether perhaps the old man had killed someone while in Texas for basic training in 1942, and whether they should open the letter to find out—in the interest of protecting the community from a murderer, of course. But the idea makes the storyteller question the sanctity of his own mail and wonder whether perhaps last year the postmaster had read his love letters to his fiancée. Such an act would be more than an invasion of privacy; it would be "stealing my life": "Each person knows how much privacy you need, and you can't accept less, not even in a small town. . . . When people watch us too closely, it turns us into an actor and kills us, because, frankly, most of us aren't good at acting. I forgave Mr. Berge for the murder he committed. Maybe it was someone who read his mail and he stabbed them with a letter opener" (206). The sketch ends on this gloomy note—almost exactly three months before the host of *A Prairie Home Companion* announced publicly that he wanted to return to the life of a private person. Twin Cities fans scoffed at him when he insisted, "If you're going to be a celebrity in the town, in your hometown, then that's unbearable, it's unbearable. . . . It's self-consciousness that really kills you as a writer."[3] But the details in "Post Office" express how strongly he felt that celebrity had violated his personal life, both as a citizen and as a writer—even as he described Mr. Berge's mail with a storyteller's pleasure in voyeurism.

Speaking in his own public voice, he treated the matter with some candor in the introductory "Letter from Copenhagen" as well as in discussions with the press in the months prior to the Farewell Performance. Consistently he pointed to a single incident: his discovery, on returning to St. Paul with his new wife Ulla Strange Skaerved after their wedding and honeymoon in Denmark, that the *St. Paul Pioneer Press Dispatch* of 27 December 1985 featured the address, selling price, and taxes of their new home on the front page. Though the event occurred more than a year before Keillor announced his resignation, it apparently continued to rankle, and he cited it whenever he was asked about his decision to leave radio.[4] Almost proving Keillor's point that the local press made him front-page news at every opportunity, his complaints to out-of-town newspapers became the subject of several feature articles and an editorial in both the *St. Paul Pioneer Press Dispatch* and the *Minneapolis Star and Tribune*.[5]

But the story at the center of the book, "David and Agnes, a Romance," suggests that the idea of leaving home may have crossed his mind as early as 17 August 1985, when his monologue hinted at his still-secret courtship with Ulla Skaerved. The tale depicts Val Tollefson's discovery of why his father had run off with Agnes Hedder forty years earlier: the couple had discovered a love so passionate that abandoning their mates and children and committing bigamy seemed their only chance at happiness, and in the imaginary town of Mount Canaan, Washington (the promised land far, far from down-to-earth Minnesota), they did fulfill their dream of a new life together. The autobiographical significance of this monologue doubtless slipped by people unaware of Keillor's courtship with Ulla, whom he first knew as a Danish exchange student at Anoka High School twenty-five years before. Certainly it antedates by nearly three months public awareness of his estrangement from Margaret Moos, the first producer of the live Saturday night version of *A Prairie Home Companion*, who had lived with Keillor for many years. The first edition of *Lake Wobegon Days*, then just appearing, carried a dedication "To Margaret, my love." In this context, "David and Agnes" hints at the complexity of Keillor's personal life as well as the danger of reading too much biography into fiction.

Not a veiled defense, the story explores different points of view and the difficulty of rendering moral and literary judgments. David realizes his dissatisfaction with his present life only after falling hopelessly in love with Agnes. The story's interest lies in its examination of basically ordinary, considerate, responsible people suddenly driven to extraordinary acts of immorality and irresponsibility (judged by conventional norms) in order to claim their happiness. Going through his father's belongings, including the love letters that chronicle David's decision to run away, allows Val to glimpse the complexity of love, though he cannot forgive his dad for abandoning him. The multiple points of view in "David and Agnes"—David's, Val's and the narrator's—make clear that the act of leaving home, always fraught with misgivings, usually connotes progressing in one's life, not just moving away. For its expression of this crucial theme, even more than for its autobiographical hints, "David and Agnes" deserves its position at the very center of *Leaving Home*. Perhaps more important, however, in the context of relations between literature and life, is the story's emphasis on writing. David's love messages to Agnes inspire her to run off with him; to his son Val they appear as unpleasant evidence that he has forever lost his chance to enjoy his father's love; but to Val's wife, Florence, and to the town librarian, they are literature. At the end of the story, "Poem, Unknown" (123) is all that remains of David's love for Agnes, but Keillor hints that it is all that counts.

Other tales point to more generalized dissatisfactions. "I'm not that old," the storyteller protests in "Lyle's Roof," suggesting that

Leaving Home also bids farewell to his own youth, "but I know a lot because I used to hang out with old people back when there used to be real old people. Now everyone is sort of my age or younger, and most people don't know much more than I do" (99). Autobiography does not have to account for the details in "Christmas Dinner," in which the forty-two-year-old Daryl—the same age as Keillor at the time of the original monologue—learns from Dr. DeHaven that his reflexes have begun to weaken with age (though the story may have some basis in fact), but the identity between author and character suggests at the very least that the writer saw his youth fading. In any event, he places himself squarely in the ranks of the older generation in "Goodbye to the Lake," the monologue delivered on the farewell broadcast. The sketch closes the volume with a misty recollection of halcyon days in Lake Wobegon "when I was little" (244), a time so long past that he can put his own contempt for the artificiality of modern life in the mouth of a town elder, Norwegian bachelor farmer Byron Tollefson. "It's getting to be like everything else," Tollefson grumbles. "You got decaffeinated coffee, soda pop with no sugar, pretty soon we'll have chemical sweet corn. Taste fresh year-round, and it'll be flat and round like a cracker. . . . You wait and see. It's coming" (243). According to Keillor's introductory "Letter from Copenhagen," however, the dreaded future has already come. Conceding that he might never have left home if he had eaten more sweet corn, the self-exiled Minnesotan prophesies that Americans will soon regret "all the good things we surrendered in favor of deadly trash" now that ballparks have roofs and shopping malls have "killed off . . . the cornfields" (xv–xvi). Whether or not Keillor complains for joy, as he claims Tollefson does, he makes clear the time has come to move on—metaphorically and literally.

The end of the monologue puts the inhabitants of Lake Wobegon in a tableau, an artfully arranged scene that stands at great aesthetic distance from the 1971 image of Jack's Auto Repair and wooded lots alongside an overgrown puddle. And its creator drops hints about other landscapes of the mind. His journey across the sea, he implies in the lyrical reverie of his conclusion, may lead to new discoveries, perhaps even revealing "what is down there around the big bend where the cottonwood trees on shore are slowly falling, bowing to the river, the drops glistening on the dark green leaves" (224). Regardless of why he is leaving home or whether he will learn Lake Wobegon's secrets, this closing passage reminds us that the journey itself, like *Leaving Home*, is partly about fiction. The landscape of Lake Wobegon is a landscape of the imagination, crafted in words as a work of art.

For all this evidence of conclusion and change, *Leaving Home* still offers fans of *A Prairie Home Companion* plenty of dependable satisfactions. The monologues' tropes had become so familiar by the time *Leaving Home* appeared that the reviewer for *Time* wrote a mock monologue in epistolary form, complete with comments about lunch at the Chatterbox Cafe, "where we stopped in for the usual (mushroom soup and a cheese sandwich)."[6] Appropriately enough for fantasies of regression into the old hometown, oral satisfactions top the list. These are not just oral tales, but oral tales of oral gratification. Keillor links storytelling with food when he describes his childhood desire for a voice like Orson Welles's, "as rich and smooth as my mother's gravy on Sunday pot roast" (xvi). As this homely description suggests, food contributes more than homespun flavor to his local-color stories.

The tales overflow with comestibles: fresh caramel rolls at breakfast, mushroom soup and grilled cheese sandwiches at lunch, pot roast with mashed potatoes at Sunday dinner, and always, *always* fresh sweet corn with butter. "That was so wonderful," Keillor imagines an immigrant Norwegian murmuring in bed after sex one night, "But it wasn't as good as fresh sweet corn" (xiv–xv). So many of the sketches extol the virtues of fresh sweet corn that one suspects Keillor of poking fun at his own corny humor, but for the most part he plays the game, if not exactly straight, at least as a straight man. His humor asserts that we are what we eat while comically contrasting the emphatically ordinary folks of Lake Wobegon with the sophisticates of the world beyond. In "Corinne," Keillor recites the whole menu of the lunch at which Hjalmar Ingqvist lends his daughter the money for her dream house: "Meat loaf, whipped potatoes, string beans, bread, and tapioca pudding—a lunch you can seal a bargain on and know it'll stay sealed" (25). The joke involves recognizing that the weight of the foods alone prevents escape—of the bargain or any party to it—but at the same time the words mean exactly what they say. No city banker could give Corinne a better deal, our storyteller warns, whatever they might have had for lunch, for strange foods present dangerous temptations. Morel mushrooms symbolize Marlys Diener's social aspirations in "How the Crab Apple Grew"; sausage pizza signifies decadence and delinquency in

"Where Did It Go Wrong?" In Lake Wobegon, wholesome food and the wholesome life go hand in hand. The Chatterbox Cafe doesn't serve madeleines.

Descriptions of food link the participants in Keillor's séance. Storyteller and audience first share memories; then they share secrets. United with his audience in a comic conspiracy against Lake Wobegon's most intimate embarrassments, Keillor knows—and tells—who hasn't changed his underwear, whose pants are torn in the crotch, who has sneaked where for what purpose. He even offers a few tidbits purportedly from his own past. "They . . . call me by a nickname that I left home in order to lose," our narrator confides. "Wild horses couldn't drag it out of me now. But I'll tell you: it was Foxfart" (148). Lake Wobegon's most cherished, most embarrassing secrets similarly tend toward the painful and scatological. Essentially instances of slapstick, banana-peel humor, these secrets boil down to how dignified people act ridiculous or smell terrible sometimes—as when the twenty-four Lutheran ministers aboard Wally's twenty-six-foot boat find that the power of faith cannot overcome the force of gravity, when flu sufferers Harold and Marlys Diener find that sharing fever, headaches, diarrhea, and vomit has added "a dimension to their marriage," or when Daryl Tollerud's gratitude to parents and God climaxes with baptism by skunk. The pleasures of the good old days—for Keillor and his audience—include lots of juvenile jokes.

That explains why some of the finest moments in *Leaving Home* involve its worst smells. Comic euphemism becomes eloquence in "Homecoming," in which poor Carl Krebsbach dutifully digs up his parents' backyard and hauls away the old Chevrolet that had served too long as a septic tank, finally becoming so overloaded that the lawn had begun to sink. Dragging "thirty years of family history" behind him, he heads straight for his destiny—the homecoming parade led by his daughter Carla coming toward him on the road:

[He] wasn't getting much oxygen to his brain, only the fumes of his heritage. . . .

. . . He and the National Guard put on the brakes and met nose to nose directly in front of the Chatterbox Cafe. The band had melted away to the side. About half the crowd began to move off toward a more distant vantage point, and the other half followed them. A strong aroma of Chev got in the ventilator of the Cafe, and the patrons silently put down their forks and emerged from the rear. Queen Carla sat in front of the tank, her eyes almost level with her father's where he sat, in front of the old family heirloom. (150–51)

Keillor relies on a favorite comic tactic when he has Carl shrug off the embarrassment of driving "the Krebsbach float" by insisting, "Who needs dignity when you can be in show business?" (151). "Homecoming" downplays moral issues and sophisticated topics while putting eloquence in the service of farce.

Of course the writer does claim redeeming moral value for his stories, although his pose of the Philosopher/Preacher first entered the monologues through the satiric context of the Powdermilk Biscuit commercials. In *Leaving Home* the comments of the Philosopher usually surface near the end of a tale, where they offer a frame for distancing and evaluating slapstick details. "Nothing you do for children is ever wasted," he notes at the end of "Easter," establishing a transition between his report of the Buehler grandchildren's antics last week and his recollection of a fishing trip with Uncle Al more than thirty years before; that trip has become "a permanent work of art in my head" (20). Similarly, he pretends to apologize for the rather limited ethical dimensions of his stories in "Pontoon Boat," where he twits his audience about the truth of his tall tales. "People are so skeptical," he complains; "they force a storyteller to spend too much time on the details and not enough on the moral" (105). But then he doesn't offer any moral to the tale of how "eight Lutheran ministers in full informal garb took their step for total immersion" (108), unless you count the implications of overloading a boat or inviting twenty-four business associates for dinner without first checking with your spouse. Keillor says that stories must have an ethical dimension to be worth the aesthetic attention of either the writer or an audience,[7] but he does not put business before pleasure. Neither parables nor object lessons, the Lake Wobegon tales use religious homilies as one more ingredient, along with gossip and apple pie, of local-color humor. References to old-time religion not only sustain the dream of childhood (when everyone still believed in God and justice) but also elevate gossip to the level of moral exemplum, all the while providing sentimental targets for comic attack.

A few tales in *Leaving Home* succeed brilliantly in balancing all these strategies. In "Life Is Good," for example, Daryl Tollerud's run-in with the skunk follows an epiphany in which he comes to terms with his place not only in his family but also in the cosmos. The man who had felt unloved by his own father now says, "Thank you, Lord," and thinks grateful thoughts about his six children; he thereby raises the tale to a point of high sentimentality, ripe for debunking. In a stroke of comic genius that we might call *deus ex skunk*, Keillor rewards Daryl for his faith. He will get his wish and inherit his parents' house—if only while they vacation in Seattle—so that our narrator can justifiably conclude, "Life is good, friends. It's even better if you stay away from Daryl, but basically life is good" (91).

"Life Is Good" has the hallmarks of Keillor's best work: a meticulously controlled narrative voice, a sympathetic but slightly ridiculous protagonist, a concern with questions of identity, a blend of high ethics and low farce. Keillor holds on tightly to every nuance of the tale as its plot swerves from the universal to the particular, from Daryl's initial fantasy that "he was adopted. That's why his dad wouldn't make out the will" (88) to his final recognition that their kinship ran deeper than he had ever realized: "If his paper plate fell apart, he'd try to save it, even if his hand was burning. Same as his dad" (90). Daryl's naïveté sustains his sense of injury even as it invites our amused superiority. If a married man with six kids seems too old to worry about his own paternity, he can reasonably resent being treated like a child, and in any event Keillor filters Daryl's thoughts through a detached, mildly ironic narrator. Such narration makes possible both poetic and comic justice at the end, when Daryl takes over his parents' stinking house. The detached observer—a variation on the Witness—represents Keillor's main strategy for keeping to the edge between sincerity and ridicule, with one foot in each camp. At his best, as "Life Is Good" makes clear, Keillor is a narrative acrobat, making the risky seem easy.

Unfortunately, not many tales in *Leaving Home* display the agility of "Life Is Good." Others indulge the sentimental impulse that prompted one reviewer to warn, "Parts of *Leaving Home* will only be suitable for people who like their sweet corn well buttered."[8] Sometimes Keillor strains for a concluding image of heart-warming affection, as in "Brethren," when family harmony is restored by the very aroma of Aunt Flo's fried chicken. On a few occasions, nostalgia yields to reverie unmediated by critical self-consciousness, as in this example from "State Fair":

> The [ferris] wheel carries us up high, high, high, and stops, and we sit swaying, creaking, in the dark, on the verge of death. You can see death from here. The wind blows from the northwest, from the farm school in Saint Anthony Park a chilly wind with traces of pigs and sheep in it. This is my vision: little kids holding on to their daddy's hand, and he is me. He looks down on them with love and buys them another corn dog. They are worried they will lose him, they hang on to his leg with one hand, eat with the other. This vision is unbearably wonderful. Then the wheel brings me down to the ground. We get off and other people get on. Thank you, dear God, for this good life and forgive us if we do not love it enough. (114–15)

At the opposite extreme, the absence of sentimentality injures "The Royal Family." The print version lacks the sympathy of the narrator's spoken voice, which (as the *Fall* recording shows) transformed ironic distance into genial ridicule:

> The Philadelphia man . . . sent them a [genealogical] chart that unfolded bigger than their kitchen table. . . . the lines led right straight to them: Earl, Marlys, and Walter. The Royal Family of Scotland living in Lake Wobegon in a green mobile home, furniture donated by the Lutheran church.
>
> They were astounded beyond words. . . . then it took hold—this was grace, pure grace that God offered them. Not their will but His. Grace. Here they were in their same dismal place but everything had changed. They were different people. . . . —and there were times in the months that followed when Walter wished he could tell somebody that he was a prince of Scotland, particularly his cousin Donna who lived in the house the Campbells lived behind and who made complex rules about who could play in her yard. (141)

Balancing the banality of the characters' life with their awe at the possibility of deliverance and their desires for petty revenge, the passage shows Keillor's careful hand at work. And taken together, the examples from "State Fair" and "The Royal Family" demonstrate that even in their disappointing moments, the sketches in *Leaving Home* are hardly contemptible, nor do they lack for quotable lines. Still, the collection as a whole cries out for the nuances of Keillor's spoken voice, whose ingenuous sincerity conceals contempt as easily as it justifies the sweetest of sentiments. Incantatory in sound and spirit, Keillor's voice was a major component of his Lake Wobegon monologues, whether or not his tones passed the test of his mother's gravy, and its absence here is a loss.

Oral humor from the radio can become mock-oral humor in print, but successful translation from one medium to the other calls for more than mere transcription. The success of *Lake Wobegon Days* stems in large measure from the literary elements superimposed on the oral material of the monologues. The mock history of Lake Wobegon has an extended first-person narrative and essentially continuous chronology as well as literary burlesque, revisionist history, and typographical jokes; the narrative stumbles when the literary structures lose dominance. *Leaving Home*, by contrast, makes few concessions to print. Instead of the visual jokes that recur throughout *Lake Wobegon Days*, for instance, the stories of *Leaving Home* offer sound effects. "*Ohhhhhhh*" (2), moans Roger Hedlund when he bumps into the outside water faucet in the dark. "*Mmmmm-hmmmm*" (24), says Hjalmar Ingqvist, considering whether his daughter Corinne, who has applied for a mortgage from the First Ingqvist State Bank, earns enough to carry the loan. "*Whack*" (47) goes the ax when Keillor's father slaughters the chickens. These have a visual dimension, to be sure—in their italics or spelling—but their main emphasis is aural. They ask us to hear, if not actually to pronounce, the represented sounds. Consequently, although Keillor alludes to the layout of the typewriter keyboard in characterizing Marlys Diener's response to flu—as visual a joke as one could ask for—the focus remains on the sound of a modern-day woman transformed by flu into a member of an "ancient tribe of hairy lowbrowed people who hunker around a cold fire and chew on rancid elk and moan to each other in a dry white tongue: *huhnnn, hwihhhhh-qwertyuiop*" (197).

Sound effects confirm Keillor's announcement in the introduction that "the stories in this book . . . were written for my voice, which is flat and slow. There are long pauses in them and sentences that trail off into the raspberry bushes" (xvi). Although the texts do not merely put the radio monologues into print—all were revised somewhat—the comment suggests Keillor's awareness that these tales belong to an oral tradition not easily translated into another medium.

Other vestiges of oral narration appear in the storyteller's self-conscious commentary, when Keillor playfully speaks directly to the audience. The commentary in *Leaving Home* reveals very little of the teller, in contrast to the first-person narration in a traditional mock-oral tale such as "Attitude" or "The Slim Graves Show," for example, which characterizes the narrator by his talk. "There's a story about Lyle's house, as there is about most houses in town" (99), he says, beginning a digression in "Lyle's Roof" with a conventional introduction. Yet his comic tone indicates that the remark has less to do with self-revelation than with twitting his audience about his tall tale. For all the humility implicit in his complaint about the shortage of "real old people" to teach him more stories, he still knows enough to get directly back to the story at hand: "I do know that Lyle's house was built in 1889 by a carpenter named Swanson who . . ." (99).

This example suggests that Keillor's commentary has more in common with the postmodernist's emphasis on the artificiality of narrative than with the dramatic monologuist's unmasking of a speaker—in itself a pretty funny anachronism for a cracker-barrel humorist. But most of the time, the direct remarks signify mainly that the narrator enjoys displaying his craft, allowing us to watch while he pulls the strings of his characters. *Leaving Home* keeps these oral elements intact, as well.

In "Hansel," for instance, the storyteller notes that he has the power to prevent an argument between Joanne and Kenny over the mess in the living room; he can send her on a walk around the block, giving Kenny two minutes to control the chaos. Two months before the display of artificiality in "Hansel," performed 22 November 1986, the yarn spinner took an opposite tack. Near the beginning of "The Killer" (based on the monologue of 20 September 1986), Keillor twits his audience about the veracity of his tales:

> Some storytellers would take one look at a little town on a cold wet fall day and tell you about a family on a vacation trip through the Midwest who wonder why this town seems so deserted and get out of their car and there on Maple Street, coming at them with a pitchfork, is a gigantic man with no eyes and chunks of his face falling off and big clods of brown dirt stuck to his bib overalls, but I am a storyteller who, for better or worse, is bound by facts, so I simply observe that nobody was out walking because it was raining, a steady discouraging rain (125).

Part of the pleasure of the tall tale involves how transparent the lies appear to the initiated, while they maintain enough realism to sustain the illusion of truth. The examples from "Hansel" and "The Killer" both show the tale-teller's explicit enjoyment in asking his audience to suspend disbelief. Keillor stands comfortably omniscient in his role as the storyteller. Even at their most deliberately artificial, however, as when he asks us to note "how gracefully I tell this story" (149) of Carl Krebsbach and the septic Chevy, his remarks point away from the teller toward the telling and tale. The tactic reveals a certain modesty in the storyteller, all the more noteworthy in contrast to the apparent self-revelation in the monologues.

The tactic works in part because of differences between oral and written first-person tales. Although oral tales seldom exploit the narrative persona as a major dramatic element, every story, oral or written, bears enough of the teller's voice to let audiences interpret his or her character and motives. Keillor's humor shows that he understands the principle perfectly. It explains why, for example, in shaping the Matter of Minnesota, he found it useful to assume aspects of Barbara Ann Bunsen's character into his own persona and adopt Lake Wobegon as his own hometown. By abandoning the conventions of the ironic epistolary narrator implicit in Barbara Ann's letters to her family and speaking instead in his own voice, the Companion could present himself as an insider initiating his friends into the secrets of Lake Wobegon life, not as an outsider sneering at the locals. It also explains why *Lake Wobegon Days* uses both first- and third-person narration. Whether he attributes the "I" to a Wobegonian ancestor or claims it for mock autobiography, the first-person narratives in *Lake Wobegon Days* all have elements of the dramatic monologue, while the third-person stories do not; in fact, we can understand the novel's difficulties by noting that the doubled third-person narratives make the first-person accounts more revealing than they otherwise would have been. Like the seasonal chapters of *Lake Wobegon Days*, *Leaving Home* mainly focuses on Wobegonians other than the narrator, but the oral quality of the tales helps *Leaving Home* evade the structural problems of *Lake Wobegon Days*.

Written stories can differentiate between first and third person more precisely than oral tales can. A first-person narrator is always a significant choice in fiction, even if the author doesn't fully exploit it (essentially the internal conflict in Keillor's novel), whereas an oral story cannot exist without its speaker. Oral narrators always characterize themselves to some degree or another, by their vocal mannerisms, if nothing else, though they needn't actually figure in their tales. The different narrative conventions of oral storytelling emphasize the telling and the tale, not the teller, and that's where Keillor puts his emphasis in *Leaving Home*.

The mixing of genres and conventions yields mixed results. *Leaving Home*, bridging the gap between radio and print, listeners and readers, ends up as neither fish nor fowl. The book's immediate success—813,000 copies in print within the first three months—confirmed that Viking Press seized on a perfect time and ready market in putting *Leaving Home* atop its list for fall 1987. In addition to building on the prior success of *Lake Wobegon Days*, published just two years earlier, the collection capitalized on the publicity attending the farewell broadcast of *A Prairie Home Companion*. Over the summer, window posters in bookstores exhorted fans to reserve their copies of *Leaving Home* before publication. Moreover, by capturing Keillor's radio audience, *Leaving Home* not only had a greater chance at success than most collections of short fiction but also poised itself to outperform *Happy to Be Here*, Keillor's first collection, which sold a respectable number of copies but apparently failed to satisfy listeners. They wanted Lake Wobegon stories. Recordings could feed their appetites even better than print, but these present rather serious problems of marketing and distribution, although the audio cassettes of *Lake Wobegon Days* and *The News from Lake Wobegon* did become best sellers in the category that publishers call spoken books. Considering the number and diversity of book outlets (including the Book-of-the-Month Club and supermarket racks), however, a volume of monologues could reach Keillor's radio fans much more effectively than either audio cassettes (sold primarily through direct mail) or the harder-to-market videotapes. As a result, maintaining the oral qualities of the stories in *Leaving Home* was crucial. In the end, the volume is neither a collection of transcripts nor an anthology of short fiction but a hybrid with troubling internal conflicts.

Although every collection suffers some degree of unevenness, here the texts convey the press of their author's departure, implying a certain fatigue with his formulas if not actual uninterest in the book. By the time he came to compose *Leaving Home*, Keillor had become willing to give up at least some of the illusions of Lake Wobegon's reality and expose its artifice for all to see. Whether he wanted to disenchant admirers who believed too intensely in his myth or to call attention to his aesthetic craftmanship, he indicated when the Disney cablecasts of *A Prairie Home Companion* began that he'd had a surfeit of his listeners' willing suspension of disbelief: "For me, to go from radio to television is to *want* to give up those illusions, and especially the personal illusions that people may have had, and to reveal myself and to reveal this show . . . in the merciless way that television does."[9] After years of invidious comparisons between television and radio, Keillor finally saw some virtue in television's ability to shrink performers below human size.[10]

In this context, the mixture of oral and written narrative forms reflect implicitly what the book's introduction says more directly. When Keillor insists, "These stories are not about my family" (xx), he takes the stories of *Leaving Home* a long way from the revelations about "my hometown" on *A Prairie Home Companion*. The introduction, ostensibly written on his arrival in Copenhagen, hints at his sense of imminent freedom in the date at the beginning, 3 July, the eve of Independence Day. The implication suits the tone and theme of the introduction, especially his dissatisfactions with Minnesota's commercialization of the landscape and its people, himself included. But taken together, all these details raise the possibility that Keillor might have seized on any opportunity to abandon Lake Wobegon without appearing to flout his fans, that he really needed to move beyond the limiting formulas of *A Prairie Home Companion*. Whatever his reasons, the decision to leave the texts as monologues rather than remake them for their new context amounted to a compromise. It satisfied radio listeners at the price of writerly success. The hybrids of *Leaving Home* offer some wonderful renderings of the Matter of Minnesota, but they lack the oral virtuosity of his performances on *A Prairie Home Companion*, on the one hand, and the narrative sophistication of the fiction in *Happy to Be Here* and *Lake Wobegon Days*, on the other.

For the differences between oral and mock-oral performance, we can look at "Aprille," a superb monologue originally composed for the grand reopening of the World Theater on Friday, 25 April 1986, and broadcast live over the American Public Radio network the following night, the regular Saturday broadcast. PBS television carried the live broadcast on the 26 April, and the Disney Channel subsequently carried the performance on cable.[11] The oral performances of "Aprille" rely on three devices for which no literary equivalents exist. How can the printed page express the unselfconscious tone of voice, the appearance of artlessness and spontaneity, or the perfectly timed pause? Not surprisingly, considering how often Keillor has been hailed as a new Mark Twain, these are the very techniques Twain singled out in "How to Tell a Story" (1897), which drew on his own triumphs as a performer and oral storyteller. "Aprille" shows that Keillor has mastered the principles of Twain's lesson quite well, although not well enough to translate his oral tales into print without the old problem expressed as *traduttori traditori*: translators are traitors.

Radio offered an ideal medium for Keillor, who modulates his voice with virtuoso precision while seeming only to chat with friends. To this illusion of artlessness, live broadcasting added both feigned and real spontaneity. Keillor's practice of plotting out his monologues but not scripting or memorizing them gave the tales elements of literary composition while fostering genuine improvisation. Keillor upped the ante in this already risky game of memory and improvisation when he structured "Aprille" around a ten-line passage from *The Canterbury Tales* and a lengthy verse from the New Testament. A printed quotation cannot convey the least degree of artlessness or spontaneity. Nor can it demonstrate Keillor's remarkable memory, which produces these effects in the first place. By contrast, in the oral performance of "Aprille," memory not only sustains Keillor through a long recitation in passable Middle English but also enables him to embellish the prepared story on the spot. Without this display of memory, on the other hand, the story loses other crucial elements: our awe of the storyteller, apparently spinning this yarn just for us as we sit enchanted by his gift; and our delight in language, perhaps the most powerful oral gratification. For this homespun Philosopher/Preacher, the beginning is most definitely the word. Seven pages of reading cannot match the rhetorical impact of Keillor's thirty-minute séance, for the very medium of print inhibits, though of course it does not entirely obscure, the tale's celebration of words—Chaucer's, Keillor's, and the Bible's.

Recitations from Chaucer and the Bible give unity to the oral tale, setting the springtime Minnesota scene for the main story: how Lois Tollerud, a young woman troubled by the existence of evil in the world, fails to find her faith on Confirmation Day, and yet nothing happens as a result. Because the anticlimactic resolution follows three other anecdotes—Keillor's visit to his missing family, Einer Tingvold's loss of his binoculars, and Keillor's childhood game of Strangers with his Aunt Lois—the resolution becomes ambiguous. It not only implies the orthodox conclusions that Lois's faith in God matters less than God's faith in her and that neither God nor faith will abandon her if she does not throw them away or try to become someone she is not, but also insinuates the downright blasphemous notion that faith is irrelevant to a good story. After all, with the story of how Einer threw away the next day's breakfast eggs and his own beloved binoculars just because he was frustrated that an unruly group of Boy Scouts wouldn't learn semaphore signals, Keillor provides a highly comic parable on the consequences of throwing away one's religious values in the heat of a moment's disappointment. At the same time, the binoculars need not symbolize faith or even integrity to provide a reason for telling the tale, since the details of the story offer the considerable pleasures of comic retribution. This sort of playing with didactic and aesthetic narration explains Keillor's appeal to both rural and urban audiences. It also suggests that the yarn spinner sometimes uses religious material as he uses tuna hot dish—as an element of local color.

In the oral performance of "Aprille," in any event, a crucial function of scripture is oral. Several times the storyteller recites parts of Lois's confirmation verse, relishing its sounds, but he gives the full text only once, when describing how Marilyn Tollerud inscribed all thirty-one words—"Be not conformed to this world: but be ye transformed by the renewing of your mind, that you may prove what is that good, and acceptable, and perfect, will of God"—in blue frosting atop Lois's cake. This gentle ridicule of the Tolleruds' celebration quite literally, and not so gently, reduces the Bible to a mouthful of words, of which Keillor's share on his square of cake reads "con but for"—a hint at the humorist's con game. The long recitation of the verse on the cake exploits the advantages of oral performance by demonstrating the teller's prodigious memory, all the more impressive at the end of the narrative when he reasserts his control over all his apparent digressions. With a fine touch of symmetry, he recites a few lines of Chaucer again in the context of Lois's and his own stories.

But no moment of "Aprille" better illustrates Keillor's genius as an oral yarn spinner than the modulations and pauses of an inspired improvisation in the middle of the monologue. Slipping from his role of observing narrator, he adopts Lois's point of view to relate her thoughts on good and evil during a solitary walk in the woods after lunch, while her family eats the cake. He continues to tell the story from Lois's perspective as he describes the girl's frantic efforts to run away from a man standing by the road, whom "she knew . . . was put there by an evil force, . . . and that this was Evil roaming the world, and looking for whomever it may devour" (26 April 1986). Tension increases as she falls, begging him for mercy. "'Please, please,' she said, 'don't do it.'" Keillor's voice drops to a whisper in the tension. Then he pauses, raises the pitch, and in a slightly bewildered tone, adds unexpectedly, "Which surprised me. . . ."[12] In the pause following this wrenching shift of perspective, we realize that our storyteller was the man standing there, that Lois made a mistake; the revelation rescues Lois and the tale comically as it evades the question of evil. Nonetheless, this exquisite moment from the oral performances, a rhetorical tour de force, does not appear in *Leaving Home*. In the printed version of "Aprille," a new paragraph just under Lois's plea begins simply and directly, "I hadn't seen her for five years" (235). Whether or not he had added the remark about his surprise, Keillor might still have revised the written text to startle his readers as he had shocked his listeners—that is, to translate the oral-aural experience into a literary one. But he didn't. Compared to the stunning oral performance, the printed yarn has the impact of *The Canterbury Tales* in modern English verse.

If the spirit of "Aprille" doesn't survive transcription intact, the written text nonetheless offers the primary aesthetic compensation of print: careful construction. Keillor included in both his performances a comment about "a pilgrimage of my own" (25 and 26 April 1986), but doubtless few listeners caught the many structural parallels among the three pilgrims of the tale—not just Lois and Keillor but Chaucer, as well. These parallels give the written tale its strong structure and theme. All three pilgrims undertake spiritual journeys that turn into occasions for storytelling. Chaucer's "Prologue" frames the narrative, which nests first Keillor's and then Lois Tollerud's stories within. And as in *The Canterbury Tales*, the Lake Wobegon pilgrims' stories eventually become more important than the religious goals inspiring them.

Not that this tale lacks humor. The narrator's own pilgrimage fails when he arrives at the family house to find nobody at home; the journey then gets transformed into a quest for a toilet (so much for the Lutheran ritual of Sunday morning coffee). But the themes emerging from the structural parallels subsume the humor of the written story; in addition, the narrative becomes much more serious in print because print invites serious reflection. Oral stories are unidirectional, unlike fiction, which allows a reader to flip back and forth among the pages. And whereas the intent listener concentrates on the last joke only at risk of missing the next gem, a reader has the leisure to explore implications between the lines. In the context of three subverted pilgrimages, the dominant context of the written tale, whether God loves Lois seems not so much paradoxical (the implication of the oral story) as irrelevant. Ultimately, the "Aprille" of *Leaving Home* characterizes religion as the narrative means to a narrative end—a subject for tales and excuse for storytelling—and this image robs the conclusion of the written story of the ambiguity that enriches the oral yarn. Perhaps the goal of the oral tale was to encourage religious faith, perhaps not: the end at once promotes and suspects piety. But in the written tale, which acquires a different emphasis, religion itself has a goal, and that goal undoubtedly is storytelling.

Perhaps the focus grew out of the writer's long and intense work on "Aprille." Certainly the five extant versions—two preperformance texts (both produced on a word processor and edited by hand), two recorded performances, and the printed version in *Leaving Home*—testify to how hard Keillor labored over this apparently spontaneous yarn even on the days of the performances. The first text (25 April 1986) contains all three of the main stories, Lois's lost faith, Einer Tingvold's lost binoculars, and young Gary's fear of being treated as a stranger, along with a fourth anecdote about the Tolleruds' agnostic Uncle Gunnar, which remained in all three written versions but was never included in an oral rendition, perhaps for reasons of time, since the performances both ran a full half-hour. But several crucial details in Lois's story changed after the first performance, and the ending of the narrative continued to evolve through the second performance, which represents the fourth version. In addition to illustrating the balance between planned and spontaneous elements in the monologues (the oral performances, like jazz improvisations, have much more detail than the written texts), the variations among the versions also reveal how the process of narration itself contributed to the development of the yarn.

The first major change involved eliminating the three suspected miracles that had inspired Lois to keep an open mind about her lost faith: the hot water had not run out as usual on Saturday night, her mother had managed to get a stain out of Lois's confirmation dress, and her father's arm had not burned from the candles on her cake. These events struck her as possible evidence that God did in fact exist. Removing them from the tale diverted it from questions of God's existence to questions of human faith. The shift allowed Keillor to emphasize the parallels between Lois and himself: she becomes terrified when her prayers echo without response, just as he had become frightened as a boy when his Aunt Lois pretended during a game of Strangers that she did not know him. The possibility of miracles, however banal, had allowed the original story to end with some optimism for Lois and for the faithful generally, so the deletion of the miracles required changes in the end. In the first performance of "Aprille" on 25 April 1986, Keillor expanded the simple conclusion of his written text—"For the fourteen year olds of this world, I'm glad to get old so they can grow up and we'll see what they do with themselves"—into a comment on how the world as a whole benefits from the courage of the young, "who having lost their faith could stand on the edge of darkness and wait for it to return."

As deleting the miracles deprived Lois's story of its optimism, so moving the Einer Tingvold anecdote altered its theme, from an example of faith sure-to-be-found to a warning about faith abandoned. In its new position after the story of playing Strangers on the bus, rather than before, the tale of how Tingvold threw away his binoculars appears more clearly as a parable of the dangers facing Lois. Keillor deflates the warning somewhat, beginning with the second text, by having her charge, "That's not true, is it?" and then conceding, "No it's not."[13] Calling attention to the falseness of this anecdote emphasizes its symbolic purpose.

Having underlined the connection between Lois's story and Einer's, the storyteller also intensifies the relations among his own, Lois's, and Chaucer's tales. After holding out the disturbing possibility that the young girl might throw her faith (and herself) away, Keillor equates the reliability of spring with the reliability of God, but it takes him several tries to work out the narrative expression that he wants. In the second typescript and the printed text in *Leaving Home*, he proposes that loss of faith has less to do with the existence of God than with forgetting who one is. Regardless of one's faith, the signs of spring remain today as they did in Chaucer's time: "the sweet breath, the tendre croppes, and the smale fowles maken melodye—God watches each one and knows when it falls, and so much more does He watch us all" (238). The insistence on faith in spite of doubt is traditionally Christian, of course, and a proper conclusion to reach in print, a durable medium that may have inclined the storyteller to greater conservatism than in his radio tale, but for whatever reason, the second performance resolves the question less doctrinally and, consequently, more in keeping with the ambivalence of Lois's experience and the secular, aesthetic structure of his tale. Apparently on an inspiration during the final performance of the story, Keillor loosens the connection between spring and reborn faith. Instead, he proposes a more generalized power in "this world, and each other, and the people in it": "Well, I'm transformed by this world, the one that I look at. It's so beautiful. I believe that it has the power to make us brave, and to make us good. . . . It has the power to give us faith, the sweet breath of the wind and the tender crops, and the smale fowles maken melodye, that slepen all the nycht with open eye." The rhymed, iambic pentameter ending of this final performance lacks the Christian humility of the version in *Leaving Home*, but it offers instead a powerful aesthetic vision of people, faith, and nature transformed by the literary imagination. The printed version of "Aprille" suffers by contrast.

The power of the monologues derived from a number of elements in their performance. Keillor's voice—intense, sincere, companionable—was a major factor, much enhanced by the intimacy of radio as a medium and Keillor's understanding of how to exploit it. In place of the Announcer (or one of the comic inversions of this pose, the Shy Person or Amateur), the monologues portrayed one colloquial, confessional voice speaking directly to the individual radio listener—one companion chatting to another.[14] The obviously live, unscripted performance added to the illusion of spontaneous conversation, as did the choice of "panned mono" technique for the stereo broadcasts, since this sound mix emulates live, directional, nonbroadcast speech.[15] But Keillor's genius lay in matching his message to the medium. As he worked out the Matter of Minnesota for oral storytelling, he borrowed techniques from oral narrative traditions. As Walter Ong observes in "Writing is a Technology That Restructures Thought," oral stories link present and past, memory and orality, knower and known—all in the "simultaneous present" created by live narration.[16] The lesser immediacy of sound recordings weakens these links, Ong notes, but even the total absence of Keillor's spoken voice cannot cancel the fundamental orality of *Leaving Home*, which not at all coincidentally helps explain the monologues' appeal: they mimic our most beloved kinds of folklore.

The weekly monologue of *A Prairie Home Companion* actually embraced many kinds of stories, a wide variety of oral genres. The published tapes suggest the range. Personal narratives such as "Tomato Butt" and "Me and Choir" spanned the historical and the confessional. A tale about rusticity such as "Uncle Ed" could offer urban folks a few lessons in pride and family loyalty, or, as in "The Living Flag," it could celebrate the simplicity of the rubes. "Bruno the Fishing Dog" and "A Day at the Circus with Mazumbo" related wondrous and ridiculous anecdotes about animals and people. "Babe Ruth Visits Lake Wobegon" provided a full-fledged tall tale, complete with narrative frame and inner yarn. Structurally, the weekly monologue grew out of the formula of the newscast and Barbara Ann Bunsen's letters home: in both predecessors two shorter anecdotes usually preceded the main tale, and the three tended to be very loosely linked. A fine sense of realism emerged from the apparently arbitrary combination of the week's events. Keillor enhanced this effect by varying the format to approximate the structure of conversation; like a friend reporting on his last visit home, he switched easily among the topics of discussion, from this Christmas to last, or one interesting character to her aged mother. However he determined the parts of the weekly installment, each one was largely discrete from the rest. The Lake Wobegon legend as a whole, if it can be said to exist at all, emerged in the minds of Keillor and his listeners as they reconstructed it—piecemeal—from the individual tales.[17]

Anthropologists loosely classify oral narratives as news (gossip, rumors, eyewitness accounts), legends (factual and mythic interpretations of experience), and lies (including fiction and jokes).[18] The monologues deliberately confused all these genres. Originally billed on *A Prairie Home Companion* as the weekly "News from Lake Wobegon," the tales' mixture of fictional and factual genres became all the funnier because every purportedly true element was invented, beginning with the eyewitness's hometown, and because even Keillor's personal history was fictionalized. Blending the genres and confusing their functions kept the narratives humorous while imbuing them with social and rhetorical seriousness.

The social dimension of storytelling has diminished in the last generation as we have relegated oratory to the limited arenas of politics and religion, and reduced even epic tales to the nineteen-inch video screen. Yet all oral stories take on certain ritualized aspects of performance, if only because listeners forgo their part of the conversational dialogue while attending to the tale. For their part, storytellers vary in their ability to fulfill their role as performers, which centers on keeping and gratifying their listeners' attention. But all storytellers try, and the truly formless anecdote probably does not exist. Even the story told spontaneously at a dinner party or to a child at bedtime attempts to grip and hold its audience. As this terminology suggests, moreover, the narrative act involves competition, aggression, and power.[19] To a certain degree all storytellers are the Ancient Mariner, detaining the Wedding Guest with an urgent tale.

Keillor created a narrative context for his stories on *A Prairie Home Companion* that gave them a strong social dimension. Like real place legends, stories about the community of Lake Wobegon emerged in a communal act of narration. As a result, few of his mock folktales subordinated the tale to the teller, in the manner of written fiction, with its greater potential for private revelation. Those stories that did focus on the teller belonged to a special class of folktale, the personal narrative or anecdote of personal experience, which has become a vital American genre in both rural and urban cultures.[20] Keillor's pseudoconfessional stories of growing up in Lake Wobegon imitate the genre almost to the letter of Sandra K. D. Stahl's description:

> The character presented in . . . [the] story is protected by the humor and the entertaining style of the storyteller. But the storyteller himself is quite vulnerable. . . . The conventions of the story make self-revelation acceptable and entertaining, but the courage of the storyteller in articulating usually covert values makes the storytelling an engaging experience for the teller and the audience. . . . Existentially, the personal experience narrator not only acts or experiences but "thinks about" his action, evaluates, it, learns from it, and tells the story—not to express his values, but to build them, to create them, to remake them each time he tells his stories.[21]

Keillor's self-revelations frame the story about Lois's loss of faith, beginning with the initial confession of his childhood worry that his mother paid other boys to be his friends to the final revelation about being reduced to tears by his Aunt Lois's silence during their game of Strangers. The confessions in "Aprille" create a bond of intimacy between the Companion and his listeners, a bond that Keiller acknowledged when he described the monologues as "an intimate form in a public place."[22] His parable of Einer Tingvold's binoculars gains intensity from this bond, since in the context of "Aprille" Keillor tells the anecdote as much to reveal what he learned from it as to pass on its lesson to Lois or to us. The humor of Einer's story, like the joke of inscribing the long confirmation verse in blue icing on the cake, prevents the tale of faith from being sanctimonious. More important, the meaning of the story emerges primarily in the narration—not the writing—of it. Compared with their written counterparts, both oral versions relate the main incidents in greater detail, and both work out the ending with greater subtlety and conviction. No more than his tone of voice can these elements of the oral performance be translated to print. However carefully worked out in advance, a monologue like "Aprille" remains authentically oral.

To this authenticity, Keillor added a large dose of universality to his depictions of Lake Wobegon by drawing on a second folklore genre. A quick look at Richard Dorson's list of topics for the genre known as anecdotal legends proves the point. Focused generally on the clever and oddball, they fall roughly into eleven groups, and *Leaving Home* has examples of every theme on Dorson's list:

> *stinginess or meanness:* Byron's tightfistedness in "A Ten-Dollar Bill"
> *stubbornness:* the unwillingness of Daryl's father to take a vacation or make out his will in "Life is Good"
> *ugliness:* symptoms of flue in "Where Did It Go Wrong?"
> *knavery or rascality:* the con artist in "The Speeding Ticket"
> *naïveté or rusticity:* the Lutheran sailors in "Pontoon Boat"
> *clever retorts:* the old jokes at the end of "High Rise"
> *degeneracy:* some of the returnees in "Exiles"
> *witty remarks:* the comic euphemism in "Homecoming"
> *laziness:* Arlen in "Darlene Makes a Move"
> *absentmindedness:* Florian's leaving Flo behind in "Truckstop"
> *general eccentricity:* "Out in the Cold."[23]

The list provides a clue to the widespread appeal of the monologues among urban *and* rural audiences, older *and* younger listeners: despite the highly defined eccentricities of the Wobegonians, the narratives have the universal themes of our most fundamental literature. And like these universal stories, the Lake Wobegon tales came to us directly, from a human voice.

Fragmentary details in *Leaving Home* demonstrate that the apparent continuity of his monologues is yet another of Keillor's illusions. Nowhere in the volume does the storyteller give us the last names of Wally or Kenny before pointing out their houses in "Hansel," nor do we ever learn the circumstances behind the narrator's casual "Myrtle gets carsick more easily now since she bumped her head on the cupboard" (133). The implicit assumption that we already share this information with him is a rhetorical legacy of the Barbara Ann Bunsen letters of the mid 1970s, and it extends to relations among the stories as a whole. The stable cast of characters and their predictable locales imply a continuity not necessarily confirmed by incidents of plot, although Keillor occasionally strung out a story over several weeks, as in "Dale," which dates from 7 and 21 June 1986. For the most part, however, the stories in *Leaving Home* barely overlap, even though most come from the same interval. Keillor suggests the insignificance of the monologues' chronology in the thematic structure of the volume, which begins with Roger Hedlund's defection, ends with Keillor's, and peaks halfway through with the middle-aged elopement of David Tollefson and Agnes Hedder.

Some of the gaps may have served as a safety device, a sort of literary moat preventing inconsistencies by preventing encroachment. Careful listeners occasionally caught Keillor in errors of consistency—forgetting that he had already given somebody's wife a different name or attributing an incident to a different character than previously.[24] But even without the kind of overlapping events and people that Faulkner worked out so carefully in the Yoknapatawpha stories,[25] the Lake Wobegon monologues managed to coalesce into a full-fledged *imitation* of a place legend, complete with the obligatory geographical landmarks and characterizing episodes, from Jack's Auto Repair and the Chatterbox Cafe to the time Roger Hedlund got the tractor stuck in the field or the day Gary Keillor threw a tomato at his sister.[26] Like other legends of other places, the tales of Lake Wobegon pretend to truth. Indeed, folklorists distinguish a legend from a tall tale on the ground that a tall tale intends to deceive and to have its practical joke exposed later, whereas legend purports to be true.[27] But Keillor's gift to his listeners was a creation that transcended even those generic differences. The

Lake Wobegon tales constitute a legend that its narrator invited us to see as a joke.

Keillor did not set out to exploit these specialized elements of folk narration, although his sketches for *A Prairie Home Companion* flaunted the occasional bit of pseudolore, as in the various rituals of the Sons of Knute or the Installation of the Storm Windows. From time to time he also drew on such authentic American folk traditions as hoopsnakes rolling on the prairie or alligators in the sewers.[28] Crafted by one person for his own performance just once or twice, the radio monologues do not belong to any authentic genre of oral lore, but they have enough in common with them to suggest that listeners felt the kinship. Like authentic folktales, probably the most important oral literature, the Lake Wobegon stories touched basic human feelings about family and place, and they acquired a profound realism as a result. Coming from a family of storytellers, Keillor learned them in the classic way, too—at the yarn spinners' knees. Keillor's uncle Lew Powell and his wife, who entertained the Keillor children every Saturday night, told tales in the classic American grain, without punch lines or "big endings" but using "mimicry and dialogue" instead.[29] The same narrative elements characterize Keillor's oral performances, particularly in such virtuoso tales of children's thought processes as "Dog Days of August."

Many of Keillor's stories also make storytelling their theme, but just about all his oral and written humor (unlike the hybrids of *Leaving Home*) exploits the interrelations among teller, telling, and tale. Indeed, Keillor's mastery of these explains the great success of *A Prairie Home Companion* and his *New Yorker* fiction, including the stories collected in *Happy to Be Here*. Differences between his radio monologues and his written fiction show how thoroughly Keillor understands that different media demand different narration, an awareness that puts *Leaving Home*, like *Lake Wobegon Days*, in the category of literary experiments that succeed in evoking his voice and developing his themes but fall somewhat short of their goals.

The genial, homespun persona that Keillor invented as the host of *A Prairie Home Companion* suits the oral medium perfectly. Live radio broadcasting and homespun homilies are equally anachronistic in these days of VCRs and insider trading; the variety hour, throwback programming from the forties, calls for a cracker-barrel philosopher as host and guide to a town untouched by time. Keillor's best fiction likewise adapts narrator and narration to the context of print. Many tales use mock-oral narration, but very few have narrators resembling Garrison Keillor. For the stories in these other contexts Keillor invents other comic personas, including the inept anthropologist of "Oya Life These Days" (1975), the professional remorse officer of "The Current Crisis in Remorse" (1983), the former Momentist of "Who We Were and What We Meant by It" (1984). But all his tellers suit their tales, of which the telling is a crucial part.

One of Keillor's earliest *New Yorker* stories is especially relevant here, since its subjects include the differences among radio broadcasts, writing, and real life. Reprinted in *Happy to Be Here*, "Friendly Neighbor" (1973) expresses these differences in its technique as well as its theme in the tale of Walter "Dad" Benson. Told by his nephew, the president of a small-town booster club, the narrative takes the form of a newsletter containing tales within tales, a structure that Keillor could only suggest in the oral performance of "Aprille." Exploiting the subtleties among nested tales is properly a technique for a written story, which allows a reader to stop and reflect, as in the "Aprille" of *Leaving Home*. Certainly the three strands of narrative comprising "Friendly Neighbor" call for close attention. Two are intertwined: the newsletter's report on the annual Dad Benson Friendship Dinner encloses the history of Benson's radio program, *Friendly Neighbor*. Taken together, however, the two stories imply a third—an ironic fable illustrating the unfriendliness of these small-towners. And as Keillor works out the problems of radio, writing, and reality in Dad Benson's career, the story becomes a paradigm for his own.

These complexities signal the rich ironies Keillor plants within what seems on the surface a simple example of rural innocence. Dad Benson's radio fans misunderstood the imaginary elements of his program, and now that it has gone off the air they continue to misunderstand the issues it signified. Broadcast during its listeners' lunch hour, Benson's *Friendly Neighbor* offered family verities from his own lunch table, where his fictional family often listened to *The Muellers*, a show-within-the-show dramatizing real problems submitted to "Dad" in his fan mail. With some comic justice, the show fell victim to its own realism. Benson drew all the socially responsible conclusions from an episode featuring the Mueller children's misery over their father's adultery, but the community's outrage at the program's explicitness drove *Friendly Neighbor* off the air. Dad then devoted the rest of his life to improving relations between North Dakotans and Minnesotans, a project eventually resulting in the annual exchange of visits known as the Friendship Dinner. Continuing after his death, this model of homespun hospitality includes tours of the local grain elevator and school as well as a meal, "an evening sing," and opportunities to trade tapes of Dad's show. The newsletter recounts these activities and Dad's "retirement" (57) with equal earnestness. A particularly disquieting story, "Friendly Neighbor" illustrates Keillor's ambivalence toward his local-color materials, especially narration by the unsophisticated. Here, as in "The Slim Graves Show" (1973) and "My North Dakota Railroad Days" (1975), two other important early short stories reprinted in *Happy to Be Here*, he draws rural characters in affectionate detail only to undercut them through incidents that expose their hostility or invite our contempt.

Keillor exploits the comic devices of mock-oral literature in "Friendly Neighbor" with much the same precision that he employed the techniques of oral yarn spinning in "Aprille." Although the story lacks the conventional structure of a frame tale with two narrators of contrasting personalities and speech, the nested stories of "Friendly Neighbor" yield many of the same humorous incongruities. First, details about the radio shows utterly confuse reality, realism, and fantasy, as do all tall tales. Who can tell the real family eating the real lunch from the radio family eating the radio lunch? Second, the narrator's clumsy prose undermines his serious tone and makes him look silly, the first step toward undercutting his reliability as a teller. Some of his more convoluted sentences require explanatory parentheses, and others contain unneeded capitals—both devices adding visual humor similar to pseudo-illiterate misspelling. A key technique of mock-oral humor, misspelling takes advantage of the visuality of print: substandard writing suggests substandard speech. Third, and most important, Keillor's mock writer can neither tell his tale well nor understand it. In this sense, the newsletter writer stands in the humorous tradition of the Simpleton, best exemplified by Mark Twain's "Celebrated Jumping Frog of Calaveras County," narrated by a straight man who doesn't get the jokes that Smiley tells him, much less the one that he's telling himself. At the same time, in moral sensitivity Keillor's narrator stands somewhere between Huck Finn, whose fractured grammar makes his sound morality appear all the more remarkable, and Petroleum V.

Nasby, David Ross Locke's Confederate sympathizer, whose spelling is as corrupt as his politics. All the rural innocents of "Friendly Neighbor" misconstrue what's going on. Benson's unnamed nephew fails to see the irony in the unfriendly treatment of his late "Uncle Dad," not to mention the absurdity of an annual Friendship Dinner in Dad's memory or, in the ultimate anticlimax, the effrontery of asking the community to help locate a tape of the offending show.

"If anyone knows the whereabouts of that show, they should contact us in care of Freeport Machine," he concludes. In the tall tale's tradition of anticlimax, the ungrammatical remark pokes fun at the narrator and the reader both. By reminding us of the newsletter parody and by reaffirming the narrator's naïveté, Keillor leaves his condemnation of the characters implicit, limiting his explicit criticism to the very moderate bewilderment of his newsletter writer. Consequently, the ending sustains all the comic incongruities of the nested tales but in a kind of narrative joke on the reader that resolves none of the serious themes. As grand moral problems fizzle into mild distractions, "Friendly Neighbor" damns only with faint praise.

Whether writing fiction or spinning oral tales, Keillor aims to amuse, not to rant, and he has restrained himself in print as well as on the air. But compared with Keillor the oral performer, Keillor the writer leaves fewer ambiguities. The tone of mild condescension in the oral tales becomes mild scorn in the written fiction. Affection therefore yields to ridicule, innocence to corruption, and sentimental portraiture to satiric caricature. Ultimately, "Friendly Neighbor" lacks the genial nature of either Keillor's radio humor or the chatty author-narrator of the newsletter, because Keillor's fiction, highly literate and highly sophisticated, finds little to admire in innocence. Indeed, in contrast to the Lake Wobegon monologues of the 1980s, most of Keillor's fifty tales before *Leaving Home* ridicule the bliss of the ignorant. And they usually do so by undercutting their narrators, whether mock-oral speakers or implied writers.

When "Friendly Neighbor" appeared in the *New Yorker* in December 1973, six months before *A Prairie Home Companion* began its live Saturday evening broadcasts, Keillor could not have imagined how much a similar confusion between radio and real life would eventually interfere with his own mythmaking and entertaining. But thirteen years later, much as Dad Benson's audience condemned him along with the miscreant in one of his parables, so Keillor's radio fans chained him to his cracker-barrel in Lake Wobegon. A writer of Keillor's gifts needs much more freedom. Not only does he need escape from the routine of producing a weekly variety show, which eats material at an alarming rate, even for a goat; he also needs protection from his own formulas or (to put it the other way around) from his listeners' expectations. *Leaving Home* marks an important point in Keillor's career in part because the book represents in print the end of his broadcasts as the Prairie Home Companion, and so represents a brief union of his work in two media. But the collection also reveals in several different ways the private writer's dissatisfaction with the demands placed on him as a public performer. Perhaps because the audience had come to appropriate them, the people and events of Lake Wobegon so impinged on their creator's life that *Leaving Home* had to chronicle his own exodus as well as those of Roger Hedlund, Dale Uecker, and Father Emil. Keillor speaks ominously in the "Letter from Copenhagen" at the beginning of *Leaving Home* of the "collapse of an American career," a bewildering characterization of a success so intense that the celebrity had to cross an ocean to avoid the press. But then what writer could continue once his imaginary creations, including the persona invented to convey them, were reduced to simple biography? In the context of "Friendly Neighbor," we might consider his defection from Minnesota as exile—that his fans, like Benson's, drove him away against his will with their confusion of the genial persona and the real person. Unlike Benson's fans, Keillor's loyal listeners do not have to search in desperation for the tape of his last show; Walt Disney Home Video has already issued it. But it remains to be seen what Keillor will choose to rescue from the "collapse" and the splendid opportunities that it offers. His remigration from Copenhagen to New York City in September 1987 suggests that he will return to the explorations begun in his earlier *New Yorker* fiction, including "Friendly Neighbor," with decidedly ungenial personifications of rural innocence. And even in exile, by the waters of Manhattan, far from the cornfields of Minnesota, Keillor will not likely forget Lake Wobegon.

Dates of Published
Monologues

Dates for the following monologues have been identified in the PHC
Archives. Times (in minutes and seconds) reflect the edited, published
versions, which may have been compressed or abridged, not the original
performances.

The Family Radio (1982)
  "News from Lake Wobegon [Uncle Ed]," 29 Aug. 1981, 11:46.

News from Lake Wobegon (1983)

Spring
  "A Day in the Life of Clarence Bunsen," 20 Nov. 1982, 13:48.
  "Letter from Jim," 13 March 1982, 11:52.
  "Fiction," 20 Aug. 1983, 3:58.
  "Me and Choir," 13 May 1983, 29:17. Used in *Lake Wobegon Days.*

Summer
  "The Living Flag," 13 June 1981, 5:19. Used in *Lake Wobegon Days.*
  "The Tollefson Boy Goes to College," 12 June 1982, 11:26. Used in
    Lake Wobegon Days.
  "Tomato Butt," 31 July 1982, 11:36. Used in *Lake Wobegon Days.*
  "Chamber of Commerce," n.d., 2:17.
  "Dog Days of August," 22 Aug. 1981, 11:13.
  "Mrs. Berge and the Schubert Carillon Piano," 16 Oct. 1982, 14:26.

Fall
  "Giant Decoys," 18 Sept. 1982, 6:08. Excerpts.
  "Daryl Tollerud's Long Day," 26 Sept. 1981, 9:35.
  "Hog Slaughter," 9 Oct. 1982, 13:42. Used in *Leaving Home.*
  "Thanksgiving," 27 Nov. 1982, 10:38.
  "The Royal Family," 13 Nov. 1982, 20:15. Used in *Leaving Home.*

Winter
"Christmas Story Re-told," 19 Dec. 1981, 11:27.
"James Lundeen's Christmas," 18 Dec. 1982, 13:38.
"New Year's from New York," 1 Jan. 1983, 15:12.
"Guys on Ice," 15 Jan. 1983, 5:21.
"Storm Home," 29 Jan. 1983, 13:41.

Gospel Birds and Other Stories of Lake Wobegon (1985)

Tape 1
"Pastor Ingqvist's Trip to Orlando," 12 Jan. 1985, 20:49.
"Mammoth Concert Tickets," 28 Jan. 1984, 18:49.
"Bruno, the Fishing Dog," 24 Aug. 1985, 22:35.
"Gospel Birds," 27 Oct. 1984, 17:49.

Tape 2
"Meeting Donny Hart at the Bus Stop," 5 Nov. 1983, 9:53. Excerpt.
"A Day at the Circus with Mazumbo," 11 Feb. 1984, 13:57.
"The Tolleruds' Korean Baby," 9 Feb. 1985, 22:25.
"Sylvester Krueger's Desk," 24 Sept. 1983, 18:32. Used in *Lake Wobegon Days*.
"Babe Ruth Visits Lake Wobegon," 13 July 1985, 28:24. Published as "Lake Wobegon Games" (1986), and reprinted as "The Babe" in *We are Still Married.*

Leaving Home (1987)

"A Trip to Grand Rapids," 17 May 1986, with parts from 18 May 1985 and 14 June 1986.
"A Ten-Dollar Bill," 8 March 1986.
"Easter," 28 April 1984.
"Corinne," 12 April 1986.
"A Glass of Wendy," 8 Feb. 1986.
"The Speeding Ticket," 21 March 1987.
"Seeds," 30 March 1985, with 13 April 1985.
"Chicken," 13 Sept. 1986.
"How the Crab Apple Grew," 10 May 1986.
"Truckstop," 23 Feb. 1985.
"Dale," 7 June 1986 and 21 June 1986. Two-part story.
"Collection," 16 March 1985.
"High Rise," 31 May 1986, with a bit from 13 April 1985.
"Life Is Good," 28 June 1986.
"Lyle's Roof," 2 March 1985, 6 Sept. 1986, and 23 Aug. 1986.
"Pontoon Boat," 19 July 1986.

"State Fair," 30 Aug. 1986.

"David and Agnes, A Romance," 17 Aug. 1985.

"The Killer," 20 Sept. 1986.

"Eloise," 4 Oct. 1986.

"The Royal Family," 13 Nov. 1982.

"Homecoming," 13 Oct. 1984.

"Brethren," 1 Nov. 1986.

"Thanksgiving," 29 Nov. 1986.

"Darlene Makes a Move," 6 Dec. 1986.

"Christmas Dinner," 24 Nov. 1984.

"Exiles," 27 Dec. 1986.

"New Year's," 3 Jan. 1987 and 10 Jan. 1987.

"Where Did It Go Wrong?" 28 Feb. 1987.

"Post Office," 15 Nov. 1986.

"Out in the Cold," 1 Feb. 1986.

"Hawaii," 16 Nov. 1985.

"Hansel," 22 Nov. 1986.

"Du, Du Liegst Mir Im Herzen," 22 March 1986.

"Aprille," 26 April 1986.

"Goodbye to the Lake," 13 June 1987.

NOTES

CHAPTER 1. *The Matter of Minnesota: An Introduction*

1. Quoted by Rosalie Miller, telephone interview with the author, 10 March 1988.

2. See, for example, "People," *Time,* 2 March 1987, 42–43; and Jack Thomas, "Weekend in Wobegon," *Boston Globe,* 9 March 1987, F8, 10.

3. Telephone calls received by the World Theater box office estimated in Minnesota Public Radio (MPR), *1987 Report to Funders* (St. Paul: Minnesota Public Radio, 1988), 6.

4. Estimate of Ilene Zatal, the MPR volunteer who handled the *Prairie Home Companion* correspondence during this period.

5. Receipts from Minnesota Historical Society to Minnesota Public Radio, 13 Jan. 1988, detail the *Prairie Home Companion* memorabilia donated after the end of the show, including a variety of advertising posters, shirts, bumper stickers, and one of the coveted staff jackets, silver nylon with the *PHC* logo on the back.

6. Items given to the O. Meredith Wilson Library at the University of Minnesota on 25 March 1988 include English and foreign-language editions of *Happy to Be Here* (1981), *Lake Wobegon Days* (1985), and *Leaving Home* (1987), texts of monologues from 1981 to 1987, copies of relevant MPR publications (*G.K. the D.J.* [1977], *Ten Years: The Official Souvenir Anniversary Program for "A Prairie Home Companion"* [1984], *World Theater Grand Opening Program* [1986], and *Minnesota Monthly Farewell Edition* [1987]), and a few manuscripts—rather complete for *Leaving Home,* less so for *Lake Wobegon Days.*

7. Caroline J. White, Assistant Editor, Penguin USA, to the author, 13 June 1990.

8. Rosalie Miller to the author, 22 July 1989 and 8 May 1990.

9. Michael Fedo, *The Man from Lake Wobegon* (New York: St. Martin's Press, 1987), 50.

10. Two of his poems won honorable mention in the 1965 Academy of American Poets Contest at University of Minnesota, "On Waking to Old

Debts" and "Nicodemus," both published in *Ivory Tower* 66 (5 April 1965):
21. The next year, as a graduating senior, he won both the Academy of
American Poets Contest and the university's Fanny Fay Wood Prize, a
hundred dollars, for "At the Premier" and "This Is a Poem, Good
Afternoon," both published in *Ivory Tower* 67 (2 May 1966): 20. "At the
Premier" was first published anonymously in *Ivory Tower* 67 (10 Jan. 1966):
14. He worked at the student station, WMMR-AM, from 1960 to 1961 and
at the university's noncommercial professional station, KUOM-AM, from
1963 to 1968 ("Fifth Estater: Garrison Keillor, an American Home
Companion," *Broadcasting* 15 [Dec. 1986]: 127).

11. David O'Neill and Kathleen McLean, "20 Years of MPR: Two Decades
at a Glance," *Minnesota Monthly* 21 (Jan. 1987): 58.

12. Garrison Keillor, interview with Leonard Lopate, *New York and
Company*, wnyc-am, 2 Dec. 1987.

13. Roy Blount, Jr., "A Conversation with Garrison Keillor", in *Farewell
to "A Prairie Home Companion"* (St. Paul: Minnesota Public Radio, 1987),
17.

14. Diane Roback, *"PW* Interviews Garrison Keillor," *Publishers Weekly*,
13 Sept. 1985, 138.

15. Peter Hemingson, "The Plowboy Interview: Garrison Keillor, the Voice
of Lake Wobegon," *Mother Earth News*, no. 92 (May–June 1985): 18.

16. Garrison Keillor, Seminar on Radio, Museum of Broadcasting, New
York City, 7 June 1988. This was the first of two seminars that Keillor gave
at the museum, 7–8 June 1990.

17. Keillor, interview with the author, 14 Sept. 1989, New York City.
According to Lois Hendrickson of the University of Minnesota Archives,
Delta Phi Lambda was an honorary education group for students having
at least a 2.2 grade point average in composition and English courses, but
it seems to have been inactive in the 1960s. A second, similarly named
group *was* active at the time—Lambda Alpha Psi, an honorary society for
Language and Literature—but Wright was not its adviser, and Keillor was
not listed among its members. Hendrickson, telephone interview with the
author, 12 July 1990.

18. The Bibliography contains complete bibliographical citations of
Keillor's writings in chronological order. This information will not be
repeated in the notes to the each chapter or in the text, except to cite
quotations from reprinted, more widely available sources.

19. [Garrison Keillor], "The Broadside of the Tower," *Ivory Tower* 65 (4
Nov. 1963): 7. Keillor identified the sketch as his own in an interview with
the author, 14 Sept. 1989, New York City.

20. "Keillor Resigns, Hyde New Tower Editor," *Minnesota Daily*, 14 Jan.
1966, 1.

21. Garrison Keillor, interviews with the author, 14 Sept. 1989 and 22 May 1990, New York City.

22. The *Minnesota Daily* reported on these issues in a series of articles: "Pub Board, Editors Recommend Changes in Committee Report," 6 Jan. 1966, 1, 3; "Committee Reports on Publications," 6 Jan. 1966, 7–8; "Tower Editor to Submit Statement of Resignation," 7 Jan. 1966, 1; "Keillor Resigns, Hyde New Tower Editor," 14 Jan. 1966, 1.

23. "Where Art Thou, Perceptive Creativity?" *Ivory Tower* 67 (7 Feb. 1966): 12–13.

24. Walter Blair, "'A Man's Voice, Speaking': A Continuum in American Humor," in *Veins of Humor*, ed. Harry Levin (Cambridge, Mass: Harvard University Press, 1973), 185–204.

25. The photo accompanied John Skow's "Lonesome Whistle Blowing," *Time*, 4 Nov. 1985, 68–73, which suggested affinities with Twain. More sweeping claims of Keillor's greatness appeared in Doug Thorpe, "Garrison Keillor's 'Prairie Home Companion': Gospel of the Airwaves," *Christian Century*, 21–28 July 1982, 793–96.

26. See Louis J. Budd, *Our Mark Twain: The Making of His Public Personality* (Philadelphia: University of Pennsylvania Press, 1983); Budd, "A 'Talent for Posturing,'" in *The Mythologizing of Mark Twain*, ed. Sara deSassure Davis and Philip D. Beidler (University: University of Alabama Press, 1984), 77–98, 167–68; and Budd, "Hiding Out in Public: Mark Twain as a Speaker," *Studies in American Fiction* 13 (Autumn 1985): 129–41.

27. Twain's introduction to the reprint of "The Jumping Frog of Calaveras County," in *Mark Twain's Library of Humor*, ed. Mark Twain, William Dean Howells, and Charles H. Clark (1888), quoted by Alan Gribben, "Autobiography as Property: Mark Twain and His Legend," in *The Mythologizing of Mark Twain*, 47.

28. Quoted by Budd, "Hiding Out in Public," 130, who notes that naïve critics following up on this assertion have sought the southern biographical details in *A Connecticut Yankee in King Arthur's Court*.

29. Gribben, "Autobiography as Property," 41.

30. Quoted in John Bordsen, "All the News from Lake Wobegon," *Saturday Review* 9 (May–June 1983): 12.

31. For a discussion of the Matter of Hannibal, see Henry Nash Smith, *Mark Twain: The Development of a Writer* (Cambridge: Belknap Press of Harvard University Press, 1962), esp. 71–75.

32. Fred Fassert composed the words and music to "Barbara Ann" in 1961. See *The Best of the Beach Boys* (Miami: Columbia Pictures Publications, 1985), 6–7.

33. [G.M. and J.M.] to Garrison Keillor, n.d. [Jan. 1987], PHC Archives; anonymous letter [postmarked Midland, Mich.], n.d., PHC. Archives.

34. Garrison Keillor, telephone conversation with the author, 28 June 1988. As Charlie Weaver, Arquette appeared regularly on Jack Paar's edition of *The Tonight Show* (29 July 1957–30 March 1962, NBC) and *The Jack Parr Program* (21 Sept. 1962–10 Sept. 1965, NBC), among many other shows. Charlie Weaver was Arquette's only comic persona, and he assumed it even as a participant on game shows such as *Hollywood Squares*. See Tim Brooks and Earle Marsh, *The Complete Directory to Prime-Time Network TV Shows, 1946–Present* (New York: Ballantine Books, 1979).

35. Garrison Keillor, "The Slim Graves Show," *New Yorker*, 10 Feb. 1973, 33–34; and "A Prairie Home Companion," *Preview* [MER] 7 (July 1973): 20.

36. Will Jones, "After Last Night," *Minneapolis Tribune*, 3 Oct. 1971, 6D.

37. Keillor, Seminar on Radio, 7 June 1988.

38. Garrison Keillor, "To the Reader," *G.K. the D.J.*, 1.

39. Thomas J. Kigin, general counsel of MPR, interview with the author, St. Paul, 1 July 1988.

40. Erica Owen, Archivist, Map Publications, American Automobile Association, telephone interview with the author, 10 July 1990. (For many years, St. Paul had two newspapers, *The St. Paul Pioneer Press*, a morning paper, and *The St. Paul Dispatch*, an evening paper. On 2 January 1985, these merged into a single all-day paper, *The St. Paul Pioneer Press Dispatch*, which continued publication until 25 March 1990, when the *Dispatch* was discontinued and the paper was renamed *Saint Paul Pioneer Press*.)

41. A report on the study offers another example of the same assumption that everyone knows about Lake Wobegon. See Daniel Koretz, "Arriving in Lake Wobegon: Are Standardized Tests Exaggerating Achievement and Distorting Instruction?" *American Educator* 12 (Summer 1988): 8–15, 46–52.

42. Peter Applebome, "Paradise Found? Close but Not Quite," *New York Times*, 23 May 1988, A14.

43. Thomas H. Middleton, "Acrostic Puzzle," *New York Times Magazine*, 28 May 1989, 58. The puzzle featured this quotation: "Vegetables fill up the . . . kitchen . . . quarts of tomatoes have been canned, still more move in. The Mister . . . pick[s] up the paper, underneath it are three zucchini. They crawled in there to get some shade, catch a few Zs, maybe read the comics," from *Lake Wobegon Days*, 154. ("The Mister" was erroneously rendered as "He Mister.")

44. Undated note accompanying a photograph of Jack's Tours. Prairie Home Companion Archives.

45. Gil Gutknecht to Garrison Keillor, 23 April 1987, PHC Archives.

46. Garrison Keillor, *Ten Years* (1984), 25.

47. Rosalie Miller to the author, 22 July 1989.

48. The mail order business, best known by its *Wireless* catalog, eventually became a separate profit-making corporation, Rivertown Trading. Rivertown is a wholly owned subsidiary of the tax-paying Greenspring Corporation, whose sole stockholder is the Minnesota Communications Group, which owns Minnesota Public Radio and the World Theater, both nonprofit corporations.

49. Garrison Keillor, Seminar on Radio, Museum of Broadcasting, New York City, 8 June 1988.

50. Fedo, *The Man from Lake Wobegon*, 55.

51. Untitled poem, [1972], PHC Archives; Garrison Keillor, interview with the author, 14 Sept. 1989. The first verse was printed on the jacket of *A Prairie Home Album* (Minnesota Educational Radio, [1972?]).

52. Philip Roth, "On *The Great American Novel*," in his *Reading Myself and Others* (New York: Farrar, Straus and Giroux, 1976), 91.

53. These factors also explain the success of the film *Big* (1988), in which a disgruntled young boy tries out all the pleasures of adulthood and gratefully returns to being a child again.

54. Garrison Keillor, interview with the author, 14 Sept. 1989.

55. First published in *Happy to Be Here* (New York: Atheneum, 1981), 119-126.

56. Hemingson, "Garrison Keillor," 17–20, 22; James Traub interviewed Keillor in the course of writing "The Short and Tall Tales of Garrison Keillor," *Esquire* 97 (May 1982): 108–17.

57. Various PHC staff members, personal interviews with the author, June 1988.

58. Keillor, *Ten Years*, 20.

59. The volume includes photographed copies of two obstructive letters. See Fedo, *The Man from Lake Wobegon*, x.

60. Rosalie Miller, interview with the author, 23 June 1988. According to MPR staffers, the first writer with whom St. Martin's signed a contract for the biography decided not to pursue a book about an unwilling subject, at which point the publishers signed up Fedo.

61. Eleanor Blau, "TV Notes: Keillor's Goodbyes," *New York Times*, 23 May 1988, C16. The slogan appeared in many ads, including a full-page *Prairie Home Companion* products spread in MPR's *Wireless* catalog, Late Spring 1988, 21.

62. The announcement came from San Francisco and promised that *American Radio Company of the Air* would broadcast live from various cities, including New York and St. Paul. (The item erroneously gave *A Prairie Home Companion* a thirteen-year history on National Public Radio.) See "Keillor on Radio," *New York Times*, 19 May 1989, C34.

CHAPTER 2. A Prairie Home Companion *Homespun and Hip*

1. The historical analysis of live broadcasts of *A Prairie Home Companion* in this chapter is based primarily on unpublished audiotape cassettes in the PHC Archives at Minnesota Public Radio, St. Paul. These tapes are cited parenthetically in my text. Published recordings, on the other hand, are cited in conventional notes. Unless otherwise indicated, all transcriptions are my own, based on principles described in the Preface.

Hinkley and Larson left the Powdermilk Biscuit Band in 1975 ("A Prairie Home Alamanac," in *Ten Years*, 9).

2. Keillor recognized the implications of the decision. "Nowadays you can't really think of radio in terms of shows, anyways," he told Bordsen in 1983. "It's formats, and ours is a throwback." See Bordsen, "All the News from Lake Wobegon," 12.

3. Sean Mitchell, "Homespun Radio's Cozy 'Companion,'" *Dallas Times Herald*, 22 Feb. 1981, 7.

4. Tom Kigin, quoted in Patricia Weaver Francisco, "The Life and Times of MPR," *Minnesota Monthly* 21 (Jan. 1987): 52; Keillor, interview with the author, 22 May 1990, New York City.

5. Fedo, *The Man from Lake Wobegon*, 60.

6. Will Jones reported the quarrel, which neither Keillor nor MPR disputes, in his column "After Last Night," *Minneapolis Tribune*, 3 Oct. 1971, 6D.

7. Untitled typescript, 9 Oct. [1971], PHC Archives. The larger archives of MPR include a few tapes of *The Morning Program*, but these are so fragile as to be essentially unavailable for research.

8. Untitled typescripts, 6, 9 Oct. [1971], and n.d. [Oct.–Nov. 1971], PHC Archives.

9. Untitled typescript, n.d. [April–May, 1972], PHC Archives. This text raises an interesting question about the creative process, for Keillor changed typewriters just at the point where he designated "the anomaly" as one of the unmentionable parts. Perhaps he thought of the anomaly between home and the office?

10. Will Jones, "After Last Night," *Minneapolis Tribune*, 9 Oct. 1971, 10A.

11. Will Jones, "After Last Night," *Minneapolis Tribune*, 31 Oct. 1971, 4D. Keillor's activities as a poet and novelist were reported in a series of articles with essentially the same material, probably printed from a news release: "Three Poets to Speak at Walker" in *St. Anthony Sun, Columbia Heights Sun*, and *Blaine, Spring Lake Park Sun*; and "Poetical Natives to Perform," *Savage, Minnesota, Sun*, all unpaginated clippings dated week of 22 Nov. 1971, MPR Publicity Archives, St. Paul. Keillor's "1871-2" remains unpublished.

12. Jones, "After Last Night," 3 Oct. 1971, 6D.

13. Garrison Keillor, "To the Reader," in *G.K. the D.J.* (1977), 1. More

than ten years and hundreds of radio hours later he said much the same thing in the Seminar on Radio, 7 June 1988.

14. See "Keillor to Quit Daily Show; Others Leave KSJN," *Minneapolis Tribune*, 24 Aug, 1973, 14B.

15. The article that resulted from the Nashville trip is "Onward and Upward with the Arts: At the Opry," *New Yorker*, 6 May 1974, 46–70. Perpetuating the story of the Nashville inspiration are, for example, Lawrence Ingrassia, "Live from St. Paul, Here's 'A Prairie Home Companion,'" *Wall Street Journal*, 21 Jan. 1981, 1; Richard Harrington, "Whimsical Satirical Miracle," *Washington Post*, 20 March 1981, K2; "Opry Visit Paid Off for Writer," *Community News* [Madison, Tenn.], 1 April 1981, 8A; "Keillor, Garrison," *Current Biography* (Aug. 1985): 28; Bill C. Malone, *Country Music, U.S.A.*, rev. ed. (Austin: University of Texas Press, 1985), 370 n. 1; Fedo, *The Man from Lake Wobegon*, 77–78; and Michael Schumacher, "Sharing the Laughter with Garrison Keillor," *Writer's Digest* 66 (Jan. 1986), 33–34. Keillor insisted in a personal interview with the author (22 May 1990) that whatever MER intended, the show remained unformed in his own mind until his visit to the Opry.

16. Keillor, interview with the author, 22 May 1990.

17. Keillor, Seminar on Radio, 7 June 1998.

18. Ibid.

19. Ibid.

20. Garrison Keillor, interview with the author, 14 Sept. 1989. This description convinced Rosalie Miller of MPR that the story is "A Corner Lot" from 13 Dec. 1975 (Rosalie Miller to the author, 8 May 1990).

21. Estimate by MPR, reported by Jeff Holman, "Of Mikes and Men: The Minnesota Public Radio Story, Part I," *MPLS, St. Paul Weekly*, 24 June 1977, unpaginated clipping in MPR Publicity Archives.

22. Except for his opening bit, Keillor did not perform any sort of monologue on 4 March 1978. On 30 Dec. 1978, when Howard Mohr read his pseudoscholarly essay "Waving," Keillor announced that he wouldn't compete by telling a Lake Wobegon tale, so he read a letter (ostensibly from a listener) on the subject of "poetry as a controlled substance," a mildly funny spoof on the question of legalizing marijuana in which possession of an illegal poem is punishable by one to ten years in jail. This show is also notable as the first time Keillor goofed in singing "Hello Love." After giving up the verse and pretending to forget that Powdermilk Biscuits were his sponsor, he said, "I always knew that was going to happen," and recited the lyrics in very good humor.

23. Betty Jean Robinson and Aileen Mnich, "Hello Love" (Nashville, Tenn.: Acuff-Rose Songs, 1970). Keillor sang only the first and last verses, often extending the "Hello" phrases to include the names of guest performers. He also wrote his own verses for the bridges, one of which ran

"I've heard it said for oh so long / live radio is dead and gone / I've heard it so often I guess it's true / But here we are, and there are you" (Rosalie Miller to the author, 8 May 1990).

24. Statistics from Marcia Pankake, interview with the author, 29 June 1988, University of Minnesota, Minneapolis. Pankake also noted that 143 listeners submitted their contributions on audiotape. Marcia and Jon Pankake's collection, *A Prairie Home Companion Folk Song Book*, (New York: Viking Press, 1988) contains selections from the "Department," which (according to Keillor's foreword) ran from 1983 to 1984.

25. *Sing Along with Mitch*, hosted by Mitch Miller, ran for one hour weekly on NBC from 27 Jan. 1961 to 2 Sept. 1966.

26. Garrison Keillor, interview with the author, New York City, 29 May 1990.

27. Keillor, *Ten Years*, 9.

28. *A Prairie Home Companion* moved to the eighty-two-seat Variety Hall Theater, KSJN's neighbor across the hall in the Park Square Court Building on Sibley Street in St. Paul, 5 Oct. 1975; from there the show moved on 1 Nov. 1975 to the St. Paul–Ramsey Arts and Science Center, where it remained for three years before moving to larger quarters. St. Thomas College in St. Paul provided a temporary home in its O'Shaughnessy Auditorium (six hundred seats) from Nov. 1977 through Feb. 1978, when the show finally acquired its own quarters. Performances began 4 March 1978 at the World Theater at Exchange and Wabasha in St. Paul. When MPR purchased the World on 7 December 1981, the auditorium seated 650. After extensive renovations, including the removal of the false ceiling covering the second balcony, the theater could hold 960 (*Ten Years*, 8–14). The official capacity listed on the 1988 fire certificate was 915. During renovations of the World, the show performed at the Orpheum Theater in St. Paul (Jan. 1984 through July 1985), at the T. B. Sheldon Auditorium in Red Wing, Minn. (Aug. through 7 Sept. 1985), and then went on tour until returning to the World in Jan. 1986.

29. Michael Anthony, "Lake Wobegon Revisited: Garrison Keillor's Greatest Hits," *Minneapolis Tribune*, 30 Jan. 1981, 2C.

30. Barbara Flanagan responded to the waltz and to a recent article that Keillor had published in the *Minneapolis Star* in an open letter designated "a bread-and-butter note to my great 'grand-nephew,' Garrison Keillor." In her "Tips from a Great Aunt," *Minneapolis Star*, 5 Aug. 1977, unpaginated clipping, MPR Publicity Archives, Flanagan makes fun of his penchant for the comic epistle while accepting the praise behind his joking criticism. Keillor's analysis of the paper had appeared the previous day as "He Digests the Star and Finds It's a Meat-and-Potatoes Meal," *Minneapolis Star*, 4 Aug. 1977, 1–2C.

31. Jesus Torres ("Bombo") Rivera, born 2 Aug. 1952 in Ponce, Puerto

Rico, played in the major leagues in the 1975–1982 seasons. Arriving in Minneapolis–St. Paul from Montreal in 1978, Rivera batted .271, .281, and .221 in his three seasons with the Twins before joining the Kansas City Royals in 1981 (Joseph L. Reichler, ed., *The Baseball Encyclopedia*, 6th ed. [New York: Macmillan, 1985]).

32. Lieutenant Governor Rudy Perpich to Garrison Keillor, 29 Nov. 1976.

33. [B.N.] to Garrison Keillor, 36 Sept. 1980, PHC Archives. Similarly, one fan from Nebraska who heard me speak on *Lake Wobegon Days* charged that I had no business taking on Keillor as a subject since I lived in New York, but he was mollified when he learned that I was born, reared, and educated in the Midwest. Both his original irritation and later acceptance are revealing about the degree to which fans of the show saw it as a local possession, to be shared among themselves but not with outsiders.

34. I am grateful to Rosalie Miller of MPR for a list of characters having street names, including Robert St. Peter, Jessamine Shepard, Raymond Como, Milton Macalester, and Ken Mackubin (Miller to the author, 22 July 1989).

35. Keillor gave reign to his imagination in playing on *Airedale* and other canine associations of *-dale* in the Kitty Boutique spots, since the actual *-dale* shopping centers have geographical associations: Ridgedale, Brookdale, Rosedale, Southdale.

36. On 16 Aug. 1980, Keillor began the show by joking about the unseasonably cold weather, "I was talking to a woman out in the St. Croix Valley today on the phone, who said she thought that she saw snowflakes falling, but of course that's impossible because it's August. Sometimes, sometimes, a person gets little motes of dust in their eye, and they'll look like snow. You didn't see snowflakes today, did you? [shouts from the audience: No!] Good. I'm glad. Because the day it starts snowing in August is the day I spend my winters in Iowa. June, and July, and August are supposed to be snow-free. That's one of the rules we live under here in Minnesota, at least no measurable snowfall. No more than an inch or two, anyway."

37. On the broadcast of 26 Aug. 1976, Keillor announced the upcoming "Second Semi-Annual Mouth-Off," implying that the first mouth-music contest was the one on the 17 Jan. 1976 broadcast—and not 17 Jan. *1975*, as reported in *Ten Years*, 9. Like the Pillsbury Bake-Off (held annually in Twin Cities, home of the Pillsbury Corporation), the Powdermilk Mouth-Off divided mouth-musicians into several classes: whistling (solo or accompanied), head music (humming, cheek thumping, etc.), and miscellaneous (yodeling, tooth-tapping, instrumental imitations, and others). Details of contest from "Powdermilk Biscuits Present: The Powdermilk Mouth Music Contest or 'Mouth-Off,'" photocopy of typescript and press-type rules for the contest on 17 Jan. 1976, PHC Archives.

38. Keillor, *Ten Years*, 6. The souvenir program claims that admission fees collected for the twelve tickets totaled less than eight dollars; by my arithmetic, then, the audience included three adults ($1 each) and nine children (50¢ each).

39. Garrison Keillor, interview with the author, 29 May 1990.

40. Erving Goffman, *Forms of Talk* (Philadelphia: University of Pennsylvania Press, 1981), 110.

41. Jeff Holman reported, "Despite the spontaneous feel of the show, most everything is scripted. The first year of the show, he wrote out everything in advance, and followed his script down to the minute. . . . As he gained more confidence, he's been able to loosen up a bit. 'I don't read my scripts any more. But I do take them with me'" ("Of Mikes and Men").

42. *The Lawrence Welk Show* ran from 2 July 1955 to 4 Sept. 1971 Saturday nights in varying time-slots on ABC: 9–10 p.m. (July 1955–Sept. 1963), 8:30–9:30 p.m. (Sept. 1963–Jan. 1971), and 7:30–8:30 p.m. (Jan. 1971–Sept. 1971). (See Brooks and Marsh, *Prime-Time Network TV*). Note that the time-slot crept earlier as the show aged and entertainment patterns changed.

43. *The Mary Tyler Moore Show* ran on CBS from 19 Sept. 1970 to 3 Sept. 1977 (See Brooks and Marsh, *Prime-Time Network TV*).

44. Garrison Keillor, Seminar on Radio, 8 June 1988.

45. John C. Gerber, "Mark Twain's Use of the Comic Pose," *PMLA* 77 (June 1962): 297–304. Gerber argues very persuasively that to require a coherent persona behind the pseudonym "Mark Twain" is "to indulge in oversimplification that obscures the intricate and successful uses Twain *does* make of the comic pose or mask while narrating." The same might be said of Keillor.

46. Ibid., 299.

47. Early in 1975, he closed the show by reporting that the Powdermilk Biscuit Band had undertaken to march in formation on stage to spell out *P-H-C* one letter at a time (18 Jan. 1975). Rosalie Miller of MPR reports another example: Wood-carver Harley Refsal performed for the theater audience 15 March 1986 while the radio audience followed Keillor's play-by-play description with what must have been amusement. Refsal's return performance on 4 April 1987 was televised, however (Miller to the author, 22 July 1989).

48. Untitled typescript, n.d., PHC Archives. On *The Morning Program*, Jack mangled the host's name as "Harrison Kelly" ("Letters," *Preview*, [MER] 6 (July 1972), 6.

49. Garrison Keillor, "The Perils of Success: Selected Letters from Jack," in *Farewell to "A Prairie Home Companion*," ed. Daniel Kelly, issued as a supplement to *Minnesota Monthly* 21 (June 1987), and separately (St. Paul: Minnesota Public Radio, 1987), 100. Keillor used more literary phrasing

when he revised and abridged the letters for inclusion in *We Are Still Married*; for the parallel passage, see 77.

50. Untitled typescript, 27 Feb. 1982 and 13 Feb. 1982, with holograph notation, "TODAY Show," PHC Archives. Revised and published as "May 1986" entry of "The Perils of Success," 104.

51. Garrison Keillor, *Ten Years on the Prairie: "A Prairie Home Companion" 10th Anniversary* (1984), 1A.

52. *A Prairie Home Companion: The Final Performance* (Minnesota Public Radio, 1987), A.

53. Rosalie Miller to the author, 22 July 1989.

CHAPTER 3. *It's All I Know: Prairie Home Postures*

1. Garrison Keillor, interview with the author, New York City, 14 Sept. 1989.

2. George Hesselberg, "Take a Bow, Keillor, and Thanks," *Wisconsin State Journal*, 22 Feb. 1987, unpaginated copy in MPR Publicity Archives.

3. Skow, "Lonesome Whistle Blowing," 70. See also, for example, Schumacher, "Sharing the Laughter," 32, who reports, "Despite his reputation for being extremely shy, he appears relaxed"; and Thomas, "Weekend in Wobegon," 8, who calls him "the notoriously shy host" of *A Prairie Home Companion*.

4. Holman, "Of Mikes and Men."

5. In the early years, Powdermilk Biscuits made you "stand up and say 'Hoo—ahhhh!!!'" By 28 Aug. 1976 Keillor was using both tags.

6. Mitchell, "Homespun Radio's Cozy 'Companion,'" 7.

7. Keillor's mock radio drama, "The Spillers," which inflated "problem spilling" into a family crisis akin to alcoholism, was performed 18 Sept. 1982.

8. A revision of "Storm Home" also appears in *Lake Wobegon Days*, 248–249.

9. Quoted in Keillor's introduction to an MPR premium, *The Selected Verse of Margaret Haskins Durber* (Lake Wobegon, MN: Jack's Press, © 1979, [St. Paul: Minnesota Public Radio]). The most famous of Durber's poems, known variously as "The Finn Who Would Not Take a Sauna" and "The Ballad of the Guy Who Came in from the Cold" (as the humorist jokingly introduced it on 9 Dec. 1978), was reprinted in the booklet as "The Ballad of the Finn Who Didn't Like Saunas," [19–20]. The poem is reprinted in *We Are Still Married*, 247–49. The volume also attributes "Song of the Exile [*sic*]," a.k.a. "The Lake Wobegon Anthem," to Miss Durber. Sprinkling some truths among the jests, Keillor distinguished his poetry from Durber's by saying, "I write serious poems, and unrhymed and very obscure so nobody would understand what they mean. I kind of like hers" (9 Dec. 1978; *A Prairie Home Companion Anniversary Album* [1980], side 2.

10. Lack of time during the broadcast seems not to have been the reason, since the rundown for the show indicates that no monologue was scheduled. Of course, overprogramming of other elements may well have contributed to the decision to forgo a monologue.

11. Untitled typescript, [Summer 1978], PHC Archives.

12. Untitled typescript, [Spring 1979], PHC Archives.

13. Untitled typescript, [Jan. 1977], PHC Archives.

14. Untitled typescript, [August 1978], PHC Archives.

15. A written version of this story, "The Babe," appears in *We Are Still Married*, 89–97.

16. The story was recorded on *Fall* and included in *Leaving Home*, 139–45.

17. Thorpe, "Keillor's 'Prairie Home Companion,'" 793–96.

18. Rosalie Miller recalls that he had in fact written a nine-page story, including an ending, but that he somehow "got lost in the telling of it." Miller to the author, 22 July 1989.

19. Keillor has generously donated photocopies of these texts and other materials to the O. Meredith Wilson (West Campus) Library at the University of Minnesota, Minneapolis.

20. Mark Twain, "Platform Readings (October 10, 1907)," in *Mark Twain in Eruption: Hitherto Unpublished Pages about Men and Events by Mark Twain*, ed. Bernard DeVoto, (New York: Harper & Brothers, 1922), 214.

21. Ibid., 224.

22. Ibid., 224, 217.

23. Mitchell, "Homespun Radio's Cozy 'Companion,'" 7.

24. According to Rosalie Miller of MPR, a single sentence in an incomplete, undated monologue script (probably from before 1982) has Duane Bunsen nearly ruin the car the first time he smokes. The incident recurs in a longer unfinished piece variously titled "A Corner Lot" and "Corner Lot Outside Town." A third version, in the monologue from 17 Nov. 1984, attributes the incident to Keillor himself when he is driving on an icy road with a girl. I am grateful to Miller for digging up these other versions.

25. Garrison Keillor, interview with the author, New York City, 14 Sept. 1989.

26. The script of the first installment, however, was titled "Buster, the Radio Dog."

27. "Dusty Fiddles," typescript, used 21 Dec. 1974, PHC Archives.

28. Untitled typescript, 25 Jan. 1986, PHC.

29. "A Prairie Home Companion," *Preview* [MER], 7 (July 1973): 20.

30. Bob Eliott and Ray Goulding, "Tippy, the Wonder Dog," in their *From Approximately Coast to Coast . . . It's the Bob and Ray Show* (Boston: G.K. Hall, 1984), 107. *The Adventures of Rin-Tin-Tin*, a movie success since

1922, had a television run from 15 Oct. 1954 to 28 Aug. 1959. *Lassie*, still running in syndicated reruns, appeared weekly on network television from 12 Sept. 1954 to 12 Sept. 1971 [*sic*], according to Tim Brooks and Earle Marsh, *The Complete Directory to Prime-Time Network TV Shows, 1946–Present* (New York: Ballantine Books, 1979).

31. Untitled "Buster" typescripts, 3 Jan. 1987, 18 April 1987, 14 March 1987, 19 April 1987, PHC Archives.

32. Rosalie Miller, interview with the author, 23 June 1988.

33. Untitled "Buster" typescript, 10 Jan. 1987, PHC Archives.

34. "Buster, the Radio Dog," typescript, 6 Dec. 1986, PHC Archives.

35. John G. Cawelti analyzes the appeal of popular formulas in *Adventure, Mystery, and Romance: Formula Stories as Art and Popular Culture* (Chicago: University of Chicago Press, 1976).

36. These were even more evident after Keillor's retirement from *A Prairie Home Companion*. In a take-off on the Lake Wobegon confessional tale and the show's letters from Jack and Barbara Ann Bunsen, Richard Schickel's review of *Leaving Home* took the form of a letter to "Gary" from "Your old pal, Rollie Hogebohm." See "Just a Few Minutes of Bliss," *Time*, 26 Oct. 1987, 118.

37. According to Rosalie Miller, the last Raw Bits spot aired 7 June 1986 and the last Minnesota Language Systems spot on 11 Oct. 1986. Miller to the author, 8 May 1990.

38. Rosalie Miller, interview with the author, 23 June 1988.

39. Rosalie Miller to the author, 8 May 1990.

40. Keillor, *Ten Years on the Prairie*, side 1.

41. Keillor, "Prairie Home Almanac," *Ten Years*, 20.

CHAPTER 4. *Lake Wobegon Days*: Doubling and Division

1. Garrison Keillor, *Lake Wobegon Days* (New York: Viking, 1985), 301. Subsequent references follow this first hardcover edition, and are noted parenthetically in my text.

2. In contrast to this rather faint echo of the pose so well polished on *A Prairie Home Companion*, Keillor explicitly adopts the pose of the Amateur in the preface to *Lake Wobegon Days*, noting "The radio show kept going, perhaps because I had no illusion that I was good at it" (ix).

3. Hemingson, "The Plowboy Interview," 22.

4. See, for example, Philip Roth's *Portnoy's Complaint* (1969) and *The Ghost Writer* (1979).

5. Conversations with a variety of readers and librarians in New York, Chicago, and Minneapolis–St. Paul.

6. Diane Roback, "*PW* Interviews Keillor," 139.

7. Ibid.

8. "I am sure that I never read any memorable news in a newspaper,"

Thoreau insists in "Where I Lived and What I Lived For," probably the most famous chapter in *Walden*, and certainly the most frequently anthologized: "To a philosopher all *news*, as it is called, is gossip, and they who edit and read it are old women over their tea. . . . If one may judge who rarely looks into the newspapers, nothing new does ever happen in foreign parts, a French revolution now excepted. What news! how much more important to know what that is which was never old!" See *Walden and Civil Disobedience*, ed. Owen Thomas (New York: W. W. Norton 1966), 63–64.

9. See Chester C. Anderson, ed., *Growing Up in Minnesota: Ten Writers Remember Their Childhoods* (Minneapolis: University of Minnesota Press, 1976), 4. Keillor is not among the writers anthologized here, but he might very well have known the book, which includes a second detail particularly relevant to the Matter of Minnesota: like Lake Wobegon, Minnesota is a name with etymological conflicts—in this case, between "sky blue water" and "milky water," neither of which describes the Mississippi River in Minneapolis.

10. Mark Twain, *Roughing It*, ed. Franklin R. Rogers and Paul Baender, vol. 2 of *The Works of Mark Twain* (Berkeley: University of California Press, 1972), 344–49. No evidence in *Lake Wobegon Days* establishes for certain whether Keillor has read *Roughing It* or even "My Grandfather's Old Ram," often anthologized on its own, but both Twain's and Keillor's novels make use of western folklore about men lost in a blizzard a few feet from the front door.

11. Both stories link the bear with defecation. Near the beginning of the episode in *Lake Wobegon Days*, student Weiss saw the bear, "turned away and fouled his pants and sat down"—essentially an inversion of the conclusion of Thorpe's story, which ends when the narrator, seeing the bear, tries to get up from the squat in which he's been defecating, trips over his pants, and accidentally shoots the animal.

12. Following an article on Keillor in *Twin Cities Reader*, 16–22 March 1988, a Dr. D. Louren of Sedan, Minnesota, complained to the editor, "in his *LWD* he falsifies and distorts history in the account he gives of the Alcott family. The religious bigotry evident in his account of the Alcotts is but part of his absolute lack of intellectual integrity as a writer. He is (quite simply) a sham and a humbug (like the Great Oz)." (Undated, unpaginated clipping, MPR Publicity Archives). The sense of injury conveyed here should remind us of the hostile undercurrent to tall tales, which are a narrative form of practical joke.

13. Most of the Phunny Phellows used pseudonyms. David Ross Locke (1833–1888) wrote ironically as Petroleum V. Nasby, the notoriously illiterate southern sympathizer who thereby promoted the Union cause; Charles Farrar Brown (1834–1867) wrote and performed on the lecture platform as Artemus Ward. For examples of Locke's work, see *Divers Views, Opinions,*

and Prophecies of Yoors Trooly Petroleum V. Nasby (Cincinnati: R. W. Carroll, 1866); a frequently anthologized sketch is "[Nasby] Shows Why He Should Not Be Drafted" (1862). Browne's writing includes *Artemus Ward: His Book* (New York: Carleton, 1862); a famous sketch is "Interview with President Lincoln" (1861).

14. On structures of oral narratives, see, for example, Richard Dorson, "Oral Styles of American Folk Narrators" (1960), rpt. in his *Folklore: Selected Essays* (Bloomington: Indiana University Press, 1972), 99–146, esp. 114–117.

15. For a discussion of Twain's Sufferer, see Gerber, "Mark Twain's Use of the Comic Pose," 300.

16. Keillor quotes only the opening quatrain and final couplet of Sonnet 73, omitting the following equally suggestive lines:

> In me thou seest the twilight of such day
> As after sunset fadeth in the west,
> Which by and by black night doth take away,
> Death's second self that seals up all in rest.
> In me thou seest the glowing of such fire
> That on the ashes of his youth doth lie,
> As the deathbed whereon it must expire,
> Consumed with that which it was nourished by.

Keillor chose to include the most ambiguous lines, those lending themselves to ironic interpretation in the context of his tall tale, which cannot easily encompass images of death.

17. Bordsen, "All the News from Lake Wobegon," 19.

18. A related comic stroke takes Keillor's story past graduation to his enrollment at the University of Minnesota—but in the opening chapter, instead of the usual last. Instead of progress, the structure of the book offers circularity.

19. Fedo, *The Man from Lake Wobegon*, 5.

20. Examples of historical fiction include E. L. Doctorow's *Ragtime* (1975) and Truman Capote's "nonfiction novel" *In Cold Blood* (1966). Historical and spurious facts intermingle in Philip Roth's *Great American Novel* (1973) and Thomas Pynchon's *Gravity's Rainbow* (1973). More self-consciously experimental blending of fiction and historical characters includes Joan Didion's *Democracy* (1984) and John Barth's *Sot-Weed Factor* (1960).

21. Jonathan Wilson, "Counterlives: On Autobiographical Fiction in the 1980s," *Literary Review* 31 (Summer 1988): 402. Wilson takes his title from Philip Roth's *Counterlife* (1986). Concentrating on literary figures including Roth, Didion, Norman Mailer, and Milan Kundera, Wilson does not take up the question of how an author/protagonist differs from such related manifestations as the celebrity persona. These—particularly as cultivated

by Mark Twain, Artemus Ward, and Will Rogers for their platform performances—have quite a long history in American popular culture.

22. J. D. Reed, "Home, Home on the Strange," *Time*, 2 Sept. 1985, 70.

23. Ruth Doan MacDougall, "Tender, Hilarious Reminiscences of Life in Mythical Lake Wobegon," *Christian Science Monitor*, 6 Sept. 1985, B4.

24. Barney Cooney, "Keillor, Garrison," in *Encyclopedia of American Humorists*, ed. Steven H. Gale (New York: Garland, 1988), 252.

25. J. Alan Youngren, "The News from Lake Wobegon: Public Radio's Small Town Has a Spiritual Dimension," *Christian Science Monitor*, 22 Nov. 1985, 233.

26. Keillor himself, born in 1942, stands just outside the group, usually defined as Americans born between 1946 and 1966. An interesting survey of the values of the generation is D. Quinn Mills, *Not like Our Parents: A New Look at How the Baby Boom Generation is Changing America* (New York: William Morrow, 1987).

27. A spate of articles on this subject appeared shortly after the publication of *Lake Wobegon Days*. See, for example, Pamela Reynolds, "Downward Mobility," *Boston Globe*, 28 Feb. 1986, 9–10; Vicky Cahan, "The Shrinking Nest Egg: Baby Boomers Will Have to Secure Their Own Futures or Keep Working," *Business Week*, 8 Dec. 1986, 114–16; and Arnold Kling, "Yuppies Must Work Harder Just to Keep Even," *Wall Street Journal*, 20 Feb. 1986, 27.

CHAPTER 5. *The Short Stories: In (and against) the American Grain*

1. The two catalogues of Rivertown Trading Corporation, *Wireless* and *Signals*, provide the chief direct-mail outlets for Keillor's tapes.

2. Garrison Keillor, "How Can I Be Happy When I Can't Play Hockey Like I Wanna?" *Ivory Tower* [68] (6 Feb. 1967): 26–28. Full bibliographical citations for Keillor's stories are listed in the Bibliography and will not be repeated here if they appeared in *Happy to Be Here*. In that case, references are to the widely available mass-market paperback edition and are cited parenthetically in the text. All other references are to the first publication and cited in notes.

3. "Who We Were and What We Meant by It," *New Yorker*, 16 April 1984, 44–45.

4. "On the Road, Almost," *New Yorker*, 19 Feb. 1972, 45.

5. Three years earlier, Philip Roth published an even more ambitious, black-humorous rendering of these same themes. See "On the Air," *New American Review* 10 (1970): 7–49.

6. Keillor, "A Prairie Home Companion," *Preview* [MER], 7 (Feb. 1973): 9.

7. "If Robert Frost Had an Apple . . . ," *New York Times Magazine*, 20

Nov. 1983, 80–84; "What Did We Do Wrong?" *New Yorker,* 16 Sept. 1985, 32–35. Further citations are noted parenthetically in the text.

8. Poor North Dakota gets quite a lot of teasing about its name, including comic aspersions cast by pseudo-scholar P. D. Q. Bach of the University of Southern North Dakota at Hoople.

9. Untitled typescript, n.d., PHC Archives.

10. Untitled typescripts, 3 Sept. 1983, 3 May 1986 (with holograph emendations), 8 March 1986, n.d. [1986?], PHC Archives.

11. Walter Blair, *Native American Humor,* 2d. ed. (Scranton, Pa.: Chandler, 1960), 121–24, describes the literary comedians in general; for description of the "amiable idiot," see 116. Blair and Hamlin Hill enlarge this basic description in *America's Humor: From Poor Richard to Doonesbury* (New York: Oxford University Press, 1978), 274–99. The ethical dimension of literary comedy is a major theme of David E. E. Sloane's *Mark Twain as a Literary Comedian* (Baton Rouge: Louisiana State University Press, 1979).

12. "Snack Firm Maps New Chip Push," *New Yorker,* 10 Oct. 1970, 45.

13. "Sex Tips," *New Yorker,* 14 Aug. 1971, 31. Harley Peters represents a link between Keillor's oral and written humor, as the character made his first appearance on *A Prairie Home Companion.* The humorist told a reporter for the *Minneapolis Tribune.* "I've really known Harley Peters ever since I was at KUOM," the broadcast station at the University of Minnesota, a fact that may account for the strain of college humor in the character's punningly ribald name. See Will Jones, "After Last Night," *Minneapolis Tribune,* 3 Oct. 1971, 6D.

14. John Phoenix, "Illustrated Newspapers," in his *Phoenixiana; or, Sketches and Burlesques,* 7th ed. (New York: D. Appleton, 1856), 116–25.

15. The clearest exposition of these categories is Walter Blair, "Burlesques in Ninteenth-Century American Humor," *American Literature* 2 (1930): 236–47.

16. For Keillor's insights on radio as a medium, see "Radio Is 'a Magical Country,'" *U.S. News & World Report,* 4 Nov. 1985, 75.

17. Keillor ridicules sports reporting in "Around the Horne" (1974), and business news in "Snack Firm Maps New Chip Push" (1970). He debunks political analysis in "U.S. Still on Top, Says Rest of World" (1971) and "Congress in Crisis: The Proximity Bill" (1973). The book review is ridiculed in "The Lowliest Bush a Purple Sage Would Be" (1981). "Local Family Keeps Son Happy" (1970) parodies the women's page.

18. "Radio Is 'a Magical Country,'" 75.

19. Walter Blair identifies the kinship in *Native American Humor,* 165.

20. Hemingson, "The Playboy Interview," 22. In response to a fan's question about influences on his work, Keillor wrote: "The NYer humorists:

White, Thurber, Benchley, et. al." Garrison Keillor to Jane Larue Beyt, [n.d.] 1987.

21. Roback, "*PW* Interviews Keillor," 138.

22. Blair, *Native American Humor*, 169–170.

23. Ibid., 169–171.

24. Roback, "*PW* Interviews Keillor," 138.

25. James Thurber, "You Could Look It Up" (1941), rpt. in *Short Story Masterpieces*, ed. Robert Penn Warren and Albert Erskine (New York: Dell, 1954), 508–24.

26. Thurber, "You Could Look It Up," 508.

27. Garrison Keillor, interview with the author, New York City, 14 Sept. 1989. For Roth's use of "You Could Look It Up" as a source, see Judith Yaross Lee, "To Amuse and Appall: Black Humor in American Fiction" (Ph.D. diss., University of Chicago, 1986), 103–7.

28. A telling example is that as late as 1985, although Keillor had placed forty-five tales in America's most prestigious magazines, sold more than 210,000 copies of *Happy to Be Here*, and seen *Lake Wobegon Days* reach the best-seller lists, one reviewer dismissed all the short fiction in a single dependent clause: "Keillor, who has been writing stories for the *New Yorker* for several years, had to go and publish a book." See James M. Wall, "The Secret Is Out about Lake Wobegon," *Christian Century*, 13 Nov. 1985, 1019.

29. Traub, "The Short and Tall Tales."

30. Thorpe, "Keillor's Prairie Home Companion," 794.

31. E. B. White, Preface to *A Subtreasury of American Humor*, ed. E. B. White and Katharine S. White (New York: Tudor, 1946), xxi.

CHAPTER 6. *If I Forget Thee, O Lake Wobegon: Exiles and Defectors in Leaving Home*

1. Garrison Keillor, *Leaving Home: A Collection of Lake Wobegon Stories* (New York: Viking Press, 1987), xvi, hereafter cited parenthetically in my text.

2. A Prairie Home Companion Archives contains files of Keillor's pre-performance monologue texts, usually typescripts with handwritten emendations; copies have been deposited with the O. Meredith Wilson Library at the University of Minnesota, along with other materials.

3. Mary T. Schmich, "Goodbye to St. Paul: Tired of Stardom, Garrison Keillor Makes a Fresh Start," *St. Paul Pioneer Press Dispatch*, 22 March 1987, 4G.

4. For a summary of the issues surrounding Keillor's retirement, see Rich Shefchik, "Keillor Vents Contempt of St. Paul Newspaper to Nation," *St. Paul Pioneer Press Dispatch*, 22 March 1987, 1G, 11G. Mary Schmich also discusses the issue in "Goodbye to St. Paul," which originally appeared in the *Chicago Tribune*.

5. In addition, see Deborah Howell, "Paper Not Solely to Blame for Keillor Decision," *St. Paul Pioneer Press Dispatch*, 22 March 1987, 2H, a defense of the paper by its executive editor; and Peg Meier, "Seeking Obscurity Again in Denmark," *Minneapolis Star and Tribune*, 22 March 1987, 1A, 8A. The *Star and Tribune* considered the humorist's criticisms front-page news.

6. Schickel, "Just a Few Minutes of Bliss," 118.

7. Garrison Keillor, interview with the author, 14 Sept. 1989.

8. Vincent Lawlor, "High Corn and Low Farce," *Times Literary Supplement*, 29 Jan. 1988, 102.

9. Thomas, "Weekend in Wobegon," F10.

10. Keillor had attributed his success in part to radio's equalizing power, which gives the newcomer and the star relatively equal production values, but his remarks also suggest the reductive power of television. "On radio, the audience isn't so aware of a show being broadcast across the nation because of the intimacy of the medium. Paul Harvey and the local announcer who follows him exist for the listener on the same scale. They are two human beings of the same size. One is not 30 feet high and the other 5 1/2 feet." See "Radio Is 'a Magical Country,'" 75.

11. Rosalie Miller to the author, 8 May 1990.

12. In the first performance, he said, "which amazed me" (25 April 1986).

13. The phrasing varied slightly on 26 April 1986: "She said, 'That's a lie, isn't it.' I said, 'Yes, it is.'"

14. Erving Goffman compares this "direct" announcing with the telephone call, an attempt "to simulate a conversation between two parties," and contrasts it to the imaginary "three-way" conversation of the talk show or interview, which casts the audience in the role of a mute participant in the conversation. See his *Forms of Talk* (Philadelphia: University of Pennsylvania Press, 1981), 234–35.

15. Charles U. Larson and Christine Oravec, "*A Prairie Home Companion* and the Fabrication of Community," *Critical Studies in Mass Communication* 4 (Sept. 1987): 234.

16. Walter J. Ong, S.J., "Writing Is a Technology That Restructures Thought," in *The Written Word: Literacy in Transition*, ed. Gerd Baumann (Oxford: Clarendon Press, 1986), 39.

17. Technically, legends are tales meant to be believed, in contrast to tall tales, whose fictionality is meant to be exposed. In this sense, then, Keillor has constructed a mock legend in the form of a tall tale.

18. For a discussion of news and other oral genres of fact, see Jan Vansina, *Oral Tradition as History* (Madison: University of Wisconsin Press, 1985), 3–26.

19. John A. Robinson, "Personal Narratives Reconsidered," *Journal of American Folklore* 94 (1981): 58–85, esp. 71.

20. The personal narrative is a growing area of study. In addition to Robinson, "Personal Narratives," see, for instance, Sandra K. D. Stahl, "The Personal Narrative as Folklore," *Journal of the Folklore Institute* 14 (1977): 9–30, in a special double issue devoted to the topic; Stahl, "Personal Experience Stories," *Handbook of American Folklore*, ed. Richard M. Dorson (Bloomington: Indiana University Press, 1983), 268–76; and Stahl, *Literary Folklonstics and the Personal Narrative* (Bloomington: Indiana University Press, 1989).

21. Stahl, "Personal Experience Stories," 274.

22. Garrison Keillor, interview with the author, 14 Sept. 1989.

23. See Richard Dorson, "Legends and Tall Tales" (1968), in his *Folklore: Selected Essays* (Bloomington: Indiana University Press, 1972), 159–76.

24. Rosalie Miller, conversation with the author, 22 June 1988.

25. In this context, it is worth noting that Twain's later Tom and Huck stories, including *Tom Sawyer, Detective* and the fragment "Huck Finn and Tom Sawyer among the Indians," do not sustain a coherent chronology, although one is strongly implied by remarks within the narratives.

26. For the requisites of the place legend, see Dorson, "Legends and Tall Tales," 160.

27. Ibid., 172.

28. Hoopsnakes, mythical beasts with a long history in American folklore, figure in the monologue recorded on *A Prairie Home Companion Anniversary Album* (1980). The more contemporary folktale of alligators in the sewers, also a feature of Thomas Pynchon's *V* (1963), appeared in the Fearmonger's spot on *A Prairie Home Companion*, 17 Nov. 1979.

29. Mitchell, "Homespun Radio's Cozy 'Companion.'"

BIBLIOGRAPHY

Works by Garrison Keillor

The following is a comprehensive list of Keillor's signed stories, sketches, poems, and journalism through 1989. In meetings with me, Keillor has claimed as his own all the unsigned items listed here. Articles and op-ed pieces from *Minneapolis Tribune* and the *Minneapolis Star* have been culled from the actual publications and may not represent a complete listing, since these newspapers are indexed by subject, not author. In keeping with my concentration on Keillor's work through the publication of *Leaving Home* in 1987, this bibliography lists only signed writing published after his return to the United States in September 1987. It does not include the unsigned pieces that he then began writing for the *New Yorker*'s "Talk of the Town."

College Publications

1962
"My Child Once Knew Who He Was." *Ivory Tower* 63 (30 April 1962): 6. Poem.
"At the Gallery." *Ivory Tower* 63 (28 May 1962): 14. Poem.

1963
"A Memo from Henry Boothe Luce to His Editors." *Ivory Tower* 64 (8 April 1963): 38. Poem.
"A Small Affair." *Ivory Tower* 64 (8 April 1963): 39. Poem.

"On the Freshness of Poetry: For (of and by) Reed Whittemore." *Ivory Tower* 64 (3 June 1963): 14. Poem.

"The Man Who Locked Himself In." *Ivory Tower* 65 (7 Oct. 1963): 18–19, 29, 31. Story.

"The Crucifix." *Ivory Tower* 65 (7 Oct. 1963): 27. Poem.

[Unsigned]. "The Broadside of the Tower." *Ivory Tower* 65 (4 Nov. 1963): 7. Two untitled items, beginning "I was invited last month to an organ recital" and "A week, or two ago, a friend came to my house."

1964

"The Poet, His Letters." *Ivory Tower* 65 (13 Jan. 1964): 28. Review of *The Letters of Robert Frost to Louis Untermeyer*.

"Walt and Lewis [*sic*] on the Road." *Ivory Tower* 65 (9 March 1964): 31–32. Review of Louis Simpson's *At the End of the Open Road*.

[Unsigned]. "God by Magic." *Ivory Tower* 66 (5 Oct. 1964): 6.

[Unsigned]. "The Man Who Loves His Children." *Ivory Tower* 66 (5 Oct. 1964): 6.

[Unsigned]. "A Handful of Murmurs." *Ivory Tower* 66 (5 Oct. 1964): 7.

[Unsigned]. "This is Me. Whom Are You?" *Ivory Tower* 66 (5 Oct. 1964): 8–9.

[Unsigned]. "Undercover." *Ivory Tower* 66 (5 Oct. 1964): 9.

"Means Magazine, Sneam Naieamgz." *Ivory Tower* 66 (5 Oct. 1964): 20.

[Unsigned]. "Gen. Birchbark and the Scandal." *Ivory Tower* 66 (2 Nov. 1964): 6.

[Unsigned]. "The Code." *Ivory Tower* 66 (2 Nov. 1964): 6–7.

[Unsigned]. "On Long Life." *Ivory Tower* 66 (2 Nov. 1964): 7.

[Unsigned]. "Hallowed Hall." *Ivory Tower* 66 (2 Nov. 1964): 7.

[Unsigned]. "Allons!" *Ivory Tower* 66 (2 Nov. 1964): 10–11.

[Unsigned]. "Whom are Us?" *Ivory Tower* 66 (2 Nov. 1964): 11.

"Off to the Smut War." *Ivory Tower* 66 (7 Dec. 1964): 8–10.

1965

[Unsigned]. "Build Me a Cultural Center, Baby." *Ivory Tower* 66 (11 Jan. 1965): 7.

[Unsigned]. "The Green Goose Award for Impenetrable Prose." *Ivory Tower* 66 (11 Jan. 1965): 13.

"Two On Hockey: A Conversation with Minnesota Center Doug Woog." *Ivory Tower* 66 (1 Feb. 1965): 19–23.

[Unsigned]. "How Incredible." *Ivory Tower* 66 (8 March 1965): 7.

[Unsigned]. "The Vulgarians." *Ivory Tower* 66 (8 March 1965): 8.

[Unsigned]. "A J. Liebling on Campus." *Ivory Tower* 66 (8 March 1965): 9.

[Unsigned]. "Halleluiah, He Said." *Ivory Tower* 66 (5 April 1965): 11.

[Unsigned]. "Commiestoppers' Textbook." *Ivory Tower* 66 (5 April 1965): 12.

[Unsigned]. "For Engineers." *Ivory Tower* 66 (5 April 1965): 12.

[Unsigned]. "Notes." *Ivory Tower* 66 (5 April 1965): 6. Editorial comment, beginning "Aprille, as someone has said."

"On Waking to Old Debts." *Ivory Tower* 66 (5 April 1965): 21. Won honorable mention in 1965 Academy of American Poets Contest at University of Minnesota.

"Nicodemus." *Ivory Tower* 66 (5 April 1965): 21. Won honorable mention in 1965 Academy of American Poets Contest at University of Minnesota.

[Unsigned]. "Hand Me Down My Old Escutcheon." *Ivory Tower* 66 (3 May 1965): 8–9.

[Unsigned]. "Notes." *Ivory Tower* 67 (1 Nov. 1965): 3. Poem.

[Unsigned]. "Correspondence: The Brian Cobb Incident." *Ivory Tower* 67 (1 Nov. 1965): 12–13. Epistolary fiction.

[Unsigned]. "Amo, Amare, Amenity." *Ivory Tower* 67 (6 Dec. 1965): 18.

1966

[Unsigned]. "Sunday." *Ivory Tower* 67 (10 Jan. 1966): 12.

[Unsigned]. "Said Freshman to Aged Graduate Student." *Ivory Tower* 67 (10 Jan. 1966): 14. Poem.

[Unsigned]. "At The Premier." *Ivory Tower* 67 (10 Jan. 1966): 14. Poem. Reprinted in *Ivory Tower* 67 (10 Jan. 1966): 15. Poem.

[Unsigned] "A Compendium." *Ivory Tower* 67 (10 Jan. 1966): 15. Poem.

"This Is a Poem, Good Afternoon." *Ivory Tower* 67 (2 May 1966): 20. First-prize poem.

"Frankie." *Ivory Tower* 67 (2 May 1966): 30–37. Story.

"Norman J. DeWitt, 1908–1966." *Ivory Tower* 68 (5 Dec. 1966): 27.

1967

"How Can I Be Happy When I Can't Play Hockey Like I Wanna?" *Ivory Tower* [68] (6 Feb. 1967): 26–28.

PROFESSIONAL PUBLICATIONS

1968

"Some Matters Concerning the Occupant." *Atlantic* 222 (July 1968): 54. Poem.

1970

"Local Family Keeps Son Happy." *New Yorker* 46 (19 Sept. 1970): 39. Reprinted in *G.K. the D.J.* and in *Happy to Be Here*.

"Snack Firm Maps New Chip Push." *New Yorker* 46 (10 Oct. 1970): 45.

1971

"How Are the Legs, Sam?" *New Yorker* 46 (30 Jan. 1971): 24–25. Reprinted in *Happy to Be Here.*

"The New Baseball." *New Yorker* 47 (15 May 1971): 35. Reprinted in *Happy to Be Here.*

"Sex Tips." *New Yorker* 47 (14 Aug. 1971): 31.

"Re the Tower Project." *New Yorker* 47 (28 Aug. 1971): 25. Reprinted in *Happy to Be Here.*

"Found Paradise." *New Yorker* 47 (18 Sept. 1971): 32–33. Reprinted in *G.K. the D.J.* and as "Happy to Be Here" in *Happy to Be Here.*

"U.S. Still on Top, Says Rest of World," *New Yorker* 47 (12 Oct. 1971): 35. Reprinted in *Happy to Be Here.*

1972

"On The Road, Almost." *New Yorker* 47 (19 Feb. 1972): 45. Reprinted in *G.K. the D.J.*

"Ten Stories for Mr. Richard Brautigan, and Other Stories." *New Yorker* 48 (18 March 1972): 37. Reprinted in *Happy to Be Here.*

"A Prairie Home Companion." *Preview* [MER] 6 (July 1972): [4–8].

"Bangor Man." *New Yorker* 48 (14 Oct. 1972): 39.

1973

"A Prairie Home Companion." *Preview* [MER] 7 (Feb. 1973): 9.

"The Slim Graves Show." *New Yorker* 48 (10 Feb. 1973): 33–34. Reprinted in *Happy to Be Here.*

"People's Shopper." *New Yorker* 49 (24 Feb. 1973): 37–39. Reprinted in *Happy to Be Here.*

"Congress in Crisis: The Proximity Bill." *New Yorker* 49 (7 April 1973): 36–37. Reprinted in *Happy to Be Here.*

"A Prairie Home Companion." *Preview* [MER] 7 (July 1973): 20.

"Friendly Neighbor." *New Yorker* 49 (31 Dec. 1973): 23–25 (Reprinted in *Happy to Be Here.*

1974

"Who's on the Right Track?" *Minneapolis Tribune,* 14 Jan. 1974, 8A. Op-ed piece.

"Ode to the Street System" *Minneapolis Tribune,* 20 Jan. 1974, 15A. Reprinted as "Ode to the Street System of Southwest Minneapolis" in *G.K. the D.J.*

"St. Paul Orchestra's Pure Sunshine." *Minneapolis Tribune,* 27 Jan. 1974, 11A. Op-ed piece.

"On Getting in Touch with Yourself." *Minneapolis Tribune,* 10 Feb. 1974, 15A. Op-ed piece. Reprinted in *G.K. the D.J.*

"The Delights That Will Beckon Myrtle and Harry to the City." *Minneapolis Tribune*, 24 Feb. 1974, 14A. Op-ed piece. Reprinted as "Me and Myrtle and Harry" in *G.K. the D.J.*

"Why Not 'Goodness' in Education?" *Minneapolis Tribune*, 14 April 1974, 13A. Op-ed piece. Reprinted as "One of the Most Outstanding Columns I Have Ever Written about Education in My Own Life" in *G.K. the D.J.*

"Onward and Upward with the Arts: At the Opry." *New Yorker* 50 (6 May 1974): 46–70. Non-fiction.

"The Sir Oracles Who Are Unable to Speak." *Minneapolis Tribune*, 19 May 1974, 14A. Op-ed piece.

"Getting Mileage Out of Metric System." *Minneapolis Tribune*, 23 June 1974, 13A. Op-ed piece. Reprinted as "Thinking Metric" in *G.K. the D.J.*

"Meeting the President in a Dream." *Minneapolis Tribune*, 28 June 1974, 6A, Op-ed piece. Reprinted as "Testimony" in *G.K. the D.J.*

"Wearing Well in a Cornerstone." *Minneapolis Tribune*, 4 Aug. 1974, 13A. Op-ed piece. Reprinted as "Uncle Don's Grounder" in *G.K. the D.J.*

"New Experience ($) Artists Must Seek." *Minneapolis Tribune*, 15 Sept. 1974, 17A. Op-ed piece. Reprinted as "Pecunia Pro Arte" in *G.K. the D.J.*

"Around the Horne." *New Yorker* 50 (30 Sept. 1974): 33–34. Reprinted in *Happy to Be Here*.

"Saving a Vanishing Species." *Minneapolis Tribune*, 6 Oct. 1974, 11A. Op-ed piece. Reprinted as "The Vanishing Republican" in *G.K. the D.J.*

"Plainfolks (a Handbook of Survival Skills, Folkways, Practical Wisdom, and Useful Information, Compiled from Original Sources and Reflecting 'The Way It Used to Be')." *New Yorker* 50 (4 Nov. 1974): 44–46.

"Ragged Streets are Nice." *Minneapolis Tribune*, 1 Dec. 1974, 19A. Op-ed piece. Reprinted as "We Shall Not be Curbed" in *G.K. the D.J.*

"A City Letter: What Do You Do? How Much Do You Earn?" *Preview* [MPR] 8 (Dec. 1974): 10, 12. Op-ed piece. Reprinted as "What Do You Do? (How Much Do You Earn?)" in *G.K. the D.J.*

"Neither the Best nor the Brightest." *Minneapolis Tribune*, 15 Dec. 1974. Letter to the editor. Reprinted in *G.K. the D.J.*

1975

"Oya Life These Days." *New Yorker* 50 (17 Feb. 1975): 31–32. Reprinted in *Happy to Be Here*.

"How It Was in America a Week Ago Tuesday." *New Yorker* 51 (10 March 1975): 32–35. Reprinted in *Happy to Be Here*.

"Your Wedding and You." *New Yorker* 51 (16 June 1975): 28–30. Reprinted in *Happy to Be Here*.

"My North Dakota Railroad Days." *New Yorker* 51 (1 Dec. 1975): 46–51. Reprinted in *G.K. the D.J.*

1976

"42nd in Hot Sauce?" *Minneapolis Tribune,* 8 Feb. 1976: 12A. Reprinted in *G.K. the D.J.*

"WLT (the Edgar Era)." *New Yorker* 52 (12 April 1976): 32–35. Reprinted in *Happy to Be Here.*

"Drowning 1954." *New Yorker* 52 (16 Aug. 1976): 27–28. Reprinted in *G.K. the D.J.*

1977

G.K. the D.J. St. Paul: Minnesota Public Radio, 1977.

"Don: The True Story of a Young Person." *New Yorker* 53 (30 May 1977): 38–43. Reprinted in *Happy to Be Here.* Reprinted as *Don: The True Story of A Young Person.* Minneapolis: Redpath Press, 1987.

"He Digests the Star and Finds It's a Meat-and-Potatoes Meal." *Minneapolis Star,* 4 Aug. 1977, 1C–2C.

1979

The Selected Verse of Margaret Haskins Durber. Lake Wobegon, MN: Jack's Press, © 1979 [St. Paul]: Minnesota Public Radio. Includes "The Ballad of the Finn Who Didn't Like Saunas."

"My Son, the Delivery Entrepreneur." *Minneapolis Star,* 25 Jan. 1979, A6.

"Midnight Meeting about Secret Meetings." *Minneapolis Star,* 13 March 1979, A4.

"If Begonias Bloom, Can Baseball Be Far Behind?" *Minneapolis Tribune,* 1 April 1979, 17A.

"Jack Schmidt, Arts Administrator." *New Yorker* 55 (30 April 1979): 36–40. Reprinted in *Happy to Be Here.*

"Be Careful," *New Yorker* 55 (6 Aug. 1979): 28–29. Reprinted in *Happy to Be Here.*

"Attitude." *New Yorker* 55 (27 Aug. 1979): 34–35. Reprinted in *Happy to Be Here.*

1980

"Nana Hami Ba Reba." *New Yorker* 55 (4 Feb. 1980): 30–31. Reprinted in *Happy to Be Here.*

"The Finn Who Would Not Take a Sauna." *MPLS-St. Paul* 8 (Dec. 1980): 102. Poem. Reprinted from *The Selected Verse of Margaret Haskins Durber* (1979). Reprinted in *We Are Still Married.*

1981

Happy to Be Here. New York: Atheneum, 1981.

"The Lowliest Bush a Purple Sage Would Be." First published in *Happy to Be Here.*

"Shy Rights: Why Not Pretty Soon?" First published in *Happy to Be Here.*

"Jack Schmidt on the Burning Sands." *Twin Cities* 4 (Jan. 1981): 43–47, 84–89. Reprinted in *Happy to Be Here*, rev. ed.

". . . To the State of Radio-Free Wobegon." *Los Angeles Times*, 12 April 1981, V5. Op-ed piece.

"The Place to Ease the Blues." *MPLS-St. Paul* 9 (April 1981): 144.

"Your Transit Commission." *Atlantic* 247 (May 1981): 18–19. Reprinted in *Happy to Be Here*, rev. ed.

"Mission to Mandala." *New Yorker* 57 (25 May 1981): 38–40. Reprinted in *Happy to Be Here*, rev. ed.

"The Tip-Top Club." *Atlantic* 248 (Aug. 1981): 50–54. Reprinted in *Happy to Be Here*, rev. ed.

"The New Washington: An Inside Story." *New Yorker* 57 (26 Oct. 1981): 48–51. Reprinted in *Happy to Be Here*, rev. ed.

1982

"My Stepmother, Myself." *Atlantic* 249 (March 1982): 77–79. Reprinted in *Happy to Be Here*, rev. ed.

"The Boy Who Couldn't Have TV." *TV Guide*, 15 May 1982, 39–42.

"After a Fall." *New Yorker* 58 (21 June 1982): 36–39. Reprinted in *Happy to Be Here*, rev. ed., and in *We Are Still Married*.

1983

Happy to Be Here. Revised and enlarged ed. New York: Penguin Books, 1983.

"Maybe You Can Too." *New Yorker* 59 (21 Feb. 1983): 40-41. Reprinted in *We Are Still Married*.

"Outrageous Opinion: Eating Without Guilt." *Cosmopolitan* 194 (June 1983): 16. Reprinted as "Down with Mealtime Guilt." *Reader's Digest* [Canadian] 124 (June 1984): 95–96.

"The Current Crisis in Remorse." *New Yorker* 59 (11 July 1983): 36–37. Reprinted in *We Are Still Married*.

"If Robert Frost Had an Apple . . ." *New York Times Magazine*, 20 Nov. 1983, 80–84.

1984

Ten Years: The Official Souvenir Anniversary Program for "A Prairie Home Companion." St. Paul: Minnesota Public Radio, 1984.

"A Little Help." *Atlantic* 253 (Jan. 1984): 83–84. Reprinted in *We Are Still Married*.

"Who We Were and What We Meant by It." *New Yorker* 60 (16 April 1984): 44–45. Reprinted in *We Are Still Married*.

"We Are Still Married." *New Yorker* 60 (14 May 1984): 42–43. Reprinted in *We Are Still Married*.

"Country Golf." *New Yorker* 60 (30 July 1984): 37–46. Nonfiction. Reprinted in *We Are Still Married*.

"End of the Trail." *New Yorker* 60 (17 Sept. 1984): 45. Reprinted in *We Are Still Married.*

1985

Lake Wobegon Days. New York: Viking, 1985.

Foreword to *The New! Improved! Bob & Ray Book.* By Bob Elliott and Ray Goulding. New York: G. P. Putnam's Sons, 1985: 9–11.

"The People v. Jim." *New Yorker* 61 (8 July 1985): 21. Reprinted as The People vs. Jim" in *We Are Still Married.*

"Lake Wobegon Days." *Atlantic* 256 (Aug. 1985): 27–34. Prepublication excerpt.

"What Did We Do Wrong?" *New Yorker* 61 (16 Sept. 1985): 32–35. Reprinted in *We Are Still Married.*

"End of An Era." *New Yorker* 61 (28 Oct. 1985): 31–32. Reprinted in *We Are Still Married.*

"Get Ready for Monday Night Mudwrestling." *TV Guide* 32 (7 Dec. 1985): 4–6.

"A Lake Wobegon Christmas—Such Were the Joys." *New York Times Book Review,* 8 Dec. 1985, 7. Postpublication excerpt from *Lake Wobegon Days.*

1986

"Whose Child Is This?" *U.S. Catholic* 51 (Feb. 1986): 27–31. Post-publication excerpt from *Lake Wobegon Days.*

"Lust on Wheels." *Esquire* 106 (July 1986): 59–61.

"Voices of Liberty." *Newsweek* 108 (14 July 1986): 33.

"Lake Wobegon Days." *Reader's Digest* 129 (Sept. 1986): 81–90, 192–224. Condensation.

"Lake Wobegon Days." *Ladies Home Journal* 103 (Dec. 1986): 74, 166. Postpublication excerpt.

"Lake Wobegon Games." *Sports Illustrated* 65 (22 Dec. 1986): 124–34. Based on monologue from 13 July 1985. Recorded as "Babe Ruth Visits Lake Wobegon" on *Gospel Birds.* Reprinted as "The Babe" in *We Are Still Married.*

1987

Leaving Home: A Collection of Lake Wobegon Stories. New York: Viking, 1987.

"Leaving Home: Lake Wobegon Stories." *Atlantic* 260 (Sept. 1987): 47–53. "The Killer," "Chicken," and "A Trip to Grand Rapids." Pre-publication excerpt from *Leaving Home.*

"How to Write a Personal Letter." Advertisement for International Paper Company. Reprinted in *Reader's Digest* 131 (Nov. 1987: 129–31, in

Reader's Digest [Canadian] 132 (Jan. 1988): 101ff, and as "How to Write a Letter" in *We Are Still Married.*

"The Perils of Success: Selected Letters from Jack." In *Farewell to "A Prairie Home Companion,"* edited by Daniel Kelley. Supplement to *Minnesota Monthly* 21 (June 1987): 100–104. Also in Collector's Edition, issued separately. St. Paul: Minnesota Public Radio, 1987: 100-104. Revised and reprinted in *We Are Still Married.*

[Unsigned]. "Home Team." "Talk of the Town," *New Yorker* 63 (2 Nov. 1987): 34–37. Reprinted in *We Are Still Married.*

"Hollywood in the Fifties." *New Yorker* 63 (16 Nov. 1987): 40–41. Reprinted in *We Are Still Married.*

"Your Book Saved My Life, Mister," *New Yorker* 63 (28 Dec. 1987): 40–41. Reprinted in *We Are Still Married.*

1988

"Three New Twins Join Club in Spring." *New Yorker* 64 (22 Feb. 1988): 32–33.

"Meeting Famous People." *New Yorker* 64 (18 April 1988): 34–36. Reprinted in *We Are Still Married.*

"Laying [sic] on Our Backs Looking Up at the Stars." *Newsweek* 112 (4 July 1988): 30–33. Reprinted in *We Are Still Married.*

"Everything's Up-to-Date in South Roxy." *New York Times Magazine*, 14 Aug. 1988, 18–20. Reprinted as "Lifestyle" in *We Are Still Married.*

"Cherished Moments." *Life* 11 n.s. (Fall 1988): 153–56.

"My Life in Prison." *Atlantic* 262 (Nov. 1988): 68–71. Reprinted in *We Are Still Married.*

"He Didn't Go to Canada." *New Yorker* 64 (7 Nov. 1988): 34–35. Reprinted in *We Are Still Married.*

"My Name is Yon Yonson: A New York Story." *New York Times Magazine*, 18 Dec. 1988, 77–78, 96–98. Reprinted as "Yon" in *We Are Still Married.*

1989

"*We Are Still Married: Stories & Letters*. New York: Viking, 1989.

"Glasnost." *Gettysburg Review* 2 (Winter 1989): 89–91. Reprinted in *We Are Still Married.*

"When You Kick a Liberal: A Post-Election Parable." *Harper's* 278 (Jan. 1989): 72–75. Prepublication excerpt, which appeared as "A Liberal Reaches for Her Whip" in *We Are Still Married.*

"The Heart of the Matter." *New York Times*, 14 March 1989, A23.

"Toasting the Flag." *New York Times*, 2 July 1989, E13.

Review of *Fred Allen: His Life and Wit* by Robert Taylor. *New York Times Book Review*, 9 July 1989, 7.

"The Chuck Show." *New Yorker* 65 (24 July 1989): 26–29.

"How the Savings and Loans Were Saved." *New Yorker* 65 (16 Oct. 1989): 42.
"A Christmas Story." *New Yorker* 65 (25 Dec. 1989): 40–42.

1990
"Lonesome Shorty." *New Yorker* 66 (5 March 1900): 36–37.
"Little House in the Big City: Smiling Through." *New York Times Magazine*, Part 2, 8 April 1990, 6–8.

RECORDINGS

A Prairie Home Album. Minnesota Educational Radio, [1972?].
A Prairie Home Companion Anniversary Album. Minnesota Public Radio, 1980. 2 records or audio cassettes. PHC 21012.
The Family Radio. Minnesota Public Radio, 1982. 2 records or audio cassettes. PHC 21022.
Tourists. Minnesota Public Radio, 1983. Record or audio cassette. PHC 808.
News from Lake Wobegon. Minnesota Public Radio, 1983. Four audio cassettes: *Spring*, PHC 909; *Summer*, PHC 910; *Fall*, PHC 911; *Winter*, PHC 912. Reissued by Minnesota Public Radio, 1989. Four compact discs. PHC 15376.
Ten Years on the Prairie: "A Prairie Home Companion" 10th Anniversary. Minnesota Public Radio, 1984. Two audio cassettes. PHC 1212C.
Gospel Birds and Other Stories of Lake Wobegon. Minnesota Public Radio, 1985. Two audio cassettes. PHC 1213.
Lake Wobegon Days. Minnesota Public Radio, 1986. Four audio cassettes. ISBN 0-942100-08-0.
A Prairie Home Companion: The Final Performance. Minnesota Public Radio, 1987. Two audio cassettes. ISBN 0-942110-16-1
A Prairie Home Companion: The Last Show. Disney Home Video, 1987. Video cassette. VHS and Beta.
Ain't That Good News. Minnesota Public Radio, 1987 [distributed by Polygram Records]. Audio cassette. PHC 21194.
A Prairie Home Companion: The 2nd Annual Farewell Performance. Minnesota Public Radio, 1988. Two audio cassettes. PHC 21272.
A Prairie Home Companion: The 2nd Annual Farewell Performance Minnesota Public Radio, 1988. Video cassette. VHS and Beta. PHC 55041.
Prairie Home Comedy: Minnesota Public Radio, 1988. Two audio cassettes. PHC 21302.
A Prairie Home Companion: The 3rd Annual Farewell Performance. Minnesota Public Radio, 1989. Two audio cassettes. PHC 14989.
Lake Wobegon Loyalty Days. Minnesota Public Radio, 1989. Audio cassette. MPR 15065.
Lake Wobegon Loyalty Days. Minnesota Public Radio, 1989. Compact disc.

MPR 15066. Reissued by Virgin Classics, 1989. Compact disc. VC7-92209-2.

More News from Lake Wobegon. Minnesota Public Radio, 1989. Four audio cassettes. PHC 14988.

More News from Lake Wobegon. Minnesota Public Radio, 1989. Four compact discs. PHC 15376.

Lake Wobegon Loyalty Days. Minnesota Public Radio, 1990. Video cassette. VHS. MPR 16000.

INTERVIEWS

Andrews, Terry. "Five Writers: 'They Bring Life to What We in Minnesota Have and Know and Care About.'" *MPLS-St. Paul* 9 (Aug. 1981): 73.

Blount, Roy, Jr. "A Conversation with Garrison Keillor." In *Farewell to "A Prairie Home Companion."* Collector's Edition. St. Paul: Minnesota Public Radio, 1987: 13–24. The volume was published simultaneously as a supplement to *Minnesota Monthly* 21 (June 1987).

Healey, Barth. "Sex and Violence in Wobegon." *New York Times Book Review,* 25 Aug. 1985, 15.

Hemingson, Peter. "The Plowboy Interview: Garrison Keillor, the Voice of Lake Wobegon." *Mother Earth News,* no. 93 (May–June 1985): 17–20, 22.

"Radio Is 'a Magical Country,'" *U.S. News & World Report* 99 (4 Nov. 1985): 75.

Roback, Diane. "*PW* Interviews Garrison Keillor." *Publishers Weekly* 228 (13 Sept. 1985): 138–39.

Schumacher, Michael. "Sharing the Laughter with Garrison Keillor." *Writer's Digest* 66 (Jan. 1986): 32–35.

Walker, Michael. "The Met Grill." *Metropolitan Home,* 17 (Nov. 1985): 26–31.

Selected Works about Garrison Keillor

"ABA to Underwrite Keillor Radio Series." *Publishers Weekly* 234 (23 Dec. 1988): 17.

Anania, Michael. "Small-town Swan Song." *Chicago* 34 (Sept. 1985): 118–24.

Anthony, Michael, "Lake Wobegon Revisited: Garrison Keillor's Greatest Hits." *Minneapolis Tribune,* 30 Jan. 1981, 2C.

Barol, Bill. "A Shy Person Says So Long: The Last Waltz for "A Prairie Home Companion.'" *Newsweek* 109 (15 June 1987): 65–66.

———. "What Now, Wobegon? Garrison Keillor Ponders the Past, Present, and Future of His Little Town." *Newsweek* 110 (5 Oct. 1987): 82–83.

Beyette, Beverly. "Fisher for Meaning in Lake Wobegon Waters: Garrison

Keillor Reflects on the Success of His Semi-Autobiographical Best Seller." *Los Angeles Times*, 18 Sept. 1985, V1.

Black, David. "Live from Wobegon." *Rolling Stone*, 23 July 1981, 8–13.

Blau, Eleanor. "TV Notes: Keillor's Goodbyes." *New York Times*, 23 May 1986, C16.

"Bookends." *Time* 133 (15 May 1989): 81. Review of *We Are Still Married*.

Bordsen, John. "All the News from Lake Wobegon." *Saturday Review* 9 (May–June 1983): 12–13, 18–19.

Bowermaster, Jon. "Fresh Voices Hope to Be Far from Wobegon." *New York Times*, 13 Dec. 1987, H43, 45.

Bromberg, Craig. "Live from Brooklyn, It's . . . Garrison Keillor." *Wall Street Journal*, 22 March 1990, A16.

Brooke, Jill. "His 'Home' Is Where Hearts Are." *New York Post*, 13 Nov. 1989, 67.

Bunce, Alan. "From a Town 'That Time Forgot,' Master Folklorist Keillor." *Christian Science Monitor* 77 (6 Sept. 1985): 1.

Christon, Lawrence. "Laugh Meter: The Ten Funniest Performers." *Los Angeles Times*, 3 Oct. 1982, Calendar section, 3–4.

"Coffee and Minnows." *Economist* 312 (16 Sept. 1989): 96.

Cooney, Barney. "Keillor, Garrison." In *Encyclopedia of American Humorists*, edited by Steven H. Gale. New York: Garland, 1988: 251–53.

Farewell to "A Prairie Home Companion." Collector's Edition. St. Paul: Minnesota Public Radio, 1987. Simultaneously published as a supplement to *Minnesota Monthly* 21 (June 1987).

Fedo, Michael. *The Man from Lake Wobegon.* New York: St. Martin's Press, 1987.

"Fifth Estater: Garrison Keillor, an American Home Companion." *Broadcasting* 15 (Dec. 1986): 127.

Galant, Debbie. "A Lost 'Companion.'" *New York* 20 (15 June 1987): 25.

Geng, Veronica. "Idylls of Minnesota." *New York Times Book Review*, 25 Aug. 1985, 15.

Gray, Spaulding. "Plenty Wholesome and a Little Perverse." *New York Times Book Review*, 4 Oct. 1987, 9.

Harrington, Richard. "Whimsical Satirical Miracle," *Washington Post*, 20 March 1981, K1, 2.

Heim, David. "Garrison Keillor and Culture Protestantism." *Christian Century* 104 (3 June 1987): 517–19.

———. "Keillor Cultivates a Natural Piety." *Christian Century* 105 (3 Feb. 1988): 126–29. Review of *Leaving Home*.

Henderson, Bill. Review of *We Are Still Married. New York Times Book Review*, 9 April 1989, 13.

Hertzberg, Hendrik. "Cross Talk." *New Republic* 199 (22 Aug. 1988): 42.

"A Home Companion Bids Farewell." *Broadcasting* 112 (22 June 1987): 39–40.

Howell, Deborah. "Paper Not Solely to Blame for Keillor Decision." *St. Paul Pioneer Press Dispatch*, 22 March 1987, 2H.

Ingrassia, Lawrence. "Live from St. Paul, Here's 'A Prairie Home Companion.'" *Wall Street Journal*, 21 Jan. 1981, 1, 14. Reprinted in newspapers nationwide.

Johnson, Dirk. "With Singing, Satire, and Sentiment, Lake Wobegon Fades." *New York Times*, 14 June 1987, 11.

Jones, Will. "After Last Night." *Minneapolis Tribune*, 3 Oct. 1971, 6D; 9 Oct. 1971, 10A; 31 Oct. 1971, 4D.

Judge, Paul. "Portrait: Garrison Keillor, Making Radio Waves from the Heartland." *Life* 5 n.s. (May 1982): 27–32.

Kaplan, Steven. "Unauthorized Keillor Bio Is No Hatchet Job, Says Author." *MPLS-St. Paul* 15 (July 1987): 13.

"Keillor, Garrison." *Current Biography*, Aug. 1985, 26–29.

Kilpatrick, James J. "Garrison Keillor's Tricks." *Washington Post*, 6 Feb. 1986, A17.

Kling, William. "Farewell to Lake Wobegon." *U.S. News & World Report* 102 (22 June 1987): 10.

Klose, Kevin. "The Keillor Instinct for the Truer-than-True: The Creator of 'A Prairie Home Companion' & His Very Real Town of Lake Wobegon." *Washington Post*, 15 Sept. 1985, K1.

Korn, Eric. Review of *We Are Still Married*. *Times Literary Supplement*, 3 Nov. 1989, 1217.

Kristol, E. "Garrison Keillor's Faux Peas." *American Spectator* 21 (Jan. 1988): 31–32.

"Lake Wobegon and Other Literary Landscapes." *Life*, 9 n.s. (Jan. 1986): 116–20. Photographs.

"Lake Wobegon's Garrison Keillor Finds a Love That Time Forgot and the Decades Can't Improve." *People Weekly*, 24 (25 Nov. 1985): 62.

Langway, L., and S. Monroe. "Meeting the Gang at Lake Wobegon." *Newsweek* 98 (7 Dec. 1981): 106.

Larson, Charles U., and Christine Oravec. "*A Prairie Home Companion* and the Fabrication of Community." *Critical Studies in Mass Communication* 4 (Sept. 1987): 221–44.

Lawlor, Vincent. "High Corn and Low Farce." *Times Literary Supplement*, 29 Jan. 1988, 102.

Letofsky, Irv. "A Prairie Cult Companion: Is Garrison Keillor as Good as Sweet Corn?" *Los Angeles Times*, 28 July 1985, C2.

Lurie, Allison. "The Frog Prince." *New York Review of Books* 35 (24 Nov. 1988): 33–34.

MacDougall, Ruth Doan. "Tender, Hilarious Reminiscences of Life in Mythical Lake Wobegon." *Christian Science Monitor*, 6 Sept. 1985, B4.

McDowell, Edwin. "Garrison Keillor's New Radio Show." *New York Times*, 11 Oct. 1989, C22.

McGrath, Anne. "Eye on Publishing: Lake Wobegon Success Story." *Wilson Library Bulletin* 60 (Nov. 1985): 32–33.

Martin, Douglas. "From Lake Wobegon to the Hudson." *New York Times*, 4 Dec. 1987, B1, 4.

Mayer, Catherine. "Lincoln, Mickey Mouse, and the Midwest." *Economist* 299 (21 June 1986): 93–94.

Meier, Peg. "Seeking Obscurity Again in Denmark." *Minneapolis Star and Tribune*, 22 March 1987, 1A, 8A.

Miller, Bryan. "Minnesota Memories of Smelts and Corn." *New York Times*, 2 March 1988, 20.

Miller, William Lee. "Sola Gratia in Lake Wobegon." *Christian Century*, 104 (3 June 1987): 526–28.

Mitchell, Sean. "Homespun Radio's Cozy 'Companion.'" *Dallas Times Herald*, 22 Feb. 1981, 7.

Mohr, Howard. "Stories Never Before Told about Garrison Keillor." *MPLS-St. Paul* 12 (July 1984): 168.

O'Neill, David, and Kathleen McLean. "Twenty Years of MPR: Two Decades at a Glance." *Minnesota Monthly* 21 (Jan. 1987): 58–60.

"People." *Time*, 2 March 1987, 42–43.

Platt, Adam. "An Interview with Garrison Keillor." *Twin Cities Reader*, 16–22. March 1988, 1, 10. Not in interview format.

Reed, J. D. "Home, Home on the Strange." *Time* 126 (2 Sept. 1985): 70.

"Return of an Above-Average Broadcaster." *U.S. News & World Report* 106 (29 May 1989): 12.

Roback, Diane. "Leaving the Shores of Lake Wobegon." *Publishers Weekly* 232 (21 Aug. 1987): 34–35.

Rothstein, Mervyn. "Keillor Recalls Town 'Time Forgot.'" *New York Times*, 20 Aug. 1985, 25.

Sanoff, Alvin P. "New and Old Voices Put the Snap Back into Radio." *U.S. News & World Report* 99 (4 Nov. 1985): 74.

Schickel, Richard. "Just a Few Minutes of Bliss." *Time* 130 (26 Oct. 1987): 118. Review of *Leaving Home*.

Schmich, Mary T. "Goodbye to St. Paul: Tired of Stardom, Garrison Keillor Makes a Fresh Start." *St. Paul Pioneer Press Dispatch*, 22 March 1987, 1G, 4G, 11G.

Scholl, Peter A. "Garrison Keillor." *Dictionary of Literary Biography, 1987 Yearbook*, edited by J. M. Brook. Detroit: Gale Research, 1988: 326–38.

———. "Garrison Keillor and the News from Lake Wobegon." *Studies in American Humor*, 4 n.s. (Winter 1985–86): 217–228.

Scotto, Barbara. Review of *Leaving Home. Wilson Library Bulletin* 62 (Dec. 1987): 83–84.

Sexton, David. "When Here is Nowhere." *Times Literary Suppplement*, 7 March 1986, 257.

Shefchik, Rick. "Keillor Vents Contempt of St. Paul Newspaper to Nation." *St. Paul Pioneer Press Dispatch*, 22 March 1987, 1G, 11G.

Shepard, Richard R. Review of *Leaving Home. New York Times*, 21 Oct. 1987, C25.

Singer, Mark. "Welcome to Lake Wobegon, the Town That Time Forgot." *Blair & Ketchum's Country Journal* 9 (Jan. 1982): 49–55.

Skow, John. "Leaving Lake Wobegon: Garrison Keillor Closes Down a Unique Radio Show." *Time* 129 (29 June 1987): 64–65.

———. "Let's Hear It for Lake Wobegon!" *Reader's Digest* 128 (Feb. 1986): 67–71.

———. "Lonesome Whistle Blowing." *Time* 126 (4 Nov. 1985): 68–73.

———. "Wild Seed in the Big Apple: Garrison Keillor Returns with a New York–Based Radio Show." *Time* 134 (11 Dec. 1989): 109.

Stuttaford, Genevieve. Review of *We Are Still Married. Publishers Weekly* 235 (24 Feb. 1989): 211.

Sutin, Lawrence. "How Lake Wobegon Has Swept America." *Sky*, May 1986, 11–19.

———. "Lake Wobegon: The Little Town That Time Forgot." *Saturday Evening Post* 258 (Sept. 1986): 42–45.

Thomas, Jack. "Weekend in Wobegon." *Boston Globe*, 9 March 1987, F8, 10.

Thorpe, Doug. "Garrison Keillor's 'Prairie Home Companion': Gospel of the Airwaves." *Christian Century* 99 (21–28 July 1982): 793–96.

Traub, James. "The Short and Tall Tales of Garrison Keillor." *Esquire* 97 (May 1982): 108–17.

Trescott, Jacqueline. "A Prairie House Companion: Garrison Keillor, on the Hill for Arts Talk and Rolled-up Chicken." *Washington Post*, 19 July 1985, B1.

Wall, James M. "The Secret Is Out about Lake Wobegon." *Christian Century* 102 (13 Nov. 1985): 1019–20.

Welshacher, Anne. "Newsworthies: Garrison Keillor." *Mother Earth News*, no. 77 (Sept.–Oct. 1982): 32.

"What's Up at Lake Wobegon." *Time* 118 (9 Nov. 1981): 95.

"Where Art Thou, Perceptive Creativity?" *Ivory Tower* [University of Minnesota] 67 (7 Feb. 1966): 12–13.

Youngren, J. Alan. "The News from Lake Wobegon: Public Radio's Small Town Has a Spiritual Dimension." *Christianity Today* 29 (22 Nov. 1985): 33–36.

Index

Abbreviations used:
APHC for *A Prairie Home Companion*
LWD for *Lake Wobegon Days*
LH for *Leaving Home*

graphical joke, 109; biography of, by Michael Fedo, 25; birth, 3; career since 1987, 7, 22, 23; childhood, 3, 4; college years, 3–5; college writing, 5–7, 26; comic poses used (See Amateur, Sufferer, Exile, Witness, Cracker-Barrel Philosopher/Preacher, Announcer.); compared to Mark Twain, 3, 10, 11, 22, 115–16, 119, 146; departure from St. Paul, 150; editor of *Ivory Tower*, 6; family background, 3; "Garrison" chosen, 4; marriage to Ulla Skaerved, 152; move to Denmark, 2, 25, 26, 149; name, 3; oral humor, compared to written, 119, 199n13; as performer, 9, 10, 179; as poet, 3, 5, 7, 8, 21, 24, 31; pseudonyms, 4; radio career, early, 3, 4, 5, 7, 44, 198n13; religious background, 3, 61, 62, 63; retirement from *The Morning Program*, 130; retirement from *APHC*, 1, 2, 15, 27, 88, 142, 151, 152; theory of fiction, 83, 157

Kigin, Thomas J., xii

"The Killer," 161, 162

Kling, William, 29, 30, 32, 34

KSJN, 12, 29, 31, 32, 33, 45, 190n28

KSJR, 3, 13, 29

KUOM, 3, 7, 44, 198n13

Lake Wobegon anthem. *See* "The Song of the Exiles"

Lake Wobegon, Minn.: bumper stickers, 19; characteristics of, 2, 30, 32, 35–36, 40, 61–62, 97, 149–50, 155–56; compared to Utopia, Tex., 17; described, 93; imaginary town, 11, 19, 20; Keillor as chronicler of, 8–9; Keillor's attitude toward, 21–22, 67–68, 95, 105–09, 117, 146, 149–50, 164; landscape of, 30, 36, 42, 103, 149, 154–55; as legend, 171–74; local customs of, 69; mock history of (See LWD.); as "my hometown," 14, 20, 29, 39, 66, 70, 76, 78, 149, 162, 171; motto, 98–99; name of, 30, 31, 99; origin, 29; pseudohistory of, 97–98; as saga, 19, 35, 36, 68; as trademark image, 147

Lake Wobegon Days, 91–117, 153; compared to *Tom Sawyer*, 92, 106–07, 120; compared to *LH*, 150, 160, 162, 175; compared to oral tales, 101–02, 160,

163, 164; compared to *Roughing It*, 115–16; conflict with radio work, 33; deconstructionist point of view in, 96, 97; evaluation of, 24, 115–16, 160, 162, 164, 175; footnotes in, 95–96; Keillor's popularity and, 90; Matter of Minnesota in, 92, 96, 117; mock autobiography in, 94, 103–04, 106, 107–10; mock history in, 100, 107, 136, 160, 196n12; narration in, 103, 106–15, 162; readers of, 25, 116–17; structure of, 94–95, 98, 101–04, 197n18; tall tale in (See tall tales.); visual humor in, 92–94, 160

Lake Wobegon stories: appeal of, 2, 89, 160, 170–75; artistically limiting for Keillor, 164, 179; autobiographical details in, 81–83, 150–54; comparison, written and oral, 96, 164–73, 120, 123, 125, 131, 146–47, 160, 162–64, 173, 178; continuity among, 172, 174; food in, 155–56; first-person narration in, 75–77, 162; genres of, 76, 171, 173–75; Keillor's voice in, 79, 102, 159–60; as legend, 172–75; as local color humor, 39, 42–43; Minnesota in (See Matter of Minnesota.);

Monologues: artfulness of, 78–81, 164–70; comparison, Keillor's to stand-up comic's, 34–35, 44–45, 75; duration, 14; as feature of *APHC*, 14, 28, 34, 70, 87 (See also "News from Lake Wobegon"; Bunsen, Barbara Ann); on first live broadcast, 28, 44–46, 50–52; genres of, 175; hallmarks of, 13–24; history of, 12–14, 28–31, 35–36, 42–43, 52, 56, 62, 64–65, 69–77, 87, 134; influence on *LWD*, 96, 102 (See also *LWD*.); performance of (See oral storytelling.); published, 66, 67–68, 163; relation to *LH*, 148–49 (See also *LH*.); relations among, 174; stages in development of, 68; structure of, 102, 171, 172; texts of, 15, 77, 149, 164; tropes of, 2, 21, 28–29, 34, 68, 70–71, 149, 155;

mythic dimension of, 3, 21, 48, 123, 154–55; narration of, 5, 7, 9, 12–13, 64–65, 79–80, 101–02 (See also Announcer, Cracker-Barrel Philosopher, Exile, Preacher, Witness, *LWD*.); popularity of, 2, 69, 118, 120, 140, 146, 163; religious elements in 6, 62–64, 66–67, 157; sentimentality in, 65–68, 87, 117, 125, 134, 140 (*See also* nostalgia.); tall tales in, 11–12, 36, 19, 80–81, 94, 99–100, 107–08

Lakota, N. D., 127, 128

Larson, Judy, 28, 33, 58, 85

Laugh-In, 47, 69

Lear, Norman, 47–48

Leaving Home, 148–79; autobiographical material in, 150–54; food in, 155–56, 158; monologues' influence on, 160–64; publication of, 2, 15, 26; readers of, 25; revisions of, 148–49, 164, 167; sentimentality in, 158–60; significance in Keillor's career, 21, 118, 179; structure of, 171, 174; themes, 149–57

Legends: defined, 171–72; Lake Wobegon stories as, 172–74; compared to tall tales, 202n17

Lehrer, Tom, 41

Leibowitz, Fran, 3

"A Letter from Copenhagen," 25, 151, 152, 154, 164

"Life is Good," 158, 173

Literary comedians: compared to Southwestern humorists, 131; techniques, compared to Keillor's, 101, 124, 131–39, 196–97n13; traditions of, 100, 120, 124, 131–32, 138

Live broadcasting: compared to recording, 171; of *APHC*, 29, 32, 36, 56, 148, 188n2; technical aspects, 170; revival in 1970s, 47

Live performance, 28, 47, 48, 53, 170

Live production, 36, 44–45, 47–49

Local-color humor: ambivalence of Keillor's, 117, 125, 126–28, 131; Matter of Minnesota as, 12, 39–43, 92, 131, 155–57, 191n36; nineteenth-century traditions of, 120, 125; religious material in, 166

"Local Family Keeps Son Happy," 8, 25, 133, 200n17

Locke, David Ross. *See* Nasby, Petroleum V.

Longstreet, A. B., 124

"The Lowliest Bush a Purple Sage Would Be," 198n17

Luther, Martin, 94, 95

"Lyle's Roof," 153, 161

McMahon, Ed, 44

Martin, Steve, 47

Mary Tyler Moore Show, 47

M*A*S*H, 56

Matter of Minnesota: ambivalence of Keillor toward, 21–22, 92, 95, 114, 116–17, 120; compared to "Buster, the Show Dog," 88; defined, 12–14, 21, 22, 39–41, 47, 196n9; development of, 16, 36, 39, 162, 170, 191n36; popularity of, 21, 24, 41; in *LH*, 164; in short fiction, 120, 146

Matter of New York, 23

"Maybe You Can Too," 140

"Meeting Donny Hart at the Bus Stop," 66, 76

"Meeting Famous People," 26

"Memo from Henry Boothe Luce to His Editors," 6

Memory: as theme, 21, 62–63, 107, 108, 114, 170; Keillor's, 14, 62–63, 165–66

Miller, Mitch, 38

Miller, Rosalie, xi, 55

Minneapolis Star, 39

Minnesota Educational Radio (MER), 15, 29, 32, 123, 124. *See also* Minnesota Public Radio

Minnesota Historical Society, 2, 183

"Minnesota Language Systems," 89

Minnesota Public Radio (MPR): Keillor's relationship with, 32, 151; network, 3, 12; producer of *APHC*, 1, 18–19, 29–30, 32, 41, 129, 130; producer of *American Radio Company of the Air*, 23; staff members of, 25, 55, 89

Misspelling, as comic technique, 101, 129, 177

Mist County, 18, 19

Mnich, Aileen, 21, 37, 89

Mock commercials. *See* Commercials

Mock ethnohistory, 101

Mock folklore, 69

Mock-oral narration, 94, 100, 101, 122, 176. *See also* Vernacular humor

Mock-oral narrators, 8, 124, 139, 143, 178

Mohr, Howard, 70, 89, 189n22

Monologues. *See* Lake Wobegon stories

Rhetoric of comic performance, 44. *See also* Comic Pose

Rivera, Jesus Torres ("Bombo"), 39, 40, 191*n*31

Rivertown Trading Corporation, 198

Robinson, Betty Jean, 37, 189*n*23

Rogers, Will, 3, 64, 119, 198*n*21

Roth, Philip, 21, 109; *Great American Novel*, 116, 143; "On the Air," 199*n*5

"The Royal Family," 76, 77, 149, 159

Russell, Mark, 41

Satire, 35–36, 39, 135–37, 140, 143–45

Saturday Night Live, 47

Scripts: of Lake Wobegon stories, 71, 148, 165; of mock commercials, 4, 30–31; for *APHC*, 37, 46, 192*n*41; of radio dramas, 4, 84–85, 87–88

Sentimentality. *See* Lake Wobegon stories

"Sex Tips," 8, 15, 132, 136, 199*n*13

Shakespeare, Keillor's use of, 108, 197*n*16

Short fiction, 118–47; subordinate status of, 118–19, 146, 200–01*n*28; as dominant humorous genre, 119; readers of Keillor's 25

Shyness, 60

Shy Person (pose), 49, 77, 170; contribution to *APHC*, 56–61; combined with Amateur, 59–60; and Cracker-Barrel Philosopher, 61, 65; combined with Preacher, 64; fictiveness of, 77, 81; success of, 57, 84

"Shy Rights: Why Not Pretty Soon?," 24

Sidetrack Tap, 18, 115; drawing of, 18

Signals catalog, 198

Simpleton (pose), 49, 50, 177

Sing-along, 11, 37, 38, 41

Sing Along with Mitch, 38

Skaerved, Ulla Strange, 5, 152, 153

Sketch: as humorous genre, 116, 119; Keillor's attitude toward, 140

"Sleepers," 6

"The Slim Graves Show," 15, 25, 75, 122–24, 126, 129, 139, 161, 177

Smith, Page, 138

Smith, Seba, 129

"Snack Firms Maps New Chip Push," 8, 132, 200*n*17

Softball, 65

"Some Matters Concerning the Occupant," 7

Songs: in *LWD*, 91–92, 101; on *APHC*, 37–38, 43, 46, 53, 141; Keillor's lyrics for, 4, 20–21, 39–41, 70, 193*n*3; in short fiction, 121–23, 129

"Song of the Exile," 193*n*3

"Song of the Exiles," 20

Southwestern humor, 24, 124, 143, 145

Space Shuttle Columbia, 19

"The Spillers," 86

Spontaneity, 46, 47, 55, 75, 81, 165

Stahl, Sandra K. D., 172

Stanphill, Ira F., 65

Starr, Harold (fictional character), 42, 68, 95, 113

"State Fair," 159

Statue of the Unknown Norwegian, 14, 98, 99

Stevenson, James, 118

Stevens, Wallace, 6

"Storm Home," 66, 76

Storyteller, relation to audience, x

Stowe, Harriet Beecher, 125

St. Paul newspapers: changes in titles of, 186*n*40; coverage of Keillor, 152, 179

Sufferer (pose): Keillor's use of, 106, 113; Twain's use of, 49

"Supper Time," 52, 65, 70

Sutton, Vern, 28, 37

Tall Tales: classic traditions of, 11, 12, 162, 177, 178, 196*n*12; compared to legend, 174, 202*n*17; Keillor's stories as, 24, 63, 80–81, 146, 157, 161–62, 171; *LWD*, 93–94, 99–100, 108; "My North Dakota Railroad Days," 125–28; "If Robert Frost Had an Apple," 125, 141–42, 145; "What Did We Do Wrong?" 125, 142–45

Tall talk, 36, 100

Tate, Allen, 5

Television: Keillor's attitude toward, compared to radio, 33; humor on, compared to *APHC*, 34, 41, 47–48, 56; *APHC* on, 2, 55, 164, 201–02*n*10; programs parodied by Keillor, 87–88

"Ten Stories for Mr. Richard Brautigan, and other Stories," 133

"The Tip-Top Club," 130, 139

Thoreau, Henry David, 96; *Walden*, 91; influence on "Found Paradise," 135; influence on *LWD*, 94, 101, 103,